DATE			

EGO®

® EV3

Exploring LEGO® MINDSTORMS® EV3

Tools and Techniques for Building and Programming Robots

Eun Jung (EJ) Park

WILEY

Exploring LEGO® MINDSTORMS® EV3: Tools and Techniques for Building and Programming Robots

Published by
John Wiley & Sons, Inc.
10475 Crosspoint Boulevard
Indianapolis, IN 46256
www.wiley.com

나의 부모님께 바칩니다.

(This book is dedicated to my parents.)

About the Author

Eun Jung (EJ) Park has been developing LEGO robotics and curricula at RoboFun since 2010. There she designs robots that are used in STEM (science, technology, engineering, and math) programs for children and youths. She hopes that her work provides students with opportunities to develop their creativity and encourages scientific curiosity through robotics and coding. Her LEGO robotics projects and building instructions are used in programs for children and youths around New York City.

EJ was born in Seoul, South Korea, and studied various art disciplines for more than 12 years, which formed the foundation for her passion in the interactive arts. EJ traveled to the United States to earn her Masters degree from the Interactive Telecommunications Program (ITP) at New York University (NYU). In the United States, she enhanced her knowledge of physical computing, programming, mechanical engineering, and a variety of other technologies. At NYU she started building mechanical moving sculptures called "automatons" and explored various mechanical elements such as gears, cams, and pulleys in her creations.

With her work at ITP—and, of course her passion for LEGO—she became the creative force behind Vision Education & Media/RoboFun's LEGO robotics curricula. At any given moment, she is probably building LEGO robots somewhere in New York City. You can see her work at www.ejpark.com.

About the Technical Editor

Dr. Damien Kee holds a PhD in robotics and a bachelor's in electrical engineering. He has been running technology-based workshops for students and professional development for teachers since 2003, both in his home country of Australia and abroad.

Damien has presented a variety of educational technology topics in places such as QSITE (Australia), Google Apps for Education Summit (Australia), RoboCupJunior (China), Jubilee Centre (Jordan), Tuffs University (USA), RoboFest (Singapore), and ATLAB (United Arab Emirates and Qatar).

Since 2001, Damien has been heavily involved with the RoboCup Junior competition, at a local, state, national, and international level. From 2009–2011, he was chairman of RoboCup Junior Australia and technical chair of the RoboCup Junior International Rescue Committee. He is the author of several teacher resource books, contributor to `theNXTstep.com`, and a member of the LEGO MINDSTORMS community program, a group of people around the world who consult with LEGO to make the MINDSTORMS system a better product.

Credits

Acquisitions Editor
Mary James

Project Editor
Jennifer Lynn

Technical Editor
Damien Kee

Production Editor
Christine Mugnolo

Copy Editor
Keith Cline

**Manager of Content Development
and Assembly**
Mary Beth Wakefield

Director of Community Marketing
David Mayhew

Marketing Manager
Carrie Sherrill

Business Manager
Amy Knies

**Vice President and Executive
Group Publisher**
Richard Swadley

Associate Publisher
Jim Minatel

Project Coordinator, Cover
Todd Klemme

Proofreader
Nancy Carrasco

Indexer
John Sleeva

Cover Designer
Wiley

Cover Image
Courtesy of Eun Jung (EJ) Park

Acknowledgments

From the day I started this book and until this moment, I wouldn't have been able to survive without support from the following people.

My editors from Wiley Publishing, Inc., Mary James and Jennifer Lynn, for encouraging me to take on this process and for keeping me on track to meet my deadlines; and also to the technical editor, Damien Kee, for providing valuable advice for the book.

Tom Igoe from NYU's Interactive Telecommunications Program made this book possible by bringing me and Wiley Publishing, Inc. together.

The RoboFun Crew, especially the CEO of the company, Laura Allen, for giving me the chance to begin my career in technology curricula development with LEGO robotics in the first place. My appreciations extends, as well, to Lisa Whitmer, as the Program Director at RoboFun, who always encourages me to develop my ideas to their fullest.

My friends Brian Cohen and Maria Tranquilli, whose creative spirits and positivity have brought me more confidence as an artist.

My roommates, Aya Takemoto and Christine McCaleb, who would check to make sure that I was okay when I was in my room writing and they hadn't heard from me for a number of hours.

My first supporters and teachers, my parents, Sun Tae Park and Soon Gil Lee, who always give me their support and only wish to make all of my dreams come true; and also my sisters, Ji Hye Park and Hyun Jung Park, who always manage to cheer me up, get me out of ruts, and believe that I can overcome any obstacle.

Lucian Reynolds who supported me through every single moment of this process with endless patience, encouragement, advice, and humor; who never stopped trusting in my ability to write this book, even when I doubted myself.

To anyone else who wasn't mentioned already. To all the people who had to get a rain check from me because I was too busy writing this book but who still keep me in their lives. I thank you all.

Contents at a Glance

Contents

Foreword

I have been in the field of LEGO robotics for 25 years. Some of my earliest experiences were working with Seymour Papert (MIT Media Lab) and colleagues designing and using curriculum with children. Since then, I've had the extraordinary opportunity to run my own company helping children and teachers use technology creatively and effectively.

About three years ago, EJ Park was recommended to me by a colleague. The moment EJ walked through the door, I knew there was something special about her. I quickly asked her to work with me, and for the past few years she has been my LEGO robotic project designer. EJ's work is always excellent. She doesn't settle for less. Above all, she is thoughtful and focused on sharing her incredible knowledge of the Mindstorms system. You are in for a treat with this book; it has been carefully created and will provide you with ideas, examples, and step-by-step instructions.

When you hear the term "Lego robotics," do you think about invention, innovation, and the vast possibilities that come with the EV3 platform and its place in the STEAM (science, technology, engineering, art and mathematics) and maker movement?

Or does "robotics" mean 600 pieces of a Lego Mindstorms set spread out across your living room as you try to join in your child's interest in robotics, despite a lack of know-how?

No matter where you are in your robotics journey, it would be hard to find a better guide than *Exploring LEGO Mindstorms EV3*. EJ is a passionate creator and maker with years of experience as an automata inventor and LEGO robotics project designer. EJ has taught all levels of robotics, and so she knows what skills can be tough for the beginner and what challenges can be exciting for the expert.

Exploring LEGO Mindstorms EV3 teaches robotics through clear and manageable step-by-step instructions. The book contains five projects to teach a reader how to build a robot, how to write code so your robot will work, and how to have fun at the same time.

Robotics, however, isn't only about following rigid steps to make moving objects. As EJ writes—and as we teach at RoboFun in New York City—we want the process and the product to be creative and influenced by its maker's ideas and passions.

Coding and making is a powerful learning combination. Many areas of thought are involved; planning, calculating, estimating, using variables, gear ratios, and much trial and error. Coding and building can allow students to develop skills in self-directed learning, which is an essential intellectual and developmental tool for children and one that is often left out of the school curriculum.

As you'll learn through *Exploring LEGO Mindstorms EV3,* the final result of this multilayered learning process is the great excitement and pride students feel when they roll out their invention and see a robotic creation— *their* robotic creature—come to life.

— LAURA ALLEN
Founder and President, RoboFun, NYC, NY

Introduction

The newest LEGO MINDSTORMS set has arrived! With EV3, you can build smarter, more powerful robots that are both autonomous and interactive. This set comes with more than 500 LEGO TECHNIC pieces, but you will also get upgraded components that enable you to robotize your LEGO creation. These include the programmable brick (mini computer), which will be your robot's brain, the motors, which will be your robot's muscles, and sensors, which make your robot aware of the world around it. One feature that makes this kit even cooler is the EV3 software, which acts as a bridge between you and your robot. You can write innumerable programs with this software and download them to the programmable brick to bring your robot to life.

I believe the EV3 set is one of the most user-friendly robotics kits available anywhere. It's amazing that building and programming with this set doesn't really require any previous experience; your passion for robots is all that you need. However, exploring the world of robotics with EV3 will be more fulfilling if you have a companion who can guide you along. This book will be your companion as you explore.

This book starts by introducing the parts that you will see when you open the EV3 box, and it ends with suggestions on how to begin your own robot. In between, the book covers a wide range of programming from basic to advanced. These lessons go along with projects that you can build with your own EV3 set. There will be a total of five robots that I hope will encourage you to challenge yourself to become a better maker throughout your EV3 journey.

Here's how the book breaks down:

- Chapter 1, "Introducing LEGO MINDSTORMS EV3," introduces you to the LEGO MINDSTORMS EV3 set.

- The starter vehicle that you will build in Chapter 2, "Building the Auto-Driver: A Starter Vehicle," is called Auto-Driver, and it will act as the core robot that you will use to begin coding in Chapters 3 through 6.

- The Spy Rabbit, whom you will meet in Chapter 7, "Building the Spy Rabbit: A Robot That Can React to Its Surroundings," will accompany you in Chapters 8 and 9 and will introduce you to sensor programming.

- In Chapters 10, "Building Mr. Turto: A Sea Turtle Robot," and 11, "Programming with Data Wires and Using My Blocks," you will build and animate Mr. Turto, the sea turtle robot.

- Advanced programming techniques are introduced in Chapter 12, "Using Data Operations Blocks."

- In Chapter 13, "Building the Big Belly Bot: A Robot That Eats and Poops," you will make the human-like Big Belly Bot, who, as you can see from the chapter title, eats and poops.

- Finally, there's Chapter 14, "Design Your Own Robot: How Did Guapo, the Robotic Puppy, Come to Be?" Not only do I introduce you to Guapo, the robotic puppy, but I also give you some tips for designing your own robot.

- I've also included an appendix that will help you download programs to your EV3 brick using Bluetooth and WiFi.

If you are a beginner, I recommend that you read through the book from start to finish. You will walk away with more confidence in your ability to build and program robots with the EV3. If you are experienced in building robots with LEGO MINDSTORMS, feel free to skip around the book as needed (but, don't miss out on the robots). This book will act as a reference for what you already know as well as a useful tool for future building and programming.

Have you ever eaten a piece of hard candy that is filled with jelly? While writing this book, I hoped that the reader would approach learning how to use EV3 like eating a piece of that candy. You work hard to melt the exterior of the candy to get to the chewy center. No matter how hard you have to work, this process will always be rewarding, because eating candy can be sweet and satisfying. Exploring EV3 to become a master robot builder may be a long journey, but I hope as you flip through this book, page by page, it is like melting candy.

Introducing LEGO MINDSTORMS EV3

Did you get a box that looks like the one shown in Figure 1-1?

Figure 1-1: The LEGO MINDSTORMS EV3 set, item number 31313

If you did, you are ready to use this book. Several versions of the LEGO MINDSTORMS set are available, but throughout this book we use the LEGO MINDSTORMS EV3 set, which has a LEGO item number of 31313. This chapter provides a brief overview of the equipment in the set and what it does.

Understanding the EV3 Set: It Begins When You Open the Box

The EV3 set consists of various components. You may have seen some of the components in other LEGO sets, but even those familiar with the previous version of LEGO MINDSTORMS will find some parts that they have never seen. Before you use your new set, it is important to know what you have. The key components include the following:

- The electronic components that come with the EV3 set
- EV3 software
- TECHNIC building parts
- Building instructions
- A test board

By understanding the various components, you will be able to design your robot more efficiently. Let's take a look at these components in more detail.

EV3 Electronic Parts

One of the most important characteristics defining a robot is that it processes commands and generates movements. The electronic components that come with your EV3 set will enable you to build robots that process the commands that you write and generate movements that are defined in those commands.

The EV3 Brick

The EV3 brick, shown in Figure 1-2, acts like the robot's brain. Like the way that our brain tells our body what to do, the EV3 brick instructs a robot how to behave. The difference between our brain and the EV3 brick is that our brain behaves on its own, whereas the EV3 brick only interprets the programs that you write. Note that you will need six AA 1.5V batteries to run the EV3 brick.

Motors

You will program the EV3 motors, shown in Figure 1-3, to create the movements of your robot. Saying that the EV3 brick is the brain of a robot, the motors are like muscles. As our muscles generate all of our body movements, the motors will power all the actions of your robot such as driving, walking, lifting, spinning, and so on.

Figure 1-2: The EV3 brick

Figure 1-3: The EV3 Motors: The large motors and the medium motor

As you can see in Figure 1-3, the large and medium motors have quite different appearances. The large motor is bigger than the medium motor, and the body size represents the strength of the motor. Also, the two motors move in different directions: The large motor's movement is parallel with the body of the motor whereas the medium motor's movement is perpendicular with the body of the motor, which allows you to effectively design a robot that can achieve your goal.

Sensors

Within the EV3 set, you will find a touch sensor, a color sensor, and an infrared sensor (see Figure 1-4). As you build the projects from this book, you will learn to use these sensors to make your robots interactive. In other words, your robot will be able to decide its action based on the inputs from its surroundings. For example, let's say you have a vehicle type robot. With an infrared sensor, it can detect how far an object is in front of it. Based on the data from the sensor, the robot can play a louder sound when it gets closer to the object.

Figure 1-4: The EV3 sensors

Remote Infrared Beacon

The remote infrared beacon, or the IR beacon, is one of the cool new features of EV3 (see Figure 1-5). You can use it as a remote control for your robot, and you can program various commands for each button or combinations of buttons. In addition, you can set your robot to detect where the IR beacon is. Note that you should not use this device with the infrared sensor.

Figure 1-5: The remote infrared beacon

Cables

This set contains two types of cables (see Figure 1-6): connector cables and a USB 2.0 cable. Connector cables are for plugging the motors and sensors into the EV3 brick. The USB cable is used to download a program to the EV3 brick from your computer.

25cm/10in Connector Cable

35cm/14in Connector Cable

2.0 USB Cable

50cm/20in Connector Cable

Figure 1-6: The connector cables and the USB 2.0 cable

EV3 Software

To give your EV3 robot instructions, you must use the EV3 software specifically designed for this set. If you are looking in the box for an installation disc, you will be looking for a while. LEGO offers its free EV3 software only as a download from www.LEGO.com/mindstorms. From the main page, click the Downloads link to display the page shown in Figure 1-7. Then click the Download button.

Don't worry if you don't have the EV3 software available when you want to test out your robot. There is an app that comes with the brick that allows you to program your robot. The program that you can create with this app will be simpler than with the EV3 software, but it is still very useful! You will see where you can find this app on the brick when we go over the EV3 brick interface in "Building the Auto-Driver: A Starter Vehicle."

Figure 1-7: Downloading the EV3 software

WHICH VERSION DO I DOWNLOAD?

The EV3 software is compatible with both PC and Mac. If you use a Windows operating system, it should be one of the following versions: Windows XP (32-bit); Vista (32-/64-bit), excluding Starter Edition; Windows 7 (32-/64-bit); and Windows 8 desktop mode, excluding Starter Edition. If you use a Mac operation system, it should be one of the following versions: Mac OS X 10.6, 10.7, or 10.8 (Intel only).

The download page contains options for choosing the operating system (Mac OS X and Win32) and language. If you download the installation file for PC, you will see a file with a .exe extension; for Mac, it will be a .dmg file. After the file downloads to your computer, just double-click the file icon and follow the instructions that pop up on your screen.

TECHNIC Building Parts

Other than the electronic parts, the box contains various parts for building robots. Before jumping into building robots, let's overview some of the main building parts that you will use often and their important features.

Studless TECHNIC Beams

When building EV3 robots, you will use studless TECHNIC beams (see Figure 1-8). The official name is quite a mouthful, so from here on out we will just refer to the part as a beam. These parts are crucial for building complex, moving robots that would not be possible using standard LEGO bricks.

Figure 1-8: Various studless TECHNIC beams

Connector Pegs

The set contains many small parts, but the majority of the pieces look like the connector pegs shown in Figure 1-9. Note that they are also called connecter pins.

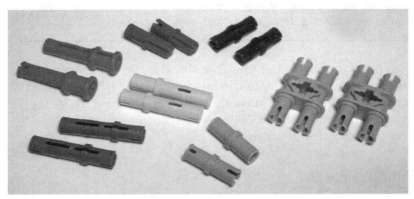

Figure 1-9: Different types of connector pegs

These components are called connector pegs because they allow multiple parts to snap together. Connector pegs come in different sizes with different features, but one of the important things that you need to know is how to distinguish the following: The connector peg and the connector peg with "friction." If you look at the regular connector peg, its surface is smooth or "frictionless" (see Figure 1-10), whereas the connector peg with friction has little bumps on the surface.

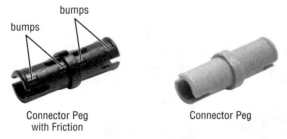

bumps

bumps

Connector Peg
with Friction

Connector Peg

Figure 1-10: Connector peg with friction versus a frictionless connector peg

If you put a connector peg on a beam, you will notice that the beam can be turned easily. However, if instead you use a connector peg with friction, it will be more difficult to turn the beam because the little bumps on the peg create more resistance.

Mechanical Pieces

When you design your robot's movements, the mechanical pieces allow for a more efficient construction (see Figure 1-11). These pieces provide, but are not limited to, mechanical advantages such as switching the direction of gear movement, building a drive train, changing the speed of gear movements, and so on.

Figure 1-11: The EV3 mechanical pieces: spur gears, double bevel gears, worm gear, cam, and so on

MAKING AN EV3 ORGANIZER

The EV3 set comes with many different pieces. Based on my experience, I prefer to have all the parts organized separately as I design a robot. I can thus see what parts I have left at a glance and not lose my thought process by spending time searching for a piece. You can probably use plastic cups or small containers, but I highly recommend that you take as your EV3 organizer an organizer that is normally used for spare parts (see Figure 1-12). This way, you can keep parts organized by size or type and store everything all together. You can find these organizers at any well-stocked hardware store or on the Internet.

Continues

continued

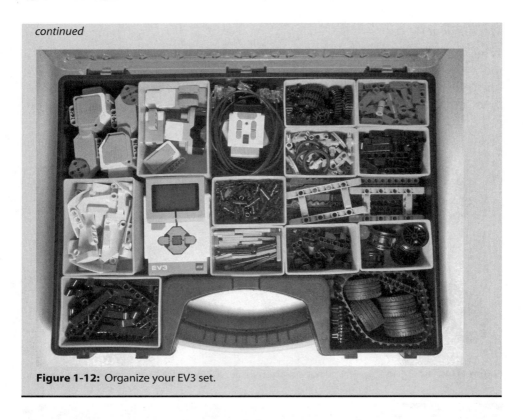

Figure 1-12: Organize your EV3 set.

The Building Instructions and the Test Board

In addition to parts, the EV3 box also contains a booklet with building instructions for one robot and simple directions for using the EV3 brick (see Figure 1-13). To augment the basic instructions in that booklet, this book provides in-depth coverage of the EV3 brick. Inside of the first layer of the package, you'll find a test board (see Figure 1-13). You use this board to test out your robot later on in this book.

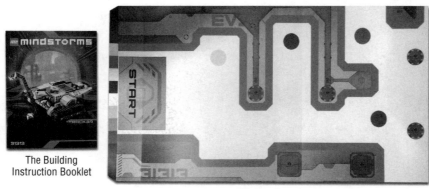

The Building
Instruction Booklet

The Test Board

Figure 1-13: The building instructions booklet and the test board

Comparing EV3 and NXT

NXT is the previous version of the LEGO MINDSTORMS set. If you use an NXT and also have an EV3, you may wonder how these two versions are comparable. In general, the EV3 equipment performs better than the NXT equipment. In terms of the brick's ability to process data, the accuracy of the included sensors, and the improved design of the electronic parts, EV3 makes for a better robot. NXT and EV3 motors are cross-compatible and work fine for either set. EV3 sensors, however, are not compatible with NXT, although EV3 can use sensors from the NXT set. Just note that using the NXT light sensor with EV3 can be quite unstable. EV3's free software is very powerful control software available for MINDSTORMS and will work with NXT (see Figure 1-14).

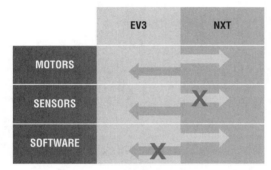

Figure 1-14: Compatibility chart for EV3 and NXT elements

Summary

In this chapter, you learned about the following:

- The electronic components of EV3
- The EV3 software download and installation process
- Characteristics of the principal building parts
- Compatibility between NXT and EV3 components

Building the Auto-Driver:
A Starter Vehicle

Now that you learned what kind of parts you have in the set, it is time to put them together to make a robot. In this chapter, starting with some of these parts, you build your first robot: Auto-Driver. In addition, you will get an introduction to working with the EV3 brick interface and use the apps in the EV3 brick to make the robot move.

Getting Started with the Auto-Driver

The Auto-Driver is a three-wheeled vehicle that can drive around (see Figure 2-1). This is one of the basic types of robot that you can have with two large motors. While building the Auto-Driver, you will learn how to follow the building instructions in this book and get a better sense of how the building system works.

What You Can Do with the Auto-Driver

The Auto-Driver will have a few of the same features that you will find in an automobile: It will be able to move forward and backward, turn right and left, and accelerate or decelerate. In Chapter 3, "Getting Started with Programming," you'll use the Auto-Driver to test out some motor-centric programs that focus on making the robot move around.

Figure 2-1: The Auto-Driver

IDENTIFYING THE PARTS ON THE BUILDING INSTRUCTIONS

The EV3 set comes with a lot of parts that vary in size and function. It also has a built-in measuring system that allows you to distinguish between different-sized pieces. Accurate sizing is crucial when you follow building instructions or create your own blueprints for others to follow.

To follow the instructions in this book, you need to understand how to measure the length of the beams and axles. As you can see in Figure 2-2, you can count the number of holes to differentiate between the various beam lengths. To measure the size of the axles, put the axle next to a beam, and then count the number of holes that the axle covers (see Figure 2-3).

Figure 2-2: Counting the number of holes on the beam to find its length

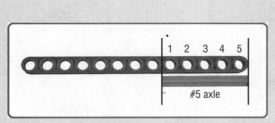

Figure 2-3: Measuring the size of an axle

I use the same template shown in Figure 2-4 for all the building instructions in this book. At the top-right corner, you will see what step you are on, and the box at the top-left corner shows you the parts you need for that step. The number next to the beam represents its specific length, and the number next to the axle starting with # refers to its relative length. Those numbers that end with x next to each piece mean how many of that specific part you'll need for that particular step.

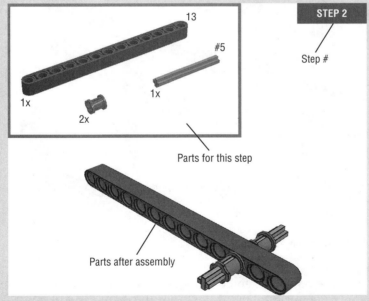

Figure 2-4: Template for building instructions

Assembling the Auto-Driver

Now that you know how to select the right parts when you read the building instructions, you are ready to assemble the Auto-Driver. Before you begin building, find all the parts that you will need (see Figure 2-5).

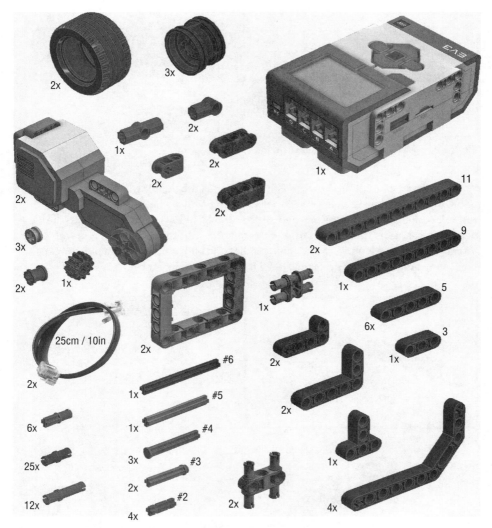

Figure 2-5: Parts list for building the Auto-Driver

After you collect all the parts presented in Figure 2-5, follow the step-by-step building instructions in Figures 2-6 to 2-25 to build the Auto-Driver.

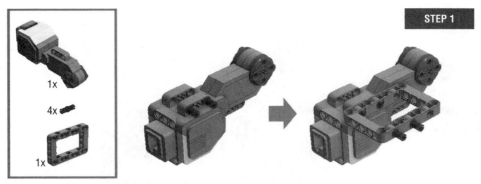

Figure 2-6: Step 1: Starting the base of the Auto-Driver

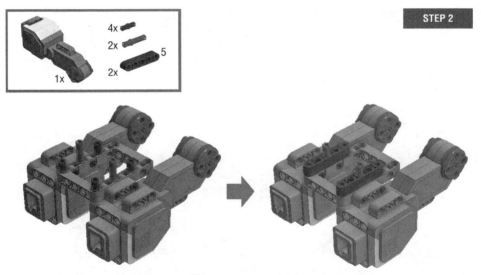

Figure 2-7: Step 2: Adding the second large motor to the base

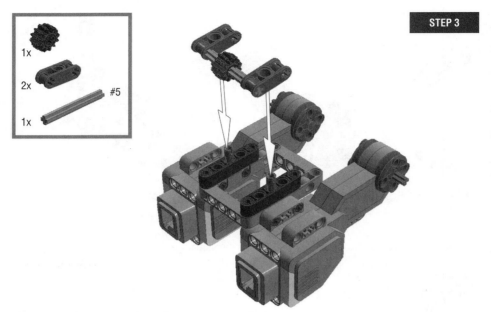

Figure 2-8: Step 3: Attaching the supporter to the base

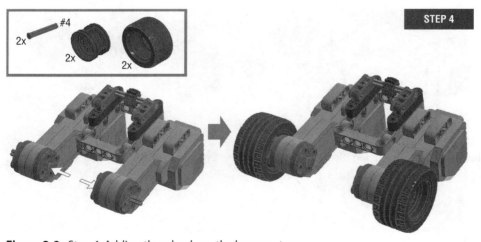

Figure 2-9: Step 4: Adding the wheels on the large motors

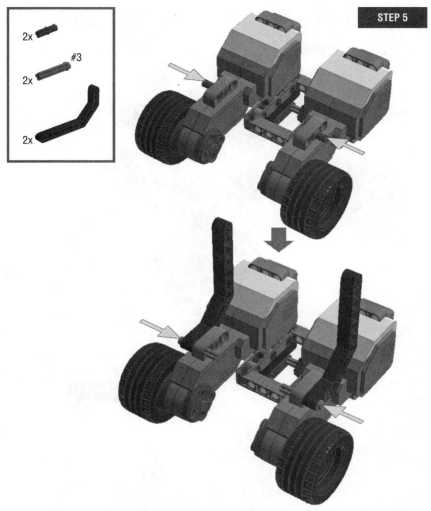

Figure 2-10: Step 5: Adding the side bars to the base

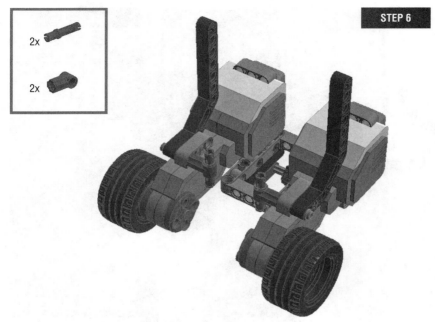

Figure 2-11: Step 6: Finishing up the base

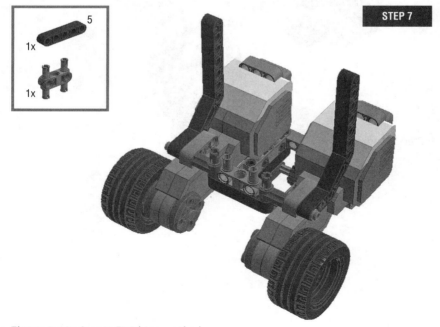

Figure 2-12: Step 7: Finishing up the base

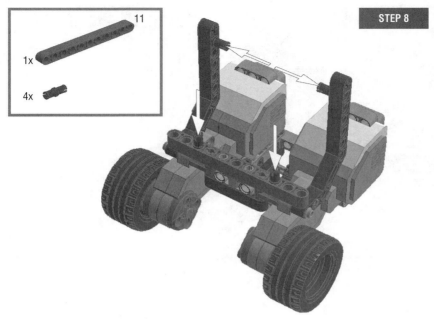

Figure 2-13: Step 8: Finishing up the base

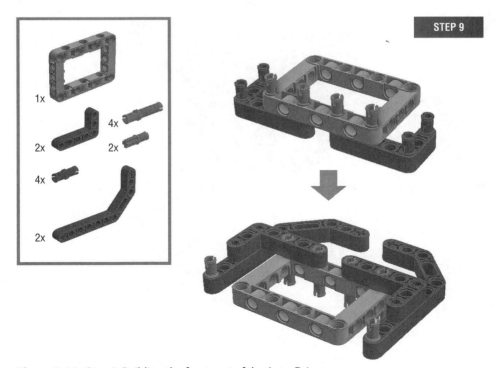

Figure 2-14: Step 9: Building the front part of the Auto-Driver

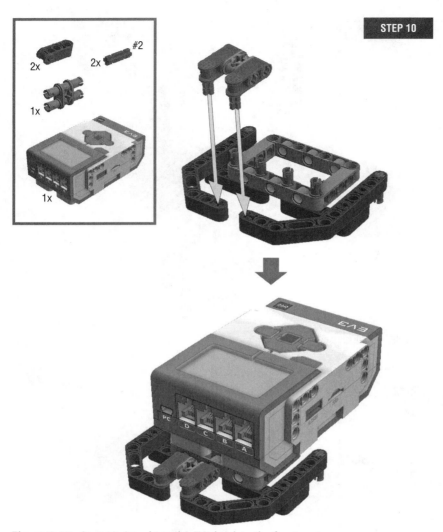

Figure 2-15: Step 10: Attaching the EV3 brick to the front part

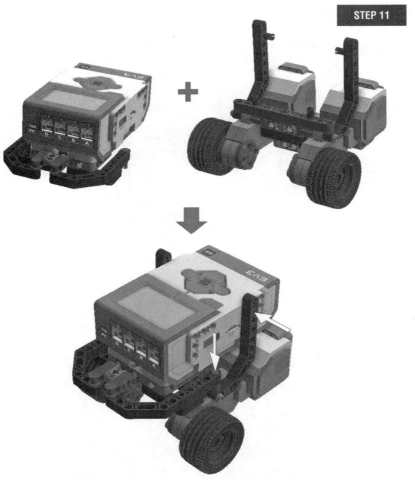

Figure 2-16: Step 11: Combining the part from step 10 and the base

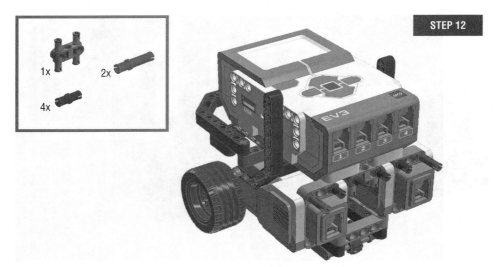

Figure 2-17: Step 12: Finishing up the body of the Auto-Driver

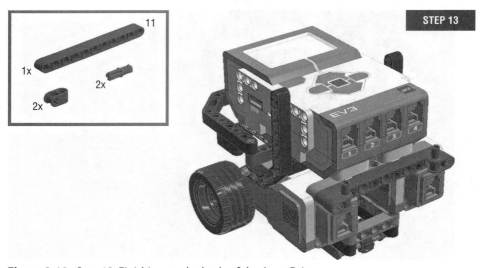

Figure 2-18: Step 13: Finishing up the body of the Auto-Driver

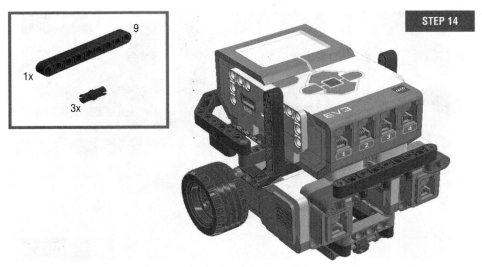

Figure 2-19: Step 14:. Finishing up the body of the Auto-Driver

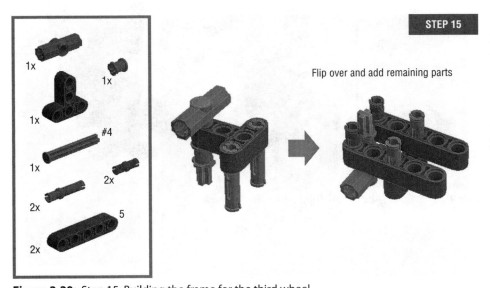

Figure 2-20: Step 15: Building the frame for the third wheel

Figure 2-21: Step 16: Building the frame for the third wheel

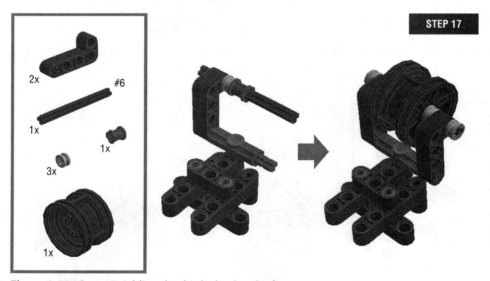

Figure 2-22: Step 17: Adding the third wheel to the frame

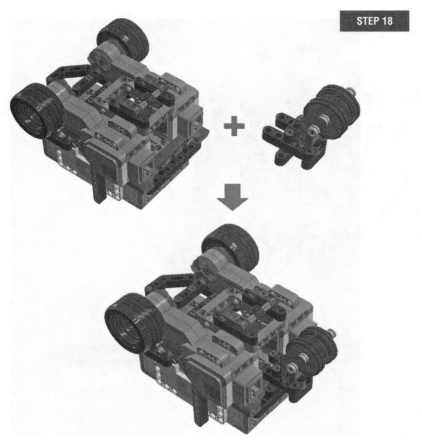

STEP 18

Figure 2-23: Step 18: Attaching the third wheel to the body of the Auto-Driver

DONE

Figure 2-24: Done

Connecting Cables

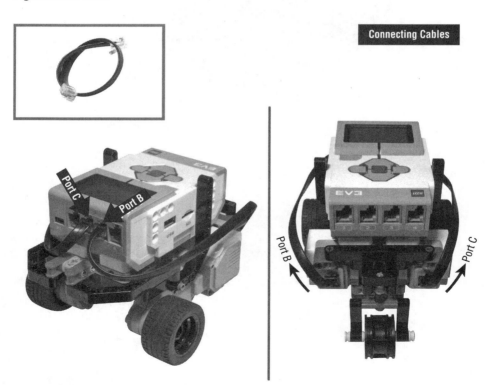

Figure 2-25: Connecting connector cables

Now that you have finished assembling your Auto-Driver, it is time to wake it up.

Understanding the EV3 Brick Interface

As discussed in Chapter 1, "Introducing LEGO MINDSTORMS EV3," the EV3 brick executes your commands to control the robot by working as its brain. The EV3 brick also works like its heart, pumping electricity into the robot to move all its electronic parts (Did you remember to fill that brick/heart with six AA batteries?) In this section, you learn how to operate the EV3 brick and get to know its built-in functions.

Using the Brick Buttons

As Figure 2-26 shows, the EV3 brick has six buttons. The center button (1 in Figure 2-26) works like the Enter/Return key on your keyboard. In other words, it is like saying the command "go" or "select." The navigation buttons around the center button (2 through 5 in Figure 2-26) are for navigating around the screen. There is one additional button beside the other buttons (6 in Figure 2-26). This button brings you to the previous screen. It is like saying "go back."

Figure 2-26: 6 Buttons on the EV3 brick

Now, let's turn on the brick. Press the center button (see Figure 2-27). The LED lights around the brick buttons will light up, and the Starting screen will display. It will take a few seconds for the brick to finish booting up, and once this process is complete, the Starting screen will disappear and the Run Recent screen, which you will look at in the next section, will appear.

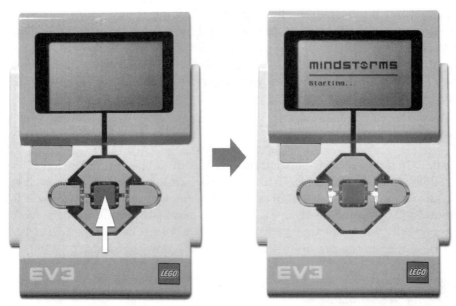

Figure 2-27: Turning on the EV3 brick

Exploring Four Basic Screens

Once the brick is on, you can toggle back and forth between four icons by using the left and right navigation buttons (see Figure 2-28). Each icon drops down a different screen. These are the four basic entry screens, and each one contains different functions or useful information about the brick. The EV3 brick can do many things, and so that you can maximize its potential, this section explains how it works and how to use it.

Figure 2-28: The four screen icons from left to right: Run Recent, File Navigation, Brick Apps, and Settings

Run Recent Screen

The first screen that you see is the Run Recent screen. This screen shows the list of recently run programs, working like the Open Recent function in other computer software that you may be familiar with. If you have never run any programs, nothing will appear on the screen (see Figure 2-29), but once you start launching the programs, the screen will begin to list the recent programs run.

Figure 2-29: Run Recent screen

File Navigation Screen

From the Run Recent screen, press the right navigation button and you will get the File Navigation screen (see Figure 2-30). This is where you can find all the items that you downloaded from your computer such as program files, sounds, images, and so on. Also, this screen shows the contents of an SD card, should you have one plugged into the EV3 brick. BrkProg_SAVE is the sample folder that comes with the EV3 brick, and once you download your projects, you will see them here.

Figure 2-30: File Navigation screen

Brick Apps Screen

Let's move on to the next screen by clicking the right navigation button again (see Figure 2-31). This screen shows four built-in apps: Port View, Motor Control, IR Control, and Brick Program.

Figure 2-31: Brick Apps screen

■ **Port View:** The Port View tells you which ports are connected to electronic parts such as motors or sensors. The top line of the boxes represents four lettered ports, *A* through *D*, and the bottom line of the boxes has four numbered ports, 1 to 4 (see Figure 2-32).

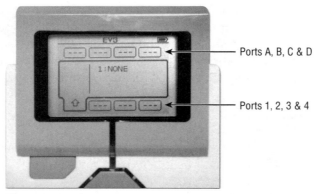

Figure 2-32: The Port View

Each box shows you the reported values from motors or sensors. For example, with the Auto-Driver, you have two motors connected into port B and C, so the Port View will look like the first image in Figure 2-33. Get to the second box on the top line (port B) by using the navigation buttons, and select it by pressing the center button. Then, try to turn the motor that is connected to port B with your hand. Do you see the number change on the screen? That is the value that you are getting from port B, which in this case is *motor degrees*. Even though you choose to view a different port on the Port View screen, the value that you get will stay in the box for port B (see Figure 2-33). If you click the center button, you will have an option to change the reading value from motor degrees to motor rotations (see Figure 2-34). We cover what those values mean later on in this book.

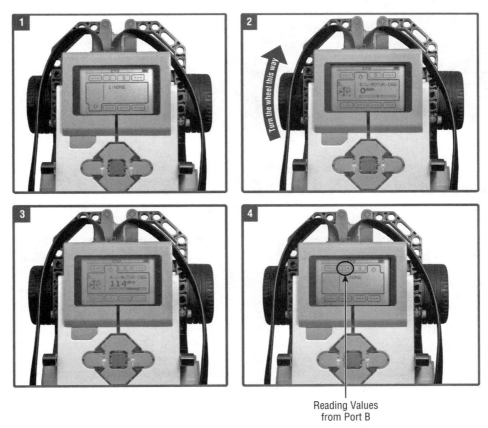

Reading Values
from Port B

Figure 2-33: Getting the value from the motor in port B

▪ **Motor Control**: Press the back button to go back to the main Brick Apps screen and select the Motor Control. This is the app that allows you to control your motors with the brick buttons.

Figure 2-35 shows two modes, and you can switch back and forth between them by pressing the center button. The first mode controls the motors that are plugged into ports A and D with the navigation buttons. A motor that is plugged into port A can be made to turn forward or backward by using the up and down navigation buttons, and a motor in port D can be turned by pressing the left and right navigation buttons. If you switch modes, motors plugged into ports B and C are controlled in the same way. Try it out.

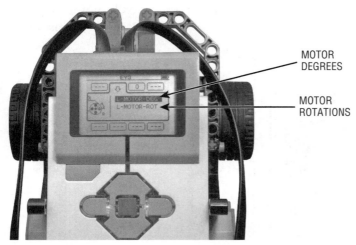

Figure 2-34: You can get two types of data from the motor: motor degrees and motor rotations

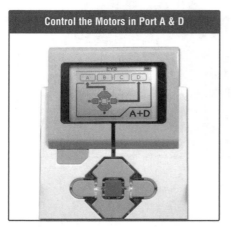 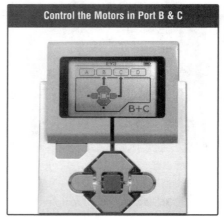

Figure 2-35: Two modes to control motors forward and backward

- **IR Control:** Eventually, you will want to drive your friends and family crazy by sending your Auto-Driver around the house, but that's difficult to do when you have to press the button on the EV3 brick the entire time. You'll probably want to use the IR Control feature to make the Auto-Driver move around remotely. Although we do not discuss IR Control setup in this chapter, you can skip ahead to Chapter 8, "Sensing the Environments: Using the Infrared, Touch, and Color Sensors," to add a remote to this project.

■ **Brick Program**: Go back to the main Brick Apps screen by pressing the back button. The last item on the list is the Brick Program. The Brick Program app can prove very useful when you don't have your computer around to program. Because it is similar to the actual EV3 software, I will come back to this function in Chapter 8, after you learn how to program with the computer.

Settings

If you haven't already done so, keep pressing the back button until you see the first main screen. Use the navigation buttons to go to the icon furthest to the right. You will see the Settings screen (see Figure 2-36).

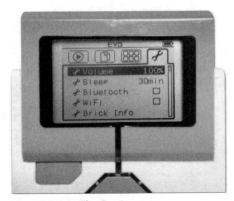

Figure 2-36: The Settings screen

On this screen, you can raise or lower the EV3 brick's speaker volume, set up times for the sleep mode, and change the status of the Bluetooth and WiFi connections. If you click the Brick Info, you will get the general information about the EV3 brick such as its operating system, its ID number, memory, and so forth.

TURNING OFF THE EV3 BRICK

As you've just learned, the EV3 brick has a sleep mode. The way sleep mode works is that after a predefined amount of inactivity, the brick shuts itself down to save power. Sleep mode is a useful feature, but it still is important to turn off the EV3 brick when you are not using it. To shut down the brick, repeatedly press the back button until you see a pop-up window like that shown on the left side of Figure 2-37. When you click the check mark, the brick will say that it is shutting down. That means the device is powering down, safely.

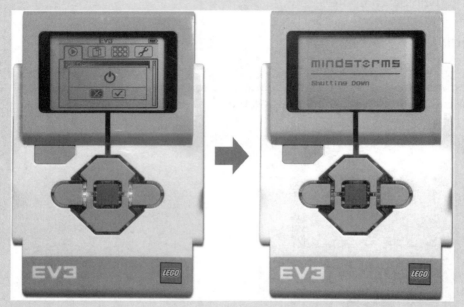

Figure 2-37: Shutting down the EV3 brick

Operating the Auto-Driver

Now that we have taken a look through the EV3 brick's operating system, let's see it in action. Go to the File Navigation screen and select the BrkProg_SAVE folder. If you click the folder by using the center button, you will find a Demo program. Get excited and click the center button (see Figure 2-38). Note that the robot will best perform on a smooth surface. Thick carpets make it difficult for little wheels to find enough friction to show off what the Auto-Driver can do.

Figure 2-38: Running the Demo program for the Auto-Driver

The Auto-Driver should go forward for a second, turn around, come back to you, and then turn around again. Congratulations!

Summary

In this chapter, you learned about the following:

- How to identify different lengths of beams and axles
- How to read building instructions for this book
- How to build the Auto-Driver
- The EV3 brick interface: the brick buttons and four basic screens
- Using the demo program to run the Auto-Driver

Getting Started with Programming

Now that you have your Auto-Driver ready from Chapter 2, "Building the Auto-Driver: A Starter Vehicle," let's make it perform more actions, such as moving forward and backward! In this chapter, you will learn about programming your robot. We start with a basic overview of programming, get your software up and running, and then delve into the essential elements of the EV3 software that you will use to bring your EV3 robots to life.

What Is Programming?

You probably have programmed a couple of things in your life. Some of you remember trying to program a VCR. Coffee pots around the world are programmed to finish brewing so that we can get up in the morning. But what is the type of programming that you hope to learn from this book? In this section, you will gain a basic understanding of programming and find out the role of programming in creating movement for your robots. In addition to the general ideas of programming, this section also covers how the EV3 programming platform is designed.

PROGRAMMING EXPERIENCE ISN'T NECESSARY!

Are you new to programming? Here is some good news: You do *not* need any programming experience to program EV3 robots. This book covers everything that you need to know to make your own robots move. With EV3's graphical interface, coding can be a fun and rewarding experience, and as you follow along, you will learn the basic concepts of programming.

If you have already done some programming in the past, don't worry; the EV3 system won't disappoint you, and you shouldn't get bored. Builders of any level can appreciate EV3's intuitive programming environment. You will be surprised at how far you can take your ideas with this software.

Communicating with Robots

Why is programming necessary? A robot won't do anything if it doesn't receive commands. You tell a robot what to do and describe how it must do it by creating a program for it. A program is a list of instructions that directs a robot's behavior, and programming is the action of writing a program. A robot follows exactly what is written down in its program; it can't read your mind, and it doesn't recognize your mistakes as mistakes. So if your creation is not performing the way that you envisioned, go back to your program—you might have to alter it slightly.

Understanding Programming Languages

Then, how do we write a program? Can we write down a set of instructions in English and have a robot read it? Unfortunately, most robots don't speak English or any languages that human beings use. To communicate with robots, we need to speak their language. This is why writing a program is also known as writing "code." A *coder* is another way of saying a *programmer*; so when people talk about *coding*, they are really talking about writing a program.

Coders use various programming languages to talk to robots. You may have heard about different types of programming languages such as C, C++, Java, Processing, and so on. (Again, don't worry if you have no idea what they are.) Some programming languages are more "machine friendly" than "human friendly." For a computer, a program written in a machine-friendly language is a lot faster to execute. However, these types of programming languages are not easy for us to learn. To do so, we would need more time to study to understand how machines work, and it would require a good amount of effort to get used to it.

In contrast, human-friendly languages are designed to allow people to use them easily. A program written in a human-friendly language may take a little bit more time for a machine to process, but will be easier for us to code.

Luckily, the EV3 programming language that we will be using for EV3 robots is a very visual, human-friendly language that you can use either with your Mac or PC.

Previewing the EV3 Software System

The LEGO MINDSTORMS EV3 set comes with its own software, which is specifically designed for the EV3 brick. An installation CD isn't in your set, but you can download it from `mindstorms.lego.com`.

The EV3 software is an icon-based programming environment. Writing instructions for the robot with the EV3 software is like designing a train. A train is a vehicle that runs in one direction down the track. The train can be long or short, depending on what it is carrying. On some trains, there are cars that carry luggage, there are cars that carry people, and there are cars that carry freight, such as food or fuel. Each car has a different function, and whether the train pulls these cars is up to the conductor.

With EV3, *you* are the conductor. There are sets of blocks that already contain certain commands, just like different cars on the train carry different cargo. Your job is to connect these blocks, as if linking train cars together. You also have to define the commands for each block, the same as choosing which cargo goes on what train car (see Figure 3-1).

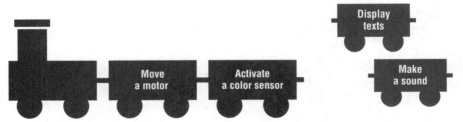

Figure 3-1: Writing a program with the EV3 software is like designing a train.

The first step is to create an EV3 program using this software on your computer. Then, by connecting the EV3 brick to the computer, you can download the program into the EV3 brick. As a brain of your robot, the brick controls the robot by executing the program that you wrote.

Launching the EV3 Software

Now that you know the basics of what programming entails and understand the core concepts of the EV3 software, it is time to launch the software. In this section, you start exploring the software with the launch page, and then learn how to start a new program. This section also introduces you to the helpful tools that you can use to manage all of your different programs.

What Do You See on the Screen?

When using any computer software, even playing computer games, it is very important to understand what elements the software displays on the screen and what they do so that you can utilize them as needed. Let's go over the pages that you will see when you use the EV3 software so that you can learn the components of each page and their functions.

Exploring the Lobby

After launching the EV3 software on your computer, you will see a screen like the one shown Figure 3-2. This page is called the Lobby, and it is the first thing that you will see when you start the software.

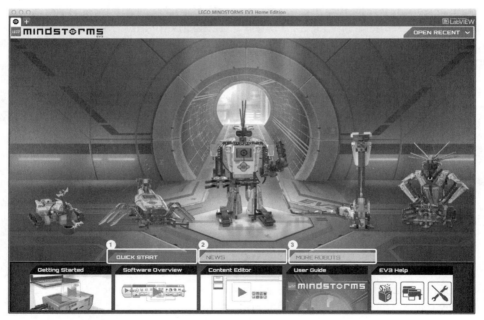

Figure 3-2: The EV3 software startup page: Lobby

> **NOTE** In the center of the Lobby, you will see five LEGO models. These are the five robot missions that come with the LEGO MINDSTORMS EV3 set. If you click a robot, it shows you instructions on how to build and program that model. Feel free to

experiment with these robots outside of the lessons that you read in this book. They are well designed and will provide extra practice.

At the very bottom of the Lobby screen, you will see three tabs: Quick Start, News, and More Robots (see Figure 3-2).

■ The Quick Start tab contains short video tutorials for using the software; if you click the arrow on the right edge, you will see a digital version of the User Guide and the EV3 Help section. The EV3 Help section is like an index for using the software. We will look into the various functions of the software in this book, but if you have questions about the software, visit the EV3 Help section.

■ The News tab brings you the latest happenings from the LEGO MINDSTORMS world. It proves useful if you want to keep up with product announcements and information about competitive events. The News tab appears to mirror information from `www.LEGO.com/mindstorms`, so if you visit that page regularly, you will have seen everything that is posted on the page.

■ The More Robots tab is a door to the EV3 online community where robot builders can share their experiences with others. There is also a fun game that involves EV3 robots and instructions for building and programming more robots apart from the five main designs that stand in the Lobby.

Let's now take a look at the top of the window (see Figure 3-3). You can find the Lobby tab in the upper-left corner of any page. Clicking it brings you back to the Lobby screen. The Add Project tab is a plus sign, and clicking it creates a new project. The Open Recent tab lets you open existing programs, and it displays a drop-down menu showing the projects that you recently opened.

Figure 3-3: Lobby tab, Add Project tab, and Open Recent tab

Creating a Project

Now you are ready to begin a new project. Click the Add Project tab. Make sure that your screen looks like the one shown in Figure 3-4.

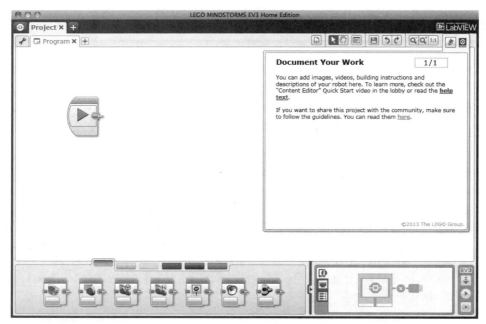

Figure 3-4: New project page

Close the Document Your Work window by clicking the Close Content Editor button on the top-right corner. (We come back to that later.) The screen you see now is the main work area when it comes time for you to write a program. Look at the top-left corner of the window (see Figure 3-5). Did you notice that EV3 automatically created a Program tab for your new project?

Figure 3-5: A Program tab is automatically generated when you begin a new project.

Now that you are looking at the Project window, I want to take a little time to explain the difference between a project and a program. Projects work like a locker that you use in a school or a gym where you save and organize your personal belongings. With your robot, the project is its assigned locker. And this locker comes with a blank container named Program by default. You will fill up the container with a set of instructions that the robot should follow. Just as you can stack up multiple containers in your locker, your robot can have multiple programs in its locker/project as well (see Figure 3-6). To create more programs, you can simply click the button with the plus sign that is right next to the Program tab.

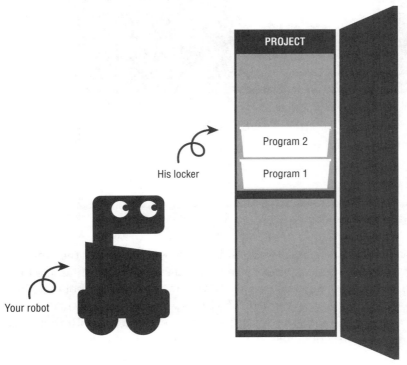

Figure 3-6: A project is like a locker, and a program is like a container in the locker.

So, do the containers in the locker hold just programs? No! The locker holds other types of containers in addition to the container for a program. Do you want to see how the locker is structured? Then let's crack open the locker and take a look inside.

Understanding Project Properties

Clicking the Project Properties button—which looks like a wrench (see Figure 3-7)and is located to the left of the leftmost Program tab—brings you to the inside of the locker. Do you see the window like the one shown in Figure 3-7?

Section A

Section B

Figure 3-7: Project Properties window

As mentioned earlier, there are more built-in containers apart from the program container. You can see them in Section A in Figure 3-7. There are containers for a project's name, a photo, a project description, and a video of the robot in action. Now take a look at Section B in Figure 3-7. This is where the program containers live. It shows you the list of programs that you created and automatically generates the various lists of elements used in your programs, such as images, sounds, and so on.

DON'T FORGET TO NAME AND SAVE YOUR PROJECT

It is very important to name your project properly and save it before you go any further. What is the best way to label your locker? Label it with your name, right? If I name my locker Human 1, how would other people know that it belongs to me? For the same reason, I wouldn't leave the project name as Project 1 either. I highly recommend that you label the project with the name of the robot to which it belongs. If you click the File tab on the menu at the top of the screen and then click Save Project, a Save dialog opens in which you can name the project.

What about a program, then? Which is the best way to organize multiple containers? We can mark a container with something to remind you of what it contains. It can be a colored tag or even a piece of masking tape with a list of its contents. I suggest doing the same thing when you save your programs. Leaving the program names as Program or Program 2 hardly distinguishes what each program does. Try to name your program based on what instructions it has. For example, if the program directs the robot though a zigzag maze, you can name this program zigzag. To change the name of a program, select the program that you want to rename and double-click the current name on a program tab. The current name will be highlighted, and you can just type in the new name.

Understanding the Programming Interface and Graphic Languages

Now that you've traveled though the first page of the software to the programming area, it is time to learn how to use it. If your Project Properties page is still open, click the Program tab to come back to the programming area. We will go over how the programming area is structured and how to use its components.

The screen shown in Figure 3-8 is the main programming area that you always see when you create a program. Its interface is made up of several sections, as follows:

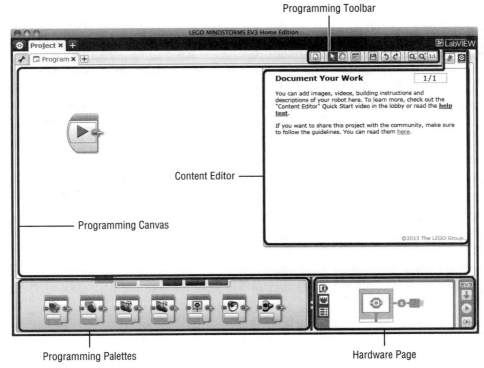

Figure 3-8: The EV3 software interface

- **Programming canvas:** The programming canvas is the work area where you will assemble lines of your program. Whenever you create a new program, you always see the block with a green Play button (Start Block) on the canvas.

- **Programming toolbar:** The programming toolbar has useful tools that can help you control and adjust your program. Figure 3-9 shows what each tool does. Note that you should choose the Select tool when you select and move around the programming blocks.

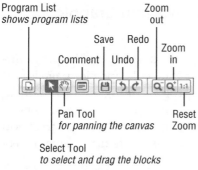

Program List
shows program lists

Zoom out

Save   Redo

Zoom in

Comment   Undo

Pan Tool
for panning the canvas

Reset Zoom

Select Tool
to select and drag the blocks

Figure 3-9: Programming toolbar

■ **Content editor:** The content editor helps you to document your work. You can use it as a working journal for yourself or as presentation material about your robot when talking to other people. When you click the Edit Mode button (see Figure 3-10) in the top-right corner of the content editor pane, the software presents you with an editing page, where you can store photos, videos, descriptions, and instructions for your robot.

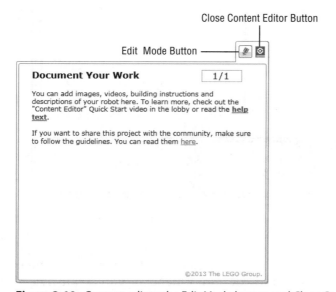

Close Content Editor Button

Edit Mode Button

Document Your Work   1/1

You can add images, videos, building instructions and descriptions of your robot here. To learn more, check out the "Content Editor" Quick Start video in the lobby or read the **help text**.

If you want to share this project with the community, make sure to follow the guidelines. You can read them here.

©2013 The LEGO Group.

Figure 3-10: Content editor: the Edit Mode button and Close Content Editor button

TIP To keep the programming canvas free of clutter, I recommend that you keep the content editor pane closed when you are programming. (You can close this pane by clicking the Close Content Editor button.) Don't worry, though; when you close the pane, it is really just minimized and out of view. So, when you reopen the content editor, all the contents that you have worked on are still there.

- Programming palettes: As mentioned previously, the EV3 software comes with sets of preprogrammed (but modifiable) blocks. Together, programming palettes function as a library for all the programming blocks that you can use in your project. The blocks are organized by color (green, orange, yellow, red, blue, and emerald blue), which lets you know what class of work that the block does. You will learn about most of the blocks throughout the rest of the book.

- **Hardware page:** If you don't already have your EV3 brick connected to your computer, you will see a graphic on the hardware page that indicates that the EV3 brick is not connected. It looks like the hardware shown in Figure 3-10. When you connect your EV3 brick to your computer, which we will try soon, the hardware page shows you how the computer is connected to the EV3 brick and into which ports the sensors and motors are plugged.

Getting Used to the Interface

Now that you're familiar with the software interface, let's take it for a spin. Clear any blocks that you may have sitting on the canvas by clicking them and pressing the Delete key on your keyboard. Here, you will practice dragging and dropping the blocks onto the canvas to create a simple line of the code for your Auto-Driver. This is just to get used to the action of using programming blocks so that you can write the example code by following the step-by-step instructions (Figure 3-11 through Figure 3-15). This code will make the Auto-Driver move forward for 2 seconds and then backward for 2 seconds.

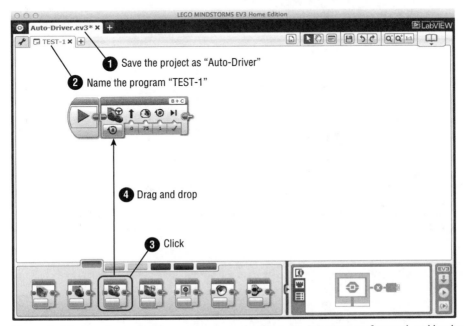

Figure 3-11: Creating a simple program to make the Auto-Driver move forward and backward (Step 1–4)

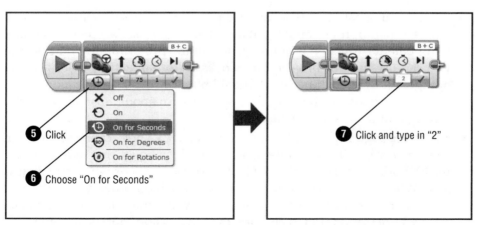

Figure 3-12: Creating a simple program to make the Auto-Driver move forward and backward (Step 5–7)

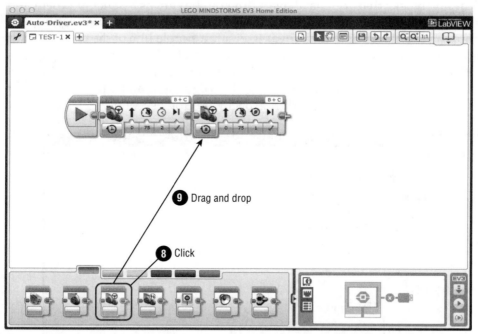

Figure 3-13: Creating a simple program to make the Auto-Driver move forward and backward (Step 8–9)

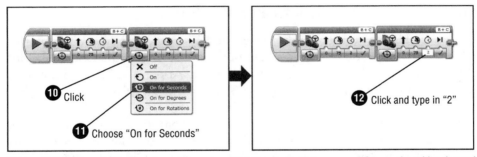

Figure 3-14: Creating a simple program to make the Auto-Driver move forward and backward (Step 10–12)

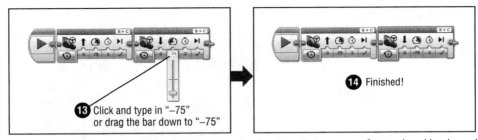

Figure 3-15: Creating a simple program to make the Auto-Driver move forward and backward (Step 13–14)

Now that you have finished writing the code, it is time to test it out with your Auto-Driver. You run the program in the following section. But before you move on, don't forget to save the project.

Downloading Programs to a Robot

Congratulations on having finished your first program. You successfully used the software to create a list of commands; to have the robot follow them, though, you need to deliver them to the robot itself. To see the program that you wrote in action, you must download it to the robot's brain (the EV3 brick). In this section, you learn about connecting your robot to the computer and downloading programs to its brain.

Connecting the EV3 Brick to a Computer

You can establish a connection between the EV3 brick and your computer in a number of ways. You can do this via Bluetooth, WiFi, or the USB cable; but in this section, you do so by using the cable. The Appendix, "Using Bluetooth and Wi-Fi with EV3," covers how to use Bluetooth and WiFi (in case you want to flip ahead).

Before going on, make sure that you have prepared the EV3 software by having the code ready on the screen and the Auto-Driver powered up. Plug the smaller end of the USB cable into the EV3 brick port that is marked PC and the larger end into the computer (see Figure 3-16).

To the EV3 brick   To the computer

Figure 3-16: Connecting the Auto-Driver to the computer with the USB cable

Once the software recognizes the Auto-Driver, you will see your EV3 brick on the hardware page (see Figure 3-17). Just note that you may have a different version of firmware from Figure 3-17.

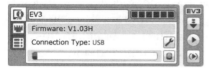

Figure 3-17: The hardware page showing the connected EV3 brick

The following section covers the kind of information that you will find on the hardware page and how to use it. Should you encounter a pop-up window about updating the firmware, see the following sidebar before you do anything else.

UPDATING THE FIRMWARE

Firmware is a general term that refers to operating software that is embedded in a small hardware device, such as the EV3 brick. LEGO will, from time to time, release a new version of the firmware to improve the EV3 brick's performance, and you'll want to update it with the newest version. If you get a pop-up window like the one in Figure 3-18, it's time to update your current firmware. Note that to update your firmware, your computer should be connected to the EV3 brick via the USB cable. You'll want to be connected to the Internet, too, so that you can actually download the new version of the firmware.

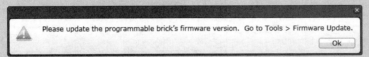

Please update the programmable brick's firmware version. Go to Tools > Firmware Update.

Ok

Figure 3-18: Firmware updating warning window

To update the firmware, go to the Tools menu at the top of the screen and choose Firmware Update (see Figure 3-19). The Firmware Update dialog box shown in Figure 3-19 will open.

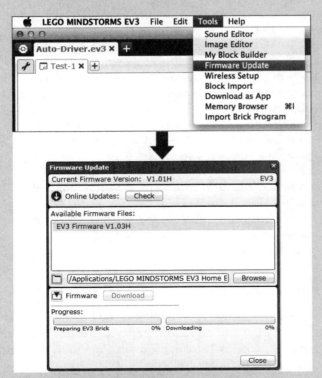

Figure 3-19: Opening the Firmware Update dialog box

Continues

continued

You will see the newer version of the firmware in the Available Firmware Files box. Select the file and click the Download button (see Figure 3-20).

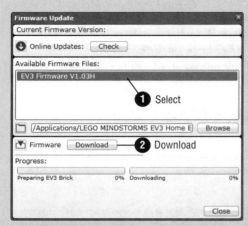

Figure 3-20: Downloading the new version of the firmware

The progress bars indicate how far along you are in the firmware update process. While the firmware is updating, the EV3 brick also shows (with a message on its screen) that it is receiving information. When the process completes, a pop-up dialog declares "Firmware update successful!"

Even if you don't get a window that warns you of an available firmware update, it doesn't hurt to manually check whether there is the newer version. To do so, click the Check button in the Firmware Update dialog box.

The EV3 software opens a new browser window that loads the LEGO MINDSTORMS website, where you can find the newest version of firmware. If you don't see any version newer than the one you have, your firmware is up-to-date. If there is the newer version, download it to your computer, and then come back to the Firmware Update dialog box and find the file that you just downloaded. Click the Browse button to do so if it doesn't show up in the Available Firmware Files box.

Once you find the file, it will show up in the Available Firmware Files box; then you can click it and download it onto your EV3 brick.

Reading the EV3 Brick on the Software

Again, the place where you can see your EV3 brick is on the hardware page. Three tabs appear on the left side of the page and carry different types of information about the EV3 brick: the Brick Information tab, Port View tab, and Available Bricks tab (see Figure 3-21).

— Brick Information Tab
— Port View Tab
— Available Bricks Tab

Figure 3-21: Three tabs of the hardware page

The Brick Information tab shows the connected brick's configuration. For example, if you have the Auto-Driver connected, this tab tells you what version of the firmware the EV3 brick has, its battery level, how it is connected to the computer, and its memory usage (see Figure 3-22).

The Name of the EV3 Brick   Battery Level

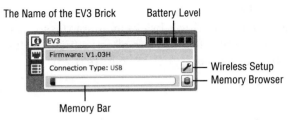

Wireless Setup
Memory Browser

Memory Bar

Figure 3-22: The Brick Information tab on the hardware page

The Port View tab automatically shows which ports are communicating with motors or sensors when you connect the EV3 brick to the computer. With the Auto-Driver connected, the Port View tab will look like the one shown in Figure 3-23.

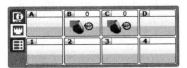

Figure 3-23: The Port View tab on the hardware page with the Auto-Driver

The top four boxes represent the lettered ports (for the motors), and the bottom four show the numbered ports (for the sensors). Similar to getting the reading values (with motors, they are either motor degrees or motor rotations) on the Port View app on the EV3 brick, you can get the live reading values here as well.

Even if the EV3 brick is not available, you can still set up the ports for the motors or sensors. If you click one of the port boxes, it gives you the available options (see Figure 3-24).

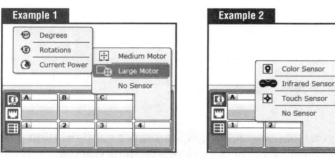

Figure 3-24: Setting up the Port View

Like its name suggests, the Available Bricks tab lists all the bricks that your computer can see one way or another. Because your computer can communicate with a brick in multiple ways, you can have multiple bricks available (assuming that your computer has USB, WiFi, or Bluetooth). You can check which brick is currently connected and change the connection type (see Figure 3-25).

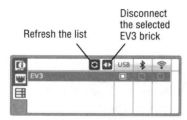

Figure 3-25: The Available Bricks tab on the hardware page

Three controller buttons appear on the right side of the hardware page. They are all for downloading the program to the EV3 brick, but each one works slightly differently. Refer to Figure 3-26 to see how each button functions.

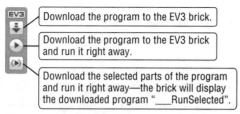

Figure 3-26: The hardware page controller buttons

You have been so patient! Now that you have the program ready to go and the Auto-Driver is connected, it is time to download it to the EV3 brick. Click the Download button on the hardware page and wait until the EV3 brick makes a noise. You can then unplug the Auto-Driver from the computer and put it on the ground. Go to the File Navigation screen on the EV3 brick and click the Auto-Driver folder. Do you see the program called TEST-1? That is the one that you've just downloaded. Click it and see what happens (see Figure 3-27).

Figure 3-27: Running the TEST-1 program on the Auto-Driver

Is your Auto-Driver moving forward and backward? You just saw the robot execute your commands. This is a taste of the complex programming skills that you will learn as you move through the lessons in this book. More fun ahead! What else can we make the Auto-Driver do?

Summary

In this chapter, you learned about the following:

- The basic concepts of programming with EV3
- The EV3 software and its user interface
- How to update the firmware on the EV3 brick
- How to connect the EV3 brick to the computer and download a program to it
- How to run a program downloaded to the EV3 and make your robot move

Exploring Action Blocks Part 1: Programming Motors

In Chapter 3, "Getting Started with Programming," you learned how to get started with the EV3 software and some basic concepts for programming. You also explored the software's user interface and made the Auto-Driver communicate with the computer. This chapter now introduces you to the key factors of block programming and then moves on to programming the motors. In this chapter, you learn how to program the motors to make the Auto-Driver move around in different ways.

Understanding the Basics of Block Programming

As mentioned in the preceding chapter, EV3 block programming is a system that allows you to complete a series of commands for the robot by linking visual code blocks. Even though the system is fairly simple and user friendly, keep in mind two basic rules when you put these blocks together. Before we jump into learning the details of the programming with the EV3 system, let's go over these rules. After that, you'll learn about the structure of the blocks themselves.

Rule 1: Use the Start Block

When you create the new program, you will always see the Start block, the block that has a green Play button graphic, on the programming palette. Do you remember dragging the programming block from the palette and connecting it to the Start block when you made the first program for the Auto-Driver in Chapter 3? Herein lies the first rule: The program will not "run" (be executable) without having the Start block in the beginning of the code.

Think about it like this: In a relay race, the first runner waits for the sound of the starting gun before she can spring forward and pass the baton to the next runner. The Start block is essentially the starting gun for your program. The next blocks in line from the Start block will be waiting to run through their instructions until the Start block begins the program. No one will run without the sound of the starting gun, and so nothing will happen without the Start block. Again, in a relay race, only the assigned runners on the track get to run, not everyone else who is around the track. The programming blocks that are connected to the Start block are like the assigned runners. You can have multiple programming blocks on the canvas, but only the ones connected to the Start block will perform (see Figure 4-1).

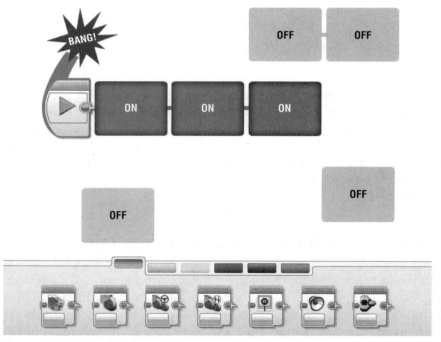

Figure 4-1: The Start block works like a starting gun at the beginning of a relay race.

NOTE If, somehow, you lost the Start block on the canvas, you can find it under the orange tab in the programming palette. You may simply click the Start block from there and drag it onto the canvas.

As you may realize, you can have more than one Start block, which means that you can have more than one sequence of code. All the tracks of code on the programming canvas that have the Start blocks in the beginning will initiate the code all at the same time when you run the program. This will prove useful when you want your robot to carry out multiple tasks simultaneously (see Figure 4-2).

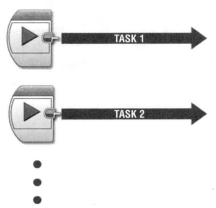

Figure 4-2: You can have more than one line of code to have the robot accomplish multiple actions.

> **TIP** Avoid writing code that tells the robot to do incompatible actions at the same time. This would be like trying to go to sleep early right after drinking four cups of coffee or telling your friend to study for a calculus exam at a heavy metal concert. Neither of these situations will have a positive result. Telling your robot to go forward and backward at the same time would be no different.

Rule 2: Respect the Program Flow

The second rule to keep in mind is that the program will always run from left to right—from the Start block to the last programming block. Going back to a relay race, after the sound of the starting gun, the first runner springs forward and passes the baton to the next runner. The same action is repeated with the next runners until the final runner gets to the finish line. They all wait for their turn and run in order. The program flow works just like that relay race.

As you build out your program, there will be a chain of programming blocks that run from one to the next in a sequence. The order of that sequence always starts on the very left of the chain at the Start block and then moves to the next block on the right until the last block's action is complete (see Figure 4-3).

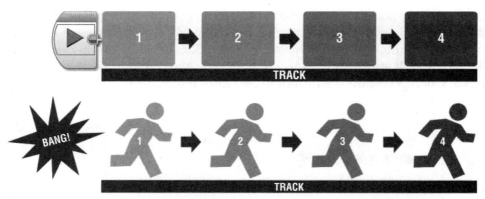

Figure 4-3: A chain of programming blocks will always run from the Start block at the left to the last block on the right.

Overview of the Programming Block's Structure

Programming blocks is more than just stringing them together in some particular order. Each block has settings that alter its function or mode. Many times, the programmer can manually set how a block operates by assigning values to different features such as motor power or duration time. Figure 4-4 shows the basic structure of the block.

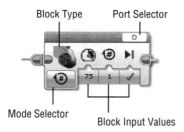

Figure 4-4: The structure of the programming block

Getting to Know the Input Values for the Motors

Now that you learned how the program flow works in the EV3 software system, it is time to learn how to control the programming blocks. Let's start with the blocks for programming the motors that are under Action blocks (green tab) in the programming palette. As shown in Figure 4-5, four programming blocks enable you to control the EV3 motors: the Medium Motor block, Large Motor block, Move Steering block, and Move Tank block.

Medium Motor   Move Steering
    Block   Block

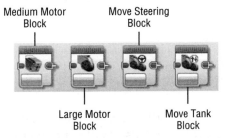

Large Motor   Move Tank
   Block   Block

Figure 4-5: Four programming blocks for the motors

Because the four blocks share the same purpose of controlling the motors, I'll group them all together as motor blocks. These blocks share a similar structure and use the same types of input values for their settings. As shown in Figure 4-6, five modes define the duration of the motor movement in all the motor blocks: Off, On, On for Seconds, On for Degrees, and On for Rotations.

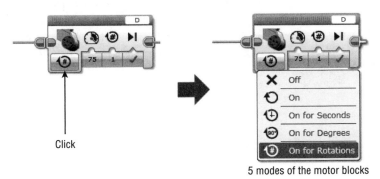

Click

5 modes of the motor blocks

Figure 4-6: The modes that control the motors

The Off, On, and On for Seconds Modes

The Off mode is to stop the motor. If you choose this mode, you will see the block change, as shown in the left image of Figure 4-7. The block input that is shown on the block is called Brake at End, and it is used to control the way the motor stops. If you click the check mark, you will get a drop-down menu with two options: Brake and Coast (as shown in the right image of Figure 4-7).

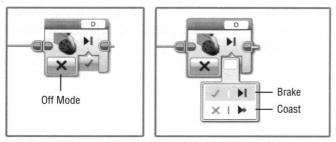

Figure 4-7: The Off mode with the Brake and Coast options

Choosing Brake (shown as Brake at End: True) will make the motor stop immediately. Choosing Coast (shown as Brake at End: False) will cut power to the motor and allow it to stop gradually on its own. You will have the Brake at End input for all the other modes except for the On mode.

The On mode is used to turn on the motor. The motor will be running until the next block occurs. The block with the On mode won't work alone; it needs another block to determine how long it should stay on (see Figure 4-8). For example, the block with the On mode can be followed by the Wait block that we will learn about in later chapters. The Wait block can say, "Wait until the touch sensor is pressed;" then the motor will be on until the touch sensor is pressed.

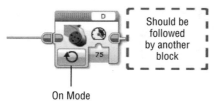

Figure 4-8: The On mode

TIP If there is no other block following the motor block set to On mode, you won't get any movement from the motor. This is a useful setting when you start including sensors into your code. For example, using On mode, you can set the motor to run until something presses a touch sensor, making it act as an "off" switch.

The On for Seconds mode always brings up the Seconds input on the block, as shown in Figure 4-9. You can simply click the number section below the clock symbol and type in how many seconds that you want to have the assigned motor to be on.

The On for Degrees and On for Rotations Modes

The next mode is the On for Degrees mode. Here, the term *degrees* means the number of degrees that the motor turns. If you select this mode, you will get the Degrees input in the block inputs section, and you can type in a number of degrees that you want the motor to be on (see Figure 4-10).

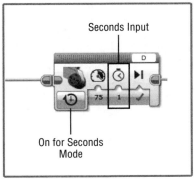

Seconds Input

On for Seconds
Mode

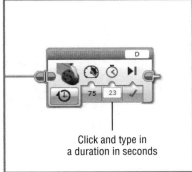

Click and type in
a duration in seconds

Figure 4-9: The On for Seconds mode

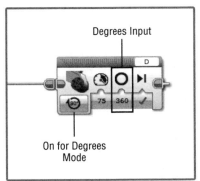

Degrees Input

On for Degrees
Mode

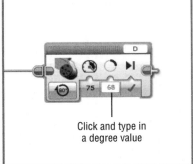

Click and type in
a degree value

Figure 4-10: The On for Degrees mode

WORKING WITH DEGREES AND ANGLES

If you aren't familiar with degrees and angles, here is a little primer. Degrees help us understand how something travels in a circle. A clock is the classic example because the minute, hour, and second hand all travel in the same direction, albeit at different speeds. The entire circle is represented by the number 360, which you'll find is easily divisible by 3 and 4. Back to the clock: If the hour hand starts at the top of the clock at 12:00 a.m., we can say it is at 0 degrees or 0°. If the hour hand travels to 3 o'clock, it has gone a quarter of the way around the clock. 360° / 4 = 90°, so that means 90° is a quarter turn. 6 o'clock is halfway around the clock: 360° / 2 = 180°, a half turn to face the opposite direction. If the hour hand makes a full revolution around the clock from its starting point at 12:00 a.m. back to the top at 12:00 p.m., it has traveled the full 360°.

See the examples of the On for Degrees mode in Figure 4-11. The dark part of the little circle on the degrees input shows approximately how far the motor will turn.

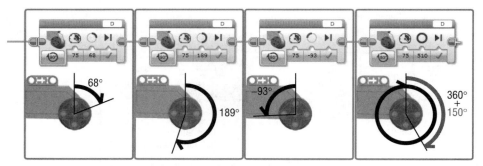

Figure 4-11: The degrees inputs and the motor movement

The On for Rotations mode works similarly to the On for Degrees mode except that you can set up how many rotations you want the motor to turn (see Figure 4-12).

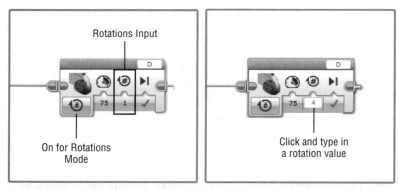

Figure 4-12: On for Rotations mode

Here, a rotation means a full motor turn, which is a 360° turn. The Rotations input doesn't always need to be a whole number; it can also be a decimal point number.

Whether you program the motor in degrees or rotations depends on your preference. Experiment with using both ways to tell the computer how far you want a wheel to turn.

Motor Power Input and the Direction of the Motor

One of the block inputs that you will always have on the motor blocks is the Power input, which looks like a gauge (see Figure 4-13). If you click the number area, you will notice that you can either type in a number or can adjust the bar.

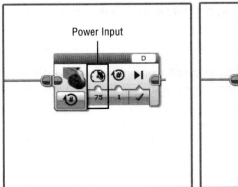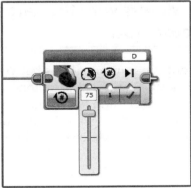

Figure 4-13: The Power input on the motor

A higher number means more power, which brings faster speed to the motor. But what do negative power numbers mean? As shown in Figure 4-14, the positive or the negative values with the Power input relates to the direction of the motor movement.

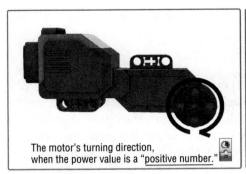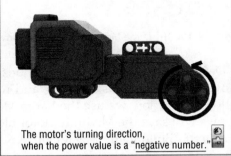

The motor's turning direction, when the power value is a "positive number."

The motor's turning direction, when the power value is a "negative number."

Figure 4-14: The motor Power input and the directions of the motors

When you use the motors for a vehicle-type robot, like the Auto-Driver, positive and negative values are not for having the robot to go forward and backward. Depending on the position of the motor on your robot, you may need a negative value to have the robot go forward and a positive value for backward or vice versa.

Controlling Motors with the Large Motor Block and the Medium Motor Block

You learned about the commonalities between motor blocks, now let's look around each block that controls the motors. We'll start with the Large Motor and Medium Motor blocks and learn about their features.

To begin, create a new program in the Auto-Driver project, and name it **Large-Motor**. Drag a Large Motor block onto the canvas and connect it to the Start block.

Working with the Large Motor Block

In Figure 4-15, you'll see what should now be painfully obvious; the Large Motor block controls a single large motor. This is opposed to the Move Tank or Steering blocks, which control two large motors. Right now we are just concentrating on controlling one solitary motor.

Figure 4-15: The Large Motor block on the canvas

Depending on what mode you choose, you will be able to control the motor's movement by seconds, degrees, and rotations, as well as by its power. In the following section, we use the Large Motor block to program the Auto-Driver, but we will save the Medium Motor block until you use the medium motor in Chapter 7, "Building the Spy Rabbit: A Robot That Can React to Its Surroundings." The Medium Motor block is designed exactly the same way as the Large Motor block, but it is for controlling the medium motor.

Creating Programs with the Large Motor Block

The Auto-Driver has two large motors in ports B and C, but we will try to program only one of them for now. Let's select port B in the port selector (see Figure 4-16). According to this block, the motor that is plugged into port B will make one rotation and then stop.

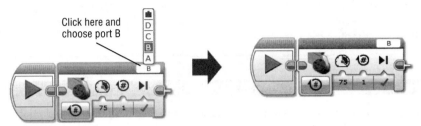

Figure 4-16: Program the motor in port B to make one rotation.

Download the code to the robot, and before you run the program, place the Auto-Driver as shown in Figure 4-17. Let's call the motor in port B the left motor and the one in port C the right motor.

Figure 4-17: The left motor and right motor on the Auto-Driver

Run the code and see happens to the Auto-Driver. Did it make an almost 90° turn to its right side? You can get the same result by controlling the left motor with the On for Seconds mode or the On for Degrees mode.

TRY IT: MAKE A FULL TURN, AUTO-DRIVER!

Try programming the Auto-Driver to make a 360° turn and come back to where it was. You will need only one Large Motor block, and you can try all three modes: On for Seconds, On for Degrees, and On for Rotations. Note that there can be various ways of programming to accomplish the same task.

TRY IT: UH-HUH, ARE YOU NERVOUS, AUTO-DRIVER?

Make a program that uses four Large Motor blocks. Have the first and third blocks to move the right motor for 1 second with the power of 50 and have the second and fourth blocks to control the left motor with the same setting. Download and run the program. Is your Auto-Driver bumbling around?

Measuring the Motor Degrees and Rotations

You may realize from the earlier Try It sidebar that instructing the robot to make a 360° turn and instructing the motor to turn 360 degrees will bring about two different results. To have the Auto-Driver make a 360° turn, you may have experimented with different modes and with multiple values. When programming, these experimental attempts are very important, but there is a tool that makes writing your final program a little bit easier. That tool is the Port View app on the EV3 brick. With it, you can measure the degrees or rotations that the motor makes when the robot make a particular turn. Here's how to use it:

1. Find the Port View app on the EV3 brick (see Figure 4-18). The screen will show you that there are two motors plugged into ports B (left motor) and C (right motor).

Figure 4-18: The Port View with the Auto-Driver

2. Navigate to port B to see the screen as shown in Figure 4-19.

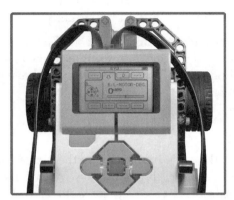

Figure 4-19: Select port B on the Auto-Driver.

3. Now pick up the Auto-Driver and set it down so that the swivel wheel is facing you. Hold down the right motor with one of your hands and manually turn the Auto-Driver until it makes a full turn. Do you see the degree numbers change on the screen (see Figure 4-20)?

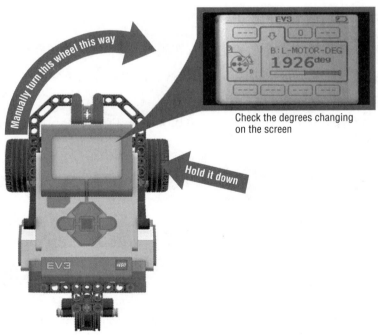

Figure 4-20: Manually turn the Auto-Driver to see how many degrees its left motor should go to make a full turn.

4. Come back to the program Large-Motor and change the mode to the On for Degrees mode. Insert the value that you observed in the degrees input. Does the Auto-Driver turn like when you turned it manually?

If you used the On for Degrees mode for the first Try It sidebar, you may realize that the number of degrees that you used is quite similar to the one that you got from the Port View. This method can be useful if you want to have your robot to make a specific movement.

Using Two Programming Sequences

You may realize that in a sequence of the code that includes the Large Motor block, you can control only one of the Auto-Driver's motors. With only one motor on, the Auto-Driver only turns. In other words, to have the Auto-Driver go straight, you need to have two motors active at the same time with the same settings. To do this with the Large Motor blocks, you must create two lines of code, each with the Large Motor block. As mentioned previously, you can have more than one line of code, and it seems like as good of a time as any to try it out:

1. Create a program called **Large-Motor-Straight**, and then line up the blocks as shown in Figure 4-21.

Figure 4-21: Program the left motor to go on for 2 seconds with the power of 75

2. Copy and paste the sequence of the blocks (follow the instructions in Figure 4-22) and change port B to C.

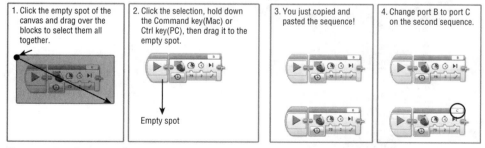

Figure 4-22: Program the Auto-Driver to move straight with two sequences of code

Once you download and run the program, these two lines of code will be executed at the same time and it will make the Auto-Driver move in a straight direction.

Using multiple lines of code can enrich your program, but it is quite a great deal of work to have this simple movement, isn't it? Luckily, there are programming blocks that enable you to control two large motors simultaneously: the Move Steering and Move Tank blocks.

Controlling Two Motors with the Move Steering Block

With the Move Steering block, you can control two large motors together. You can use this block to program a vehicle-type robot that has two driving wheels and have the robot drive straight, turn, or stop. With the Large Motor block, you can only get a tight turn, but with the Move Steering block, you can create a wider range of turns.

Working with the Move Steering Block

Before trying some programs with the Move Steering block, in this section, you'll learn its features and how they control the large motors. As you can see in Figure 4-23, the Move Steering block has a special input, a steering value that determines the angle of a turn.

Figure 4-23: The Move Steering block on the canvas

How does the steering work with a two-motor controlled robot vehicle like the Auto-Driver? (It doesn't have a steering wheel!) You steer this type of robot vehicle by setting different power levels for each motor. The motor that has more power will go faster than its counterpart, and it will be outside of the turning arc that the robot makes. If the difference of the power between two motors is higher, the curve that the robot creates will be tighter. When we used the Large Motor block, one motor was energized and the other was not even on. This created a power difference and is why the Auto-Driver turned. If the difference of the power between two motors is smaller, the curve that the robot makes will be looser (see Figure 4-24). Well, what if there is no power difference between two motors? If the both motors' power levels are the same, the vehicle will go straight without any curve.

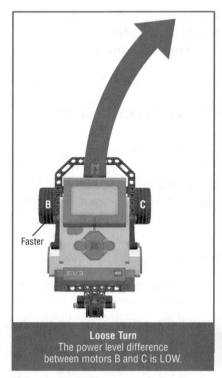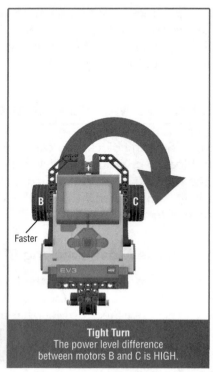

Figure 4-24: Tight turn vs. loose turn

When you use the steering value, the orientation of the two motors should be the same, as shown in Figure 4-25.

It is important to define which of the motors will be the left motor or the right motor, because it will make it easier to visualize the direction of the curve. When you place the Auto-Driver so that it is pointed away from you (the swivel wheel is in the back), the motor on your left is the left motor, and the other one is the right. When you choose the ports in the block, the port that your left motor is plugged into should be on the left side in the port selector, and the port of the right motor should be on the right side (see Figure 4-26).

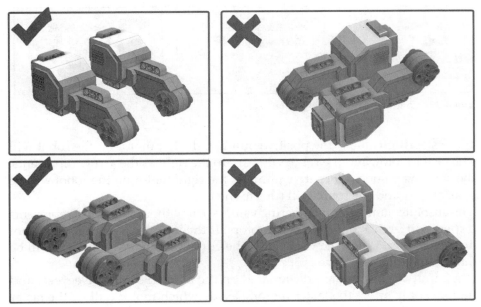

Figure 4-25: The orientations of two motors on the robot vehicle should be the same.

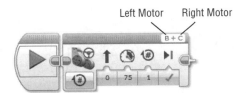

Figure 4-26: Setting the ports in the Move Steering block

When you click the steering value input, you will get the control bar that you can move left to right or right to left. As you move the bar, you will see the symbol of the Steering input change, from a straight arrow to a bended arrow, which shows how the vehicle will turn (see Figure 4-27).

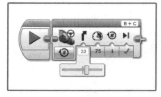 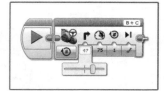 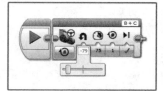

Figure 4-27: Controlling the steering value

If the steering value is the positive number, the left motor on the robot will be the faster motor, and the robot will turn to the right as the arrow represents. If the steering value is a negative number, the right motor on the robot will be the faster one, and the robot will turn to the left.

The absolute number of the steering value (see it without the – sign) represents the speed difference between two motors. If the number is higher, the robot will steer tighter. When the value is 60, the curve that the robot makes will be tighter than when the value is 30.

The input values that are designated on the block (Seconds, Degrees, and Rotations) only affect the faster motor. Decide which motor will be the faster motor by setting up the steering value first, then set up the duration of that motor by seconds, degrees, or rotations. The settings of the other motor will be adjusted accordingly to embody the turn that the Steering input delivers (see Figure 4-28).

Seconds   Degrees   Rotations

Figure 4-28: Controlling other input values

Creating Programs with the Move Steering Block

Now that you know how steering works and how to control the Move Steering block, let's visualize various steering values with the Auto-Driver:

1. Create another program in the Auto-Driver project and name it **Move-Steering-10**.

2. Create an additional program and name it **Move-Steering-50**.

   We will try to make the Auto-Driver change its position (like in Figure 4-29; it doesn't matter how far it moves as long as it changes its position in a 90° angle) by using two different steering values, 10 and 50. Let's see how they make for different turns.

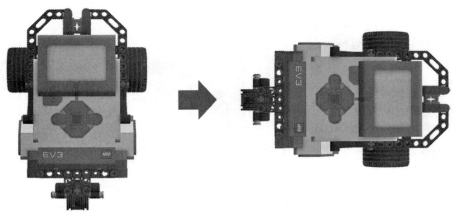

Figure 4-29: Changing the Auto-Driver's position in a 90° angle

3. Create the codes for the Move Steering-10 and the Move-Steering-50 programs to resemble the image in Figure 4-30. The mode and input values of the Move Steering block for each program should be same (Power: 75 and Rotations: 2). The steering values, however, will be different.

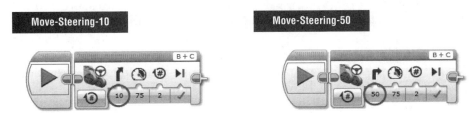

Figure 4-30: Programming the Motor Steering Block with different steering values

4. Download both programs to the Auto-Driver and check the results. Did you get movements from each program that looked like the image in Figure 4-31? As discussed before, the program with the lower steering values made a smooth, wide arc, and the one with the higher steering value made a quick, tight arc.

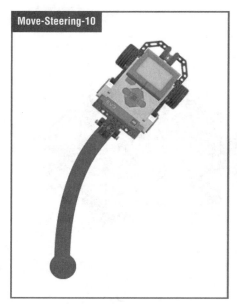

Figure 4-31: The outcomes of the programs Move-Steering-10 and Move-Steering-50

NOTE Note that if the surface upon which you run your Auto-Driver is not smooth, you might get a different outcome.

The Move-Steering -10 program stopped the Auto-Driver too soon before it got to a 90° angle. However, the Move-Steering -50 program let the Auto-Driver go too long, and so it passed the point where it was supposed to stop. You can solve these problems in various ways. You can try a new steering value, reset the seconds that the motor should be on, and adjust the degrees or rotations that the motor should make. Figure 4-32 shows some modification examples.

Figure 4-32: Modify the programs to get the correct result.

As the preceding exercise shows, even if the Steering block makes it easier to program turns, you will still need to experiment with various steering values or adjust the other input values in the block to have a robot turn the way that you want.

Breaking Down a Task into Several Actions

Each programming block can have multiple functions, but it can execute only one action at a time. For example, the Move Steering block has the capability to program the robot to go forward, backward, turn, or stop; but Move Steering can execute only one of these actions for each time that it occurs in the program. So when you plan the code for your robot, it is helpful to break the task down into several segments that correspond to the job that each programming block should process. For instance, when you program the robot to go around the shape like the left image in Figure 4-33, it will be helpful to break it down as the image on the right side of Figure 4-33.

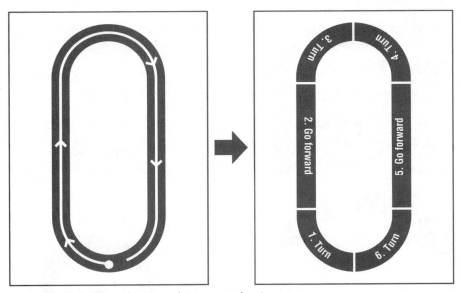

Figure 4-33: Breaking down a task into several actions

Keep in mind that one programming block can only do one job at a time! This method will be useful to solve more complicated challenges.

TRY IT: BE CAREFUL AUTO-DRIVER! YOU'RE DRIVIN' ON THE EDGE

Set up a low, rectangular-shaped table or outline a rectangle on the floor with masking tape (safer). Program the Auto-Driver to go around the edges of the table (or tape shape) and come back to the starting point. The programming order should be "go forward for a certain duration" and then "steer to a certain angle" for the first edge, then "go forward" and "turn" again for the second edge. Repeat this until the fourth edge. You will need eight Motor Steering blocks in total. Try to program an accurate turn at each corner, because if you don't the Auto-Driver may fall off (or deviate from the tape outline). Keep a close eye on your robot and catch it if it falls from the table. The idea is for you to make a series of accurately tuned programming blocks, not to break your friend the Auto-Driver.

Creating a Spiral Turn

With the Motor Steering block, you can make the robot go in circles fairly easily. Depending on the steering values, the robot can make circles of various diameters. See the two examples in Figure 4-34.

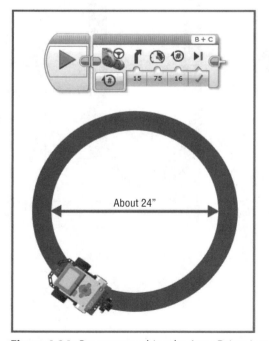
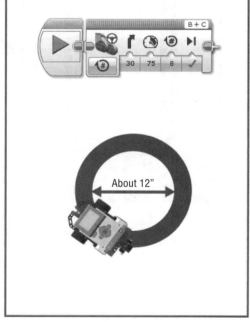

Figure 4-34: Programs to drive the Auto-Driver in two different sized circles

As you may realize, if the steering value is higher, most likely the size of the circle will be smaller, and the robot's travel time is shorter to finish the circle. Conversely, if the steering value is smaller, the size of the circle will be bigger and so the robot needs to travel more to complete the circle.

Can you make the Auto-Driver follow the spiral shape shown in Figure 4-35, from the outermost point to the innermost point?

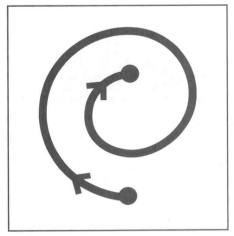

Figure 4-35: The spiral shape

Let's begin by thinking how many program blocks you will need. If you can break down this spiral shape like the image in Figure 4-36, you'll see that you can program Auto-Driver to drive three half circles that are progressively smaller from the outside in.

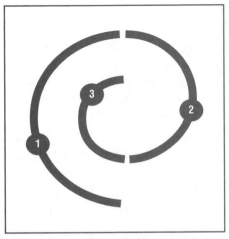

Figure 4-36: Breaking down the spiral shape into three half circles

Create a new program called **Move-Steering-Spiral** and make a line of code with three Move Steering blocks. You'll need to use a different steering value and adjust other input values for each block to keep the motor on until the robot completes the corresponding half circle. Following this reasoning, I created the program shown in Figure 4-37. The half-circles in Figure 4-36 are getting smaller, so the steering value should be increasing from the first block to the last block. For the same reason, the duration of the motor for each block should be getting smaller. Also I chose the Coast for the Brake at End input to have smoother connections between the half-circles.

Figure 4-37: The program for the Auto-Driver to go though the spiral shape

Try to design your own spiral shape. Don't worry, the Auto-Driver is a tough robot. It won't get seasick if you make it drive in circles over and over again.

Using the Move Tank Block to Control the Power Level of a Motor

The next block to explore is the Move Tank block. With this block, you can control each motor's power level. You can change two motor's speeds and turning directions by adjusting their power level separately. Let's begin by creating a program called **Move-Tank** in the Auto-Driver project.

Working with the Move Tank Block

If you use this block to program the vehicle that has two motors with the same orientation, it can be used similarly to the Move Steering block. It can control the vehicle robot as it goes forward, backward, turns, and stops, just like the Move Steering block. But the difference is the control system that makes the robot turn.

As always, defining the left motor and the right motor on the robot is important:

1. Make sure that the left (right) motor is the motor on your left (right) side when you have the swivel wheel facing toward you. Then set up the ports in the port selector so that the left port is the port that has the left motor plugged in and the other one is for the right motor.

2. Drag the Move Tank block from the palette, and then connect it to the Start block, as shown in Figure 4-38.

You will find that there are two Power inputs. (Reminder: The power input affects the speed and the turning direction of the motor.) The Power input on the left is for the motor that is plugged in the port that is on the left side in the port selector, and the other Power input is for the motor that is in the right port in the port selector.

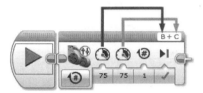

Figure 4-38: The Move Tank block

3. You can now define how aggressively your robot turns by controlling the power level for each motor.

As you learned in "Controlling Two Motors with the Move Steering Block," the difference between the power levels between the motors defines the shape of the arc that the robot will make. When you use the Move Steering block, it decides how to power the motors according to the "steering value" that you set. With the Move Tank block, however, you must manually control the power level of both motors to turn.

Creating Programs with the Move Tank Block

Let's see how the other standard block inputs work along with the two Power inputs in this block. When you choose the On for Seconds mode, both of the motors will be energized with their corresponding power level for the length of time that you define. When you choose On for Degrees or Rotations modes, the motors will be on until one of the motors reaches that duration. See the examples in Figure 4-39.

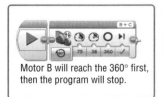

Motor B will reach the 360° first, then the program will stop.

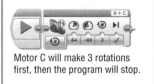

Motor C will make 3 rotations first, then the program will stop.

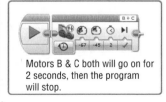

Motors B & C both will go on for 2 seconds, then the program will stop.

Figure 4-39: How the block inputs work in the Move Tank block

TRY IT: MAKE AN OBSTACLE COURSE WITH THE OBJECTS AROUND YOU

Now that you know all the ways to control your Auto-Driver, let's have a go through an obstacle course. Set up a start point and end point in your room, and then place some objects as obstacles between them and see whether you can program the Auto-Driver to go though to the end point without bumping into the obstacles.

Summary

In this chapter, you learned about the following:

- The basics of block programming
- The input values that control the motors: power level, seconds, motor degrees, and rotations
- How to use the motor blocks: the Large Motor, Medium Motor, Move Steering, and Move Tank blocks
- How to use the Port View with the motors

Exploring Action Blocks Part 2: Using Display, Sound and Brick Status Light Blocks

In Chapter 4, "Exploring Action Blocks Part 1: Programming Motors," you learned how to use the motor blocks to move the Auto-Driver. By now, you've seen that there are more than just motor blocks in the Action blocks palette (green tab). Let's say that you want to add custom images or text to the EV3 brick display or make a robot play a sequence of tones. Then this would be the moment that you have been waiting for. Venture forth and add a little character to that robot.

The Display Block

You've learned that the EV3 screen allows you to run programs, use the brick apps, and check the brick's info. You can actually program the robot to display different things on the screen, such as text, shapes, stock images, and even custom images. The programming block that allows you to do all of these things is the Display block. You can find it in the Action blocks palette (green tab) and it looks like the image shown in Figure 5-1.

Figure 5-1: The Display block on the palette (left) and on the canvas (right)

This block has several modes to display custom content on the screen, and each mode brings up corresponding block inputs. You will always see three inputs with all the modes: Clear Screen, X, and Y (see Figure 5-2).

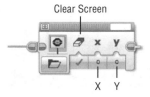

Figure 5-2: Common block inputs on the Display block

If you click the box under the icon of the Clear Screen input, which looks like an eraser, you will get two input values: True or False. If the input value is True, the screen will be cleared up before this block displays anything. If it is False, the contents that you program will be added on top of whatever is already on the screen.

Before we take a look at the X and Y inputs, let's check out the dimensions of the screen on the EV3 brick. It is a small, rectangular-shaped, black-and-white screen—178 pixels in width and 128 pixels in height. Wait, but what is a pixel? The definition of a pixel may vary depending on the context, but pixels can be broadly defined as the smallest elements of a screen or digital image. (Imagine graph paper; each square is like a pixel.) If you could enlarge the EV3 screen as shown in Figure 5-3, you would see rows of small pixels.

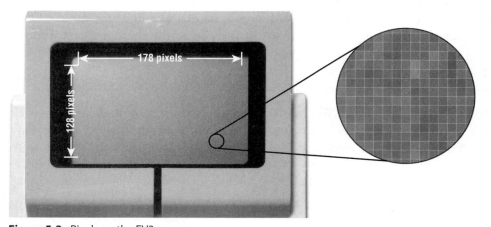

Figure 5-3: Pixels on the EV3 screen

When we talk about groups of pixels, we refer to them in "rows" and "columns." A row is a horizontal line of pixels (left to right), while a column is a vertical stack (top to bottom). Each pixel in a row has its own assigned number.

They start with pixel 0 on the left of the row and go up by increments of 1 as you move to the right. The number of the pixel within a row is called the X-coordinate. Each row of pixels also has a number, which begins with 0 at the top and increases in increments of 1 for each row as you move toward the bottom. The number that we use to identify each row is called the Y-coordinate (see Figure 5-4), which also tells us when a pixel is located within its column.

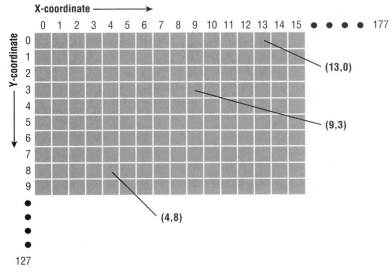

Figure 5-4: The X- and Y-coordinates on the EV3 screen

Using this convention, each pixel will have one X-coordinate value and one Y-coordinate value, which will indicate the position of the pixel on the screen. These coordinates will be written as an ordered pair (X, Y). On the EV3 screen, the range of the X values run from 0 to 177 (a sum of 178 pixels), and the Y values go from 0 to 127 (a sum of 128 pixels).

TIP The Display block has a helpful feature that enables you to preview what your program will display on the EV3 brick screen. If you click the Display Preview button in the upper-left corner of the block, you will see a small screen pop up right above the block (see Figure 5-5). I highly recommend you to open the Display Preview when you program with the Display block.

Displaying Text: The Text-Pixels and Grid Modes

With the Display block, you can set simple text characters, numbers, and symbols to show on the EV3 brick's screen. It supports most of the common characters, but not all of them. See Figure 5-6 to see the supported symbols and text. If you use unsupported characters, they won't appear on the EV3 screen or on the Display Preview.

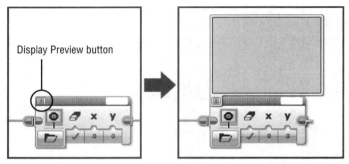

Figure 5-5: The Display Preview shows how items will be shown on the screen.

```
! " # $ % & ' ( ) + * , - . / 0 1 2 3 4 5 6 7 8 9 : ; < = > ? °
@ a b c d e f g h I j k l m n o p q r s t u v w x y z [ \ ] ^ _ √
A B C D E F G H I J K L M N O P Q R S T U V W X Y Z { | }
```

Figure 5-6: Symbols and text that are supported by EV3

Two modes on the Display block enable you to put text on the brick's screen. If you click the mode area and move your cursor over to the Text option, you'll find two options: Pixels and Grid. Let's take a look at the Text-Pixels mode first.

Text-Pixels Mode

To explore Text-Pixels mode, start by creating a new program in the Auto-Driver project and name it **Displaying Text**. Then complete the following steps:

1. Drag and connect the Display block to the Start block. If you choose the Text-Pixels mode, the block will look like Figure 5-7.

Figure 5-7: The Text-Pixels mode

2. Click the Display Preview button to turn on the preview screen. Do you see MINDSTORMS on the preview? The box on the upper-right corner of the block also shows the same text.

3. Click the box and type in something new. The text on the preview should change along with the new input (see Figure 5-8). You can type a long sentence, but only the part that fits in the screen will be shown, so be concise.

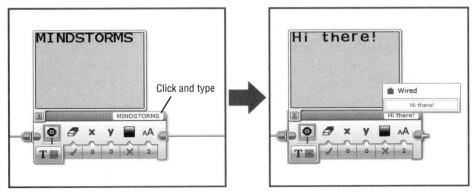

Figure 5-8: Type into the text box and see the content change in the Display Preview.

When you click the Text box, you'll see the Wired option. This option let you pull input values from other blocks. In addition to block connecting, in EV3 programming there is another technique called *data wiring*. (You'll learn more about this in Chapter 11, "Programming with Data Wires and My Blocks," and even use the Wired option.)

Other than the Clear Screen input, there are four inputs that define the position and formatting of the onscreen text: X, Y, Color, and Font. As discussed earlier, the X and Y values mean the X- coordinate and the Y-coordinate of a pixel. In this mode, (X, Y) refers to the coordinate of the pixel that is on the top-left corner of the text (see Figure 5-9). By changing the X and Y values, you can alter the position of the text.

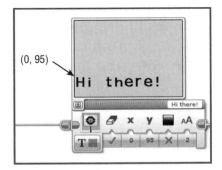

Figure 5-9: Setting the position of the text on the screen

The input next to the X and Y inputs is the Color. There can be two values, White (true) and Black (false). If you choose White, the text will be white with a black background, like the left image in Figure 5-10. Conversely, choosing Black will display the text black with a clear background.

Figure 5-10: Black and White color options for the text

The last input in this mode is the Font. This input decides the formatting of the text by changing its size and thickness. There are three values, which go from 0 to 2. The 0 value will display the text in the normal size; the 1 value will keep the text at the normal size, but make the text bold; and the 2 value will enlarge the text to greater than normal size. See the example in Figure 5-11.

 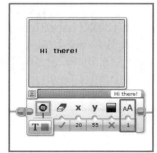 

Figure 5-11: Formatting text

4. Let's change the input values on the block to display your name on the center of the screen.

5. Download the program to the EV3 brick and try running it.

Did anything happen? Did nothing happen? Don't worry—this is normal. The reason why it seemed like nothing happened is because the EV3 brick immediately clears up the screen when the program ends. With only one block, your program was over in an instant, and the evidence of your work was immediately wiped from the brick's screen.

To keep your new display message on, you must make the program run for a longer duration by adding other blocks after the Display block. If the Display block is followed by a motor block, for example, the text will stay on the screen for as long as the motor stays running (see Figure 5-12).

Figure 5-12: The Display block with the Move steering block; the name will remain on the screen until motors B and C make three full rotations.

In life, there is always more than one way to complete an action. Programming is often the same way. You will almost certainly hit a roadblock while you are coding and be forced to find another way to get the results that you want. This is problem solving, and it is a necessary skill for programmers, engineers, and everyone in the world. Keeping the text on the screen by using a motor block certainly does work, but there are other ways to do so. The Wait block is a simple solution to the text display problem. You can find it under the orange tab, second block from the left (see Figure 5-13).

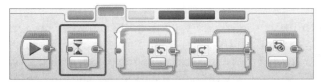

Figure 5-13: The Wait block

This block is equipped with various modes, but in this chapter we use only the Time mode, the default setting when you drag the block to the canvas. The Wait block with the Time mode set will make the program wait for the assigned time until the next action.

6. Drag the Wait block and connect it next to the Display block that you created and put **3** in its input section to have a program that looks like the one in Figure 5-14.

Figure 5-14: The Display block with the Wait block

In this program, no other block follows the Wait block, which means that the next action after the 3-second wait will be to "end the program." When you run this program, the EV3 brick will show your name (or whatever you write) on the center of the screen for 3 seconds and then end the program.

Text-Grid Mode

Another way to display the text on the screen is by using the Text-Grid mode. Let's clear up the canvas and have just one Display block connected to the Start block. If you choose the Text-Grid mode, you will see two new inputs: Column (X) and Row (Y) (see Figure 5-15).

Figure 5-15: The Text-Grid mode

With this mode, you can think of the screen with a grid system as shown in Figure 5-16. Instead of breaking down the screen with pixels, it divides the screen with 22 columns and 12 rows. The X value refers to the column numbers, which determines how far from the left side of the screen the text should begin. The Y value is the row number, which defines how far down from the top of the screen the text should go.

The height of the row corresponds to the height of a normal-sized (font: 0) or a bolded (font: 1) text character. This means the Y values become the line numbers of the text. It makes it easier to set up multiple lines of the text on the screen because instead of calculating how many pixels you need between the lines; you can just set up the line number.

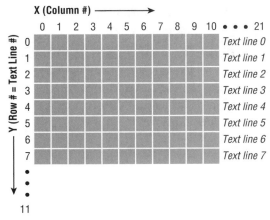

Figure 5-16: The EV3 screen with the grid: The number of the row represents the number of the text line.

TRY IT: BE MY MESSENGER, AUTO-DRIVER

Now that you know how to make the Auto-Driver display the text, let's have him deliver messages. First of all, you need to program the Auto-Driver to drive to the receiver using the motor blocks, then, have the Display block show the message on the screen. Don't forget to add the Wait block after the Display block to set up how long the text should be staying on the screen. If you want to have multiple lines, you need more than one Display block, and the following blocks after the first one should have the false value for the Clear Screen input.

TRY IT: SLIDING TEXT EFFECT

Can we try to have your name rise from the bottom of the screen and move to the top? It would be just like the ending credits for a film, but with your name. Here are some steps that you can follow (but feel free to try your own way):

1. Connect the Display block and choose the Text-Pixels. Type your name into the Text box and keep the Font value as 2.
2. Adjust the X value to have the name almost in the middle of the horizontal side.
3. Use 127 for the Y value.
4. Connect the Wait block and give it 0.5 seconds to wait.

You'll want to repeat this procedure four times, which means connecting eight more blocks in the order of D (Display block) – W (Wait block) – D – W – D – W – D – W, each with the same text and X settings, but different Y values. The Y values should be getting smaller, say 98, 66, 27, and –14.

Drawing Shapes: The Line, Circle, Rectangle, and Point Modes

In addition to showing text, you can also draw different shapes such as a point, line, circle, or rectangle on the screen. Go back to the EV3 software and create a new program. Name it **Displaying-Shapes** and then drag over a Display block and connect it to the Start block. If you click the mode area and hover your cursor over Shapes, you will see the list of the shapes that you can create (see Figure 5-17). We'll take a look at each of these shapes next.

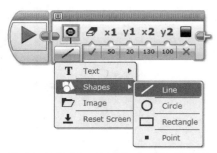

Figure 5-17: The Shapes mode on the Display block

Line Mode

If you choose the Shapes – Line mode, you will get the block with the inputs as shown in Figure 5-18.

Figure 5-18: The Shapes – Line mode

You may better understand how these inputs work if you imagine how you draw a line with a pencil. You would start from one point and move the pencil to the second point. The X1 and Y1 coordinate refers the position of the first or starting point, and the X2 and Y2 coordinate represents the location of the second or ending point of the line (see Figure 5-19).

The last input to the right, Color, is to set the color of the line. It has two values, True and False, and they present two colors, white and black. Once again, anticipating what your drawings will look like on the screen will be easier if you keep the Display Preview open.

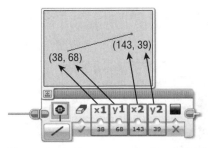

Figure 5-19: How to use the inputs to draw a line

Circle Mode

Now let's take a look at the Circle mode. Does your block have inputs like the block in the left image of Figure 5-20? Programming the brick to draw a circle is like drawing a circle with a compass. When using a compass, you will first adjust the distance between the pencil and the needle. The longer the distance, the larger the circle will be. Then, you hold down the needle and rotate the pencil side around the needle until you have a complete circle. As you can see in the right image of Figure 5-20, the X- and Y-coordinates mark where the compass needle sat, specifying the center of the circle. The radius is the measure of the distance between the needle and the pencil, defining the size of the circle.

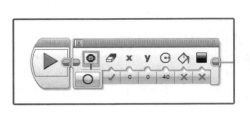
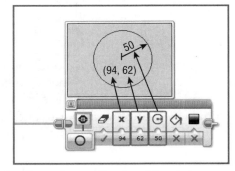

Figure 5-20: The Shapes – Circle mode and defining the center and the size of the circle

To review, the Color input (the last input to the right) sets the color of the outline of the circle. The True value will give you a white outline, and the False value will display a black outline. The value next to the Color input is the Fill input. It can also have two input values, True or False. When it is True, the circle will be filled with the color that you choose for the Color input, black or white.

The False value will leave the circle clear, and you will only see the outline of it (see Figure 5-21).

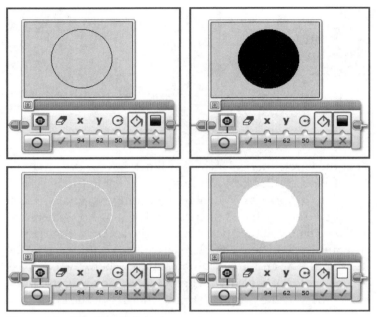

Figure 5-21: The Fill and Color inputs

Rectangle Mode

If you choose the Rectangle mode, you will see some new inputs. As Figure 5-22 shows, the X and Y values specify the top-left corner of the rectangle, which determines its position on the screen. You can set up the dimensions of the rectangle by changing the width and height values. If you use the same values for both the width and height, you will get a square.

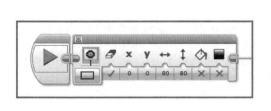

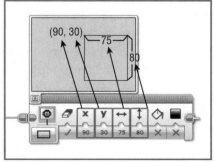

Figure 5-22: The Shapes – Rectangle mode and setting up the dimensions of the rectangle

You will also get the Fill and Color inputs, and they work exactly the same as they did with the Circle mode.

TRY IT: MAKE PATTERNS

Now that you know how to create different types of shapes, let's give the Auto-Driver cool patterns. Figure 5-23 shows some patterns that you can try.

Figure 5-23: Patterns on the EV3 screen

See what patterns you can make. Here are some tips that can help you when you program your design:

1. The Clean Screen input value should always be False in all the Display blocks except the first one.
2. The shape that goes in the back should be programmed first.
3. After all the Display blocks, there should be the Wait block to tell how long the shapes should last.

Point Mode

The last shape you can draw is the simplest one of all, a point. Choose the Point mode and you will get the inputs shown in left image of Figure 5-24. Don't they all look familiar? Basically, the point is a single pixel on the screen, and with this mode, you can pick a pixel to fill in by setting up the X- and Y-coordinates and then coloring it with either white or black. The point is very small, smaller than salt and pepper flakes, so open your eyes wide when you use this mode. By controlling the colors (white or black) of individual points, you can present some unique effects on the screen. For example, you can make the screen dissolve in and out or visualize the data from a sensor as a graph. They require advanced programming skills, so it won't be easy to try now, but soon!

Displaying Images: The Image Mode

Did you have fun with playing with the shapes? More fun is coming in this section. Other than drawing shapes, you can also display predrawn images on the screen. Like Figure 5-25 shows, the inputs of this mode should all be familiar to you.

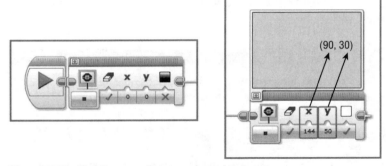

Figure 5-24: The Shapes – Point mode and its inputs

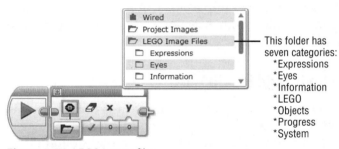

Figure 5-25: The Image mode and its inputs

The Clear Screen input either clears the screen before showing any other contents or let the contents from the previous block stay. The X- and Y-coordinates determine the location of the top-left corner of the image, thus enabling you to position the image. Then how do you get the images? If you click the File Name box on the top-right corner of the block, it will open a small window.

Pulling the Image from the LEGO Image Files Folder

After you open the little window, do you see the LEGO Image Files folder? This folder has the images that come with the EV3 brick. All the images are organized in seven different categories, and each has a variety of images (see Figure 5-26). You will only see the filenames in the image folders, but if you look at the User Guide that comes with the set (page 51~55), you will find all the images with the names.

Figure 5-26: LEGO image files

When you click the image file that you want to put on the screen, the Display Preview window pops up automatically and shows the image that you picked, as shown in Figure 5-27. I picked the Love file in the Eyes image folder.

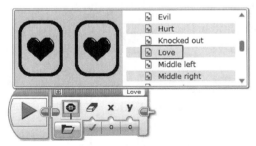

Figure 5-27: Image showing in the Display Preview

Let's connect another Display block and click the File Name box. Do you see the filename that you used for the first block in the Project Image folder? For your convenience, the software will save the recently used files in the Project Image folder. They will also be listed in the Images section in the Project Properties (see Figure 5-28).

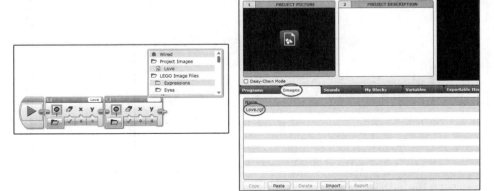

Figure 5-28: You will find the recently used files in the Project Image folder as well as in the Project Properties.

TRY IT: AUTO-DRIVER HAS EYES

Try creating fun face expressions on the Auto-Driver with the LEGO image files. How about some blinking eyes? You can switch back and forth between the Neutral image and Sleeping image in the Eye folder. Create various combinations with these images and give the Auto-Driver a chance to express its emotions.

Using the Image Editor

LEGO has a lot of cool images, but wouldn't it be more fun if you could use the image that you created? Fortunately, the EV3 software has a tool that enables you to design and edit your own image to make it suitable for the screen:

1. Go to Tools on the menu bar and choose the Image Editor. Did you get this new window to pop up (see Figure 5-29)?

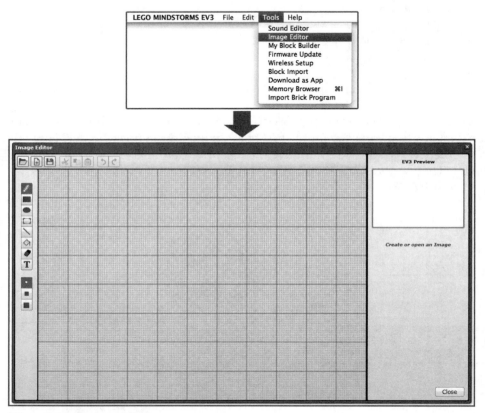

Figure 5-29: The Image Editor

Figure 5-30 shows you how the Image Editor is designed. There are many tools that let you draw your own graphics that can also be used to edit an image that you import from your computer.

If you only want to draw your own image, you can just start drawing as soon as you open the Image Editor. If you want to edit an existing image, though, you need to complete a few more steps:

2. Click the Open button and find the image on your computer that you want to edit; it will then appear in the editing area (see Figure 3-31).

You can zoom in and out to have the image fit in the EV3 screen. Note that monochromatic images work best when importing. An image with many colors and shades won't be displayed well when it's converted to the EV3 screen.

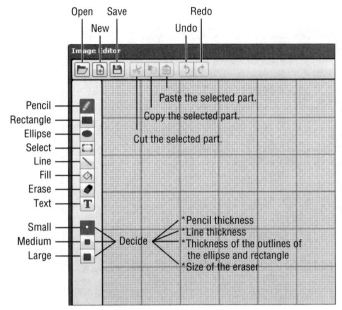

Figure 5-30: Editing tools in the Image Editor

Figure 5-31: Open the image file and adjust its size by using the Zoom-In and Zoom-Out buttons.

3. Click the Next button. Doing so will bring you to the page where you can adjust the contrast of the image. At this point, the image will become black and white.

4. Click the Next button again to display the editing page where you may customize the image (see Figure 5-32).

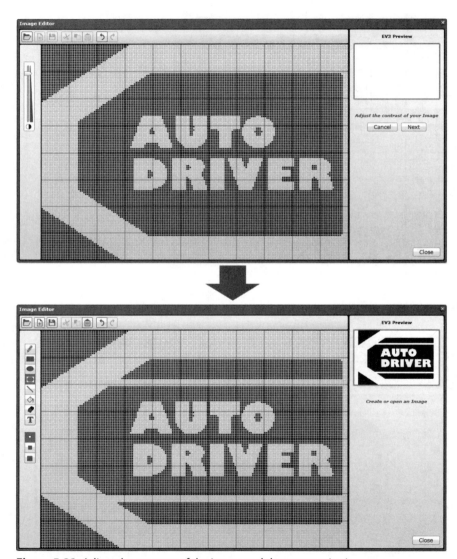

Figure 5-32: Adjust the contrast of the image and then customize it.

5. When you have finished editing, click the Cave button on the top menu, give it a name, and then save it.

This image file will be listed on the Images tab in the Project Properties, and it will also show up in the Project Images folder (see Figure 5-33). If you draw graphics without any image importing, you can just save the final graphic, and it will also appear in the Project Properties and in the Project Images folder.

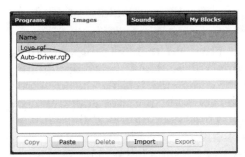
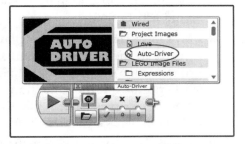

Figure 5-33: The customized image will be listed in Project Properties and in the Project Images folder.

Resetting the Display: The Reset Screen Mode

At some point after all of this image display exploration, you may want to go back to the default setting. You can use the Reset Screen mode to do this. It is the last mode on the Display block. When this mode executes in a program, the screen will reset and show the default information.

The Sound Block

You might have noticed that the EV3 brick makes sounds when you turn it on and off or download programs. It has a built-in speaker, and you can program it to play prerecorded sounds or a sound that you compose. Let's create another program and call it **Playing-Sound**. Drag the Sound block into the canvas and connect it to the Start block. There are four different modes, and each one has two common inputs, except for the Stop mode (see Figure 5-34).

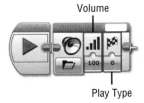

Figure 5-34: The Sound block and the Volume and Play Type inputs

The first common input is Volume, which controls the loudness of the sound, and the range of that value goes from 0 to 100. It works just like a volume control for any speaker.

The second one is the Play Type input. When you click this input section, it shows you three options (see Figure 5-35):

- **Wait for Completion**: This option plays the sound once completely before the program moves to the next block. In other words, it isn't affected by other blocks, and no matter what, the next block should wait until the sound is complete.

- **Play Once**: This option starts playing the sound; then the program moves directly to the next block. Unlike the Wait for Completion option, the program won't wait for the sound to be completed. It is like the next block starts running at the same time as the sound begins. The sound will go on and be played once while the next block is running. If there are no following blocks, you won't hear a sound.

- **Repeat**: This one works like the Play Once option but it plays the sound over and over again until the program sees the next Sound block.

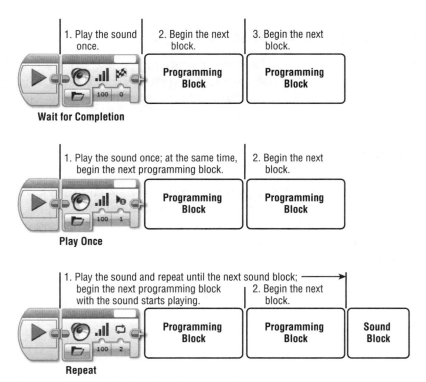

Figure 5-35: How the Play Type inputs work

Play File Mode

Let's go over the Play File mode first. The EV3 software offers various sounds that you can choose for your robot. This mode is similar to the Image mode in the Display block, but the images are replaced with sounds. If you click the File Name box, you will see the Project Sounds and LEGO Sounds file folders.

Using the Prerecorded Sounds

In the LEGO Sounds folder, all the prerecorded sounds are organized in nine categories. As a convenience, when you click any sound file, the software plays that sound for you (just like the Display Preview shows the image that you choose in the Display block). Once you use the sound, all of the recently played sounds will be saved in the Project Sounds Folder. You can also find them in the Sound section in the Project Properties. Try to have your Auto-Driver play some sounds (see Figure 5-36).

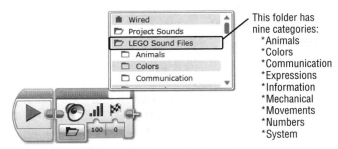

Figure 5-36: Playing the LEGO sounds

Creating Your Own Sounds: Using the Sound Editor

Just like you can design your own image for the Display block, you can also create your own sounds. This time we will use a tool called the Sound Editor:

1. Go to the Tools menu and select Sound Editor. Did you get a pop-up window that looks like the one in the bottom image in Figure 5-37?

You can use this tool in two ways. First, you can use it to record sound and edit it. Alternatively, you can import sounds or music that you have in your computer and then edit that.

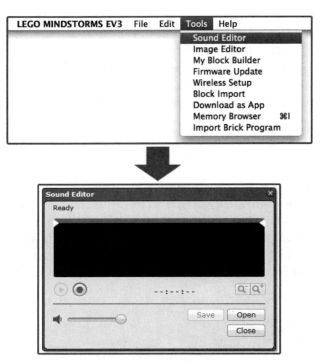

Figure 5-37: Opening the Sound Editor

If you have a built-in or line-in microphone on your computer, you can record your own sound. Click the Record button, the one with the red circle on, and it will start recording for a maximum of 10 seconds. After that, it stops automatically. You can edit the recorded sound if necessary and save it for your project. Let's walk you through the editing process with the example of importing an existing sound. Try following the steps:

2. Click the Open button and find a compatible music file. When you open the file, you will see the waveforms appear in the black window (see Figure 5-38).

If the Save button is grayed out, the current sound file is too big to be saved onto the brick. However, you can solve this problem by editing the sound. You can select the part of the sound that you want to use by moving the two sliders on the top corners of the wave window. The Zoom-In and Zoom-Out buttons can help you make an accurate selection:

3. If necessary, move the sliders or zoom in and out, and the duration of the sound will be changed accordingly (see Figure 5-39).

4. Press the Play button to hear the selected part.

Figure 5-38: The sound file opened in the Sound Editor

Figure 5-39: Editing the sound

Once the sound file is small enough to be saved onto the brick, the Save button becomes available. You can then save the file and have it show up in the Project Sounds folder in the Sound block and in the Sound section in the Project Properties.

Play Tone Mode

The next mode is the Play Tone mode, which allows you to control the tone of a sound. It uses a unit called the hertz (Hz). Let's take a moment to see what it is.

Sounds are waves that travel through the air. Waves are all around us. Some waves we can see, and others we cannot. Light waves can be visible, which means we sense them with our eyes. Sound waves are invisible to the human eye, but we have a pair of ears that can sense them. Visible and invisible waves are remarkably similar in their most basic form. To create a visible wave at home, take a heavy string, phone chord, or jump rope and attach one end to a chair or some other heavy object. Hold the other end in your hand. You will use your hand to produce mechanical energy, which will travel along the line. Moving the line quickly up and down, you will create peaks and valleys, which will travel along the line until they reach the end. Together, those peaks and valleys form a wave. Unlike your jump-rope wave, sound waves are much smaller, and the speed at which peaks and valleys are created is much, much faster.

Not only does your ear pick up the height of the peaks, but also how quickly one peak follows the one before it. The time between peaks is called the frequency. The pitch of a sound is defined by its frequency. High frequencies make higher pitches, and low frequency makes for low pitches.

The unit for frequency is the hertz. Frequencies are written out in the same way you would write out any other unit measurement, with the number and then the unit. So, the frequency of a sound is written as 68Hz, or 218Hz, or 2Hz, and so on. As you can see in the right image in Figure 5-40, when you click the Hz input, it will give the list of the frequencies and their equivalent notes. You can either choose a note or just type in a frequency. The Duration input lets you decide how long you want to have the tone play, measured in seconds.

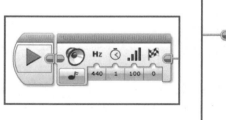
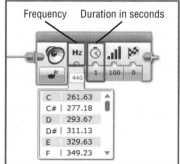

Figure 5-40: The Play Tone mode and the sound Frequency and Duration inputs

Play Note Mode

After Play Tone comes the Play Note mode. You can use this function to play a specific musical note. If you click the Note input section, it will provide a piano keyboard control like that shown in the right image of Figure 5-41, and you will get to choose one of the notes. The letter (C-B) means the name of the musical note, and the number (4-6) next to it represents the octave that that note is in. You can also control the note's duration in seconds.

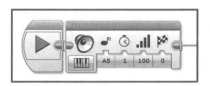
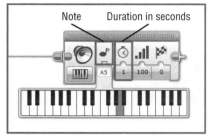

Figure 5-41: The Play Note mode and the Note and Duration inputs

TRY IT: PLAY A SIMPLE SONG

Now that you know how to make musical notes in the EV3 brick, try playing a simple song, like one that would be in a movie about a giant shark. You can imitate the beginning of the song by following these instructions:

E4 (1 sec)
F4 (0.2 sec)
Wait (0.8 sec)
E4 (1 sec)
F4 (0.2 sec)
Wait (0.8 sec)
E4 (0.2 sec)
F4 (0.2sec)
E4 (0.2 sec)
F4 (0.2sec)
E4 (0.2 sec)
F4 (0.2sec)
E4 (0.2 sec)
F4 (0.2sec)
E4 (1 sec)

What do you think? Does it feel like a shark is close by? Try to program the Auto-Driver to perform along with the song.

Stop Mode

If you want to stop all the sounds that you have programmed, you can simply connect another Sound block with the Stop mode. With that, all the sound that was playing previously will stop. However, if you have a block with the Wait for Completion input, it will still finish playing the sound first, and then stop.

The Brick Status Light Block

When you run the Auto-Driver, you might notice that the light around the buttons of the EV3 brick stay on or are blinking. This light is called the Brick status light and it can illuminate itself in red, orange, or green. The light may be set to stay on or blink.

Per the default setting, each light behavior indicates a different brick status:

- When the red light stays on, it means the brick is starting up, updating, or shutting down. When the brick is busy, the light blinks.

- When the brick has any alerts, such as low battery, or when the brick is ready, the orange light stays on. If you see a pulsing light, that either indicates an alert or means that something is running on the brick.

- When the brick is ready for any action, the green light stays on. When the brick is running a program, the light blinks.

You can actually control the light's performance by using the Brick Status Light block.

The On Mode

The first step to control the light is to choose the On mode. With this mode, you can pick the color and its outcome action. As you can see in Figure 5-42, it comes with two inputs, Color and Pulse. In the Color input, you can use numbers that represent green (0), orange (1), or red (2). The Pulse input controls how to present the light. The True value will make the light pulse, and the False value makes the light stay on.

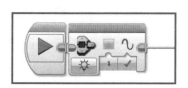 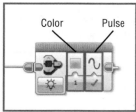

Figure 5-42: The On mode and its inputs

The Off and Reset Modes

The Off mode simply turns off the brick status light. If you want to have no light on your brick whatsoever, you can choose this mode. The Reset mode brings back the default setting. So, when you run the program with this mode, the green light will blink (see Figure 5-43).

Figure 5-43: The Off and Reset modes

Summary

In this chapter, you learned about the following:

- How to display text, shapes, and images on the EV3 brick's screen with the Display block
- How to use the Image Editor
- How to program the sound and musical notes on the EV3 brick with the Sound block
- How to use the Sound Editor
- How to program the brick status light on the EV3 brick

Exploring Flow Blocks

In Chapter 4, "Exploring Action Blocks Part 1: Programming Motors," and Chapter 5, "Exploring Action Blocks Part 2: Using Display, Sound, and Brick Status Light Blocks," we looked through the Action blocks, which are found under the green tab in the programming palettes. We used the Action blocks to program the Auto-Driver to move around, play sounds, and display images on its screen. Under the orange tab next to the green tab, you'll find the Flow blocks. Unlike many of the previously discussed blocks, Flow blocks do not enable the robot to perform an action. Instead, they control the flow of the code.

If you think of the Action blocks as cars on a road, the Flow blocks are the traffic signs. They can make the program start, wait, repeat, or simply follow one line of the code or the other. The Start and Wait blocks that we briefly used in previous chapters are examples of this traffic management. Like traffic signals in the real world, Flow blocks can work with sensors to tweak how the Action blocks behave in the code. This chapter covers Flow block basics like Switch and Loop; more advanced operations such as linking the Flow block with an infrared sensor are discussed in Chapter 8, "Sensing the Environments: Using the Infrared, Touch, and Color Sensors."

The Start Block

As your robot's builder, you have the responsibility of giving it lots of things to do. You know by now that a crucial step in EV3 programming is to connect any and all blocks to the Start block. You will always see this block whenever you create a new program, but if you lose one or accidentally delete it, you can find it in the orange palette (see Figure 6-1).

Figure 6-1: The Start block

You've already read about most of the features of the Start block in previous chapters, so the summary here recaps that information and throws in a few new tips about how to use this block.

Starting the Program

The sequence of the code must begin with the Start block. Blocks that are not connected to this block on the canvas will just sit around and collect digital dust.

You can have multiple lines of code on the canvas, and each one will run along with the others if it has a Start block at the beginning. Even though each line of code begins at the same time, they will run independently and not interact with each other.

Demonstrating the Line of Code

If your robot is connected to the computer via USB cable, Bluetooth or WiFi, you can demonstrate an individual line of the code by clicking the Play button on the Start block. Let's take a look at the example in Figure 6-2.

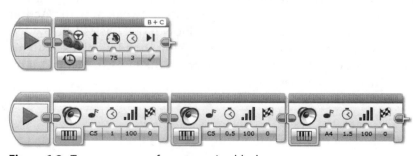

Figure 6-2: Two sequences of programming blocks

The top line of the programming blocks makes the Auto-Driver go forward for 3 seconds, and the bottom line plays musical notes while the robot moves. Let's see whether the bottom line of programming blocks makes a decent tune. Connect the robot to the computer and click the Play button on the Start block on the bottom line. Only this line of the code will be downloaded and run immediately. In the meantime, you will see the Play button on the hardware page controller change to the Stop button, as shown in Figure 6-3.

Figure 6-3: The Stop button on the hardware page controller

After the line of code that you run is finished, the Stop button may stay, and the EV3 brick status light may continue to blink, so make sure that you click the Stop button when you have finished testing.

The Wait Block

The second block in the orange palette is the Wait block. It should look familiar because we already used it to display the image on the EV3 screen in Chapter 5. The command of Wait raises questions such as "for how long?" or "until when?" These questions are basically asking, "When should I stop waiting?" For this reason, when you ask someone to wait, you might give him a condition of when to stop. Let's take a look at the following scenarios.

I went to the baseball game with Lou. After the seventh-inning stretch, he wanted to get a hot dog but I wanted to ask him to wait. I came up with three wait conditions that I could choose from:

Scenario 1. For 5 minutes

Scenario 2. Until he saw the player come up to bat whose uniform had a number that was greater than 33

Scenario 3. Until the current pitcher left the mound

If I go with the first scenario, Lou simply needs to wait for 5 minutes and then get a hot dog. If I choose the second scenario, he needs to keep comparing upcoming players' numbers with 33 until a player whose number is higher that 33 comes out of the dugout. If I ask him to follow the last scenario, he should watch who the current pitcher is and keep track of whether he stays on the field; then he can leave for a hot dog.

Each scenario has a different condition that can allow Lou to get his hot dog. You can use the Wait block to apply these same types of conditions to your robot. To have your robot wait for a certain amount of time, like the first condition, you can simply choose the Time mode and set up the time in seconds (again, like you did to keep the image on the EV3 screen in Chapter 5). How might we apply the second or third conditions to the robot? Read on.

The Compare Mode in the Wait Block

To end the great hot dog wait in the second scenario, Lou kept comparing the upcoming players' numbers with the given number. Once he saw the number that met the given condition (greater than 33), he could stop waiting and go get a hot dog. Here, the given number of 33 is the value that triggered a certain action (Lou leaving to buy a hot dog); this is called a threshold value.

You can design a similar set of instructions for your robot using the Compare mode with the Wait block. But first you need to decide the following:

- What type of data the robot should collect (Lou collected players' uniform numbers.)
- What the threshold should be (It was 33 for Lou.)
- What type of comparison you want to apply between incoming values and the threshold value (It was "higher [greater] than" in Lou's case.)

You can choose between the different types of data in the mode selector when you choose the Compare mode, and most of the time the block will have inputs for the threshold and types of comparison. The types of comparison will be represented by signs that you probably will recognize from elementary school. These operators are = (equal), ≠ (not equal), > (greater than), ≥ (greater than or equal to), < (less than), and ≤ (less than or equal to). Figure 6-4 shows how they appear on the block.

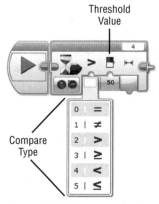

Figure 6-4: The compare type and the threshold value inputs in the Compare mode

You can apply the basics of the Compare mode covered in this section in various programming blocks, especially when you use sensors. So, you need to understand what the threshold is and how the comparison is evaluated.

The Change Mode in the Wait Block

In the third scenario, Lou needed to wait only until another pitcher replaced the current pitcher. Lou's waiting was over as soon as the new pitcher walked onto the mound. Once he finished waiting for the pitcher, he moved to his next action, yum.

Lou was basically waiting until he saw the pitcher leave the game, and that change finished his waiting. You may also use this kind of condition with the Wait block with the Change mode. With this mode, the Wait block will hold the program until it detects a certain change.

Now that you know how to set up the different types of waiting conditions that you can create for your robot by using the Compare and Change modes (thanks to the previous broad and general explanation), the following section explains more specifics about the Wait block with selected sensors. Because the sensors have yet to be discussed, this coverage focuses on just the brick buttons and Time modes. You will not read about all the features of the Wait block here, but you learn about the rest in Chapter 8, which introduces the sensors.

THE WAIT BLOCK DOESN'T FREEZE THE WHOLE PROGRAM!

While the Wait block processes its commands, either by waiting for 5 seconds or waiting to get a certain value, or even waiting for one of the brick buttons to be pressed, the blocks before the Wait block keep doing what they were doing before the program started to wait. The Wait block is telling the previous blocks to "continue what you are doing until I finish processing my job!" and asking the next blocks to "wait to begin your task until I finish what I am doing!" The whole program will still be running while the Wait block is standing by. As you can see from the program in Figure 6-5, motors B and C will keep turning as the Wait block is processing the action of "waiting for 3 seconds." After 3 seconds, motor B and C will stop.

Figure 6-5: Motors B and C will be running for 3 seconds and then stop.

The Time Mode

When you drag the Wait block to the canvas, its default will be set to the Time mode. This setting doesn't have the Compare or Change modes and is simply to tell your robot to wait for a number of seconds. Remember that "waiting for a certain amount of time" doesn't mean "stop the whole program for that amount of time"; the previous blocks of the Wait block run during the wait. You've already used this mode in Chapter 5, but take a look at Figure 6-6 for a reminder.

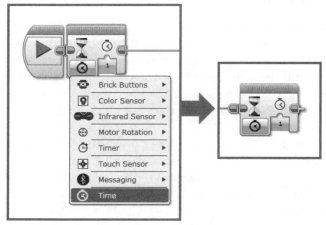

Figure 6-6: The Time mode in the Wait block

The Brick Buttons Mode

Now let's take look at the Brick Buttons mode on the Wait block. In this mode, the five buttons in the center of the EV3 brick (brick buttons) are used to control the wait period. With this block, your program will wait to proceed until one of the buttons is pressed, released, or bumped.

PRESSED, RELEASED, OR BUMPED

These terms will keep coming up when you program the brick buttons or the touch sensor. How do these three activations differ from each other? *Pressed* means that the button is being held down and will report back the number 1 for as long as it takes to be released. *Bumped* means that the button just gets pressed down and released almost immediately, producing an output of 2. *Released* refers to a button in its natural state of not being pressed or bumped. When the button is not pushed, it reports back the number 2. If your program is waiting for that value to proceed, it will wait until the button is no longer being pressed.

The Compare-Brick Buttons

As Figure 6-7 shows, if you click the mode selector, you will see the Brick Buttons – Compare – Brick Buttons mode.

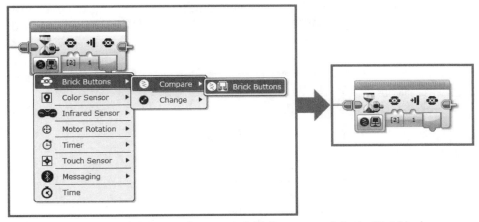

Figure 6-7: Choose Brick Buttons – Compare – Brick Buttons mode in the Wait block.

Note that each brick button has its own button ID number that refers to its position on the EV3 brick. This ID number is what the software recognizes when the brick button is activated in one way or another. Figure 6-8 shows the button ID numbers.

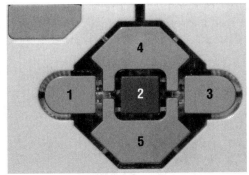

None of them is activated: 0

Figure 6-8: The button ID numbers

In terms of coding your robot, this mode tells the program to wait until one of the assigned brick buttons is activated. The first input (Set of Brick Button IDs) allows you to choose one or multiple buttons. The program will wait until one of them is activated. The second input (State) determines how you define *activated*. The buttons may be pressed (represented by 1), released (represented by 0), or bumped (represented by 2) to satisfy the conditions of the Wait block and allow the program to proceed (see Figure 6-9).

You'll find that there is yet another section next to the inputs. It is a block output, which allows one block to tell another programming block which of the five buttons has been pressed. For the moment, we aren't going to cover this, but you will learn more about block outputs in Chapter 11, "Programming with Data Wires and Using My Blocks."

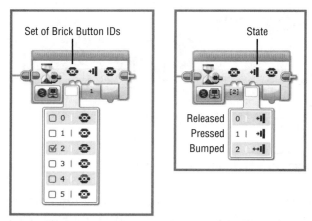

Figure 6-9: The inputs with the Brick Button mode

Let's try using the Wait block with this mode in your program! We will have the Auto-Driver wait until the center button (button ID: 2) is pressed, then move forward for 2 seconds when the center button is pressed. Create a project called **Flow Blocks** and make a new program named **Brick Buttons** then make it look like Figure 6-10.

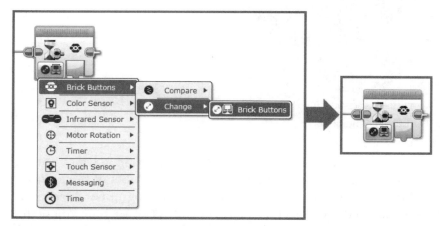

Figure 6-10: A program with the Wait block with the Compare – Brick Buttons mode

Download this program to the Auto-Driver. The Auto-Driver won't be moving until you press the center button!

The Change-Brick Buttons

Let's click the mode selector again and choose the Change – Brick Buttons. Did you select the block that looks like the one in Figure 6-11?

Figure 6-11: The Brick Buttons – Change – Brick Buttons mode in the Wait block

This mode looks simpler than the Compare mode because it has only one section for an output whereas the Compare mode has three sections for two inputs and one output. With this setting in place, the Wait block will be seeking any changes from the current status of the brick buttons. If none of the brick buttons is pressed when the program gets to the Wait block, it will wait for any of the buttons to be triggered.

Let's open the Brick Buttons program so we can mess with it a bit. Click the mode selector and try changing the mode in the Wait block to the Change – Brick Buttons. The program will look like Figure 6-12.

Figure 6-12: A program with the Wait block with the Compare – Brick Buttons mode

When you run this program on the Auto-Driver, it won't move and wait to get a change from the current status of the brick buttons. If none of the buttons are pressed when the program begins, the program will wait until any of the buttons are pressed. What if the center button is pressed when the program started? Then, the program will wait for either the center button to be released or another button(s) to be pressed in addition to the center button.

The Loop Block

Here's another programming block that you can use to beef up your code: the Loop block. As the name suggests, with it you can repeat a sequence of code. This can be useful when you want to make your robot perform a certain action over and over again. For example, let's say you want to program the Auto-Driver to move forward for a second and stop for a second and then repeat the action.

First, you need to create a sequence of code that makes the Auto-Driver move forward for a second and stop for a second. Then, maybe you'd want to copy this sequence and paste it over and over again on the canvas, however many times that you'd want to repeat this action. Save yourself from the hassle! You can achieve the same thing, in a much simpler way, with the Loop block. The Loop block looks different from the other blocks on the canvas, so let's review its structure in Figure 6-13.

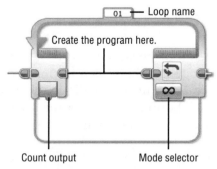

Figure 6-13: The structure of the Loop block

You can create a line of the blocks that you want to repeat inside of the Loop block. Then, the program will repeat the code inside of the Loop block until the mode selector tells the program under what conditions the loop should continue repeating and when it should stop and move on to the next block.

The Loop block automatically stretches to fit new blocks as you drag them inside, and it will also contract if you take blocks away. Should you want to manually adjust the Loop block, click it; points should then appear around the block, as shown in Figure 6-14. By dragging these points, you can adjust the size.

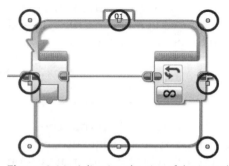

Figure 6-14: Adjusting the size of the Loop block

Like many other blocks covered so far, the Loop block has many modes. You can see them if you click the mode selector. The modes of the Loop block tell the program under what conditions the loop should continue repeating and when it should stop (see Figure 6-15).

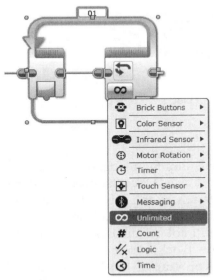

Figure 6-15: The modes in the Loop block

By using different modes, you can set up the repeating action to last for a certain number of seconds, to complete the loop a certain number of times, or to continue looping until a specific condition is met. For example, you can tell the Loop block to repeat the code contained within it for 5 seconds or until one of the brick buttons is pressed. It also has an output section called the Count output, and its value will be the number of the repetition that the Loop block makes. You can have more than one Loop block, so it is important to label each of them with different names or numbers because you may want to have one Look block interact with other blocks. This block has many sensor modes, and in this chapter we cover the Brick Buttons, Unlimited, Count, and Time modes. To see how to use other sensor modes, see Chapter 8.

The Unlimited, Count, and Time Modes

The Unlimited, Count, and Time modes are straightforward because they don't require collecting any data from the sensors. Let's create a new program called Loop. Make the program resemble the one in Figure 6-16. The line of the code inside of the loop will make the Auto-Driver go forward for a second, and the block that comes after that will make it move backward for a second.

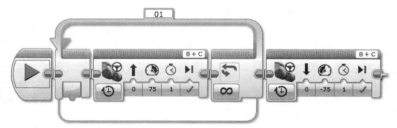

Figure 6-16: The program with the Loop block and Motor blocks

The Unlimited Mode

The Loop block shown in Figure 6-16 has the Unlimited mode, the default setting when you drag the Loop block onto the canvas. Once the program starts and moves along to the Loop block, it will stay there and repeat the sequence inside of it forever. Will the program ever reach the blocks that come after the loop? No. Unfortunately, following blocks will not get their chance to shine. Create a new program named **Loop** in the Flow Blocks project that you created in the previous section. Try downloading this program to the Auto-Driver and see what happens. The Auto-Driver will go forward forever.

The Count Mode

Click the mode selector in the program shown in Figure 6-16 and choose the Count mode. Did you see the block change like in Figure 6-17? When the Loop block starts, the program will count how many times it repeats. You can put any number in its Count input. So, if the number is 4, the Loop block will repeat the code inside for only 4 times, and then the program will move to the next block.

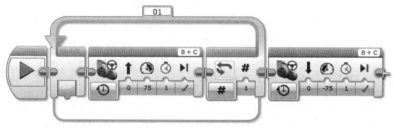

Figure 6-17: The Loop block with the Count mode

The program in Figure 6-17 shows a loop that will take 1 second to complete 1 repetition because the Move Steering block that is inside of the loop says to run the motors for 1 second. If you put 6 in the loop's Count input, it will take 6 seconds for the Loop block to complete 6 repetitions, after which the robot will move backward for 1 second.

Change the Unlimited mode in the Loop block to the Count mode in the Loop program and feel free to change the Count input, as you want. Download the program to the Auto-Driver and time it while it goes forward to see whether the count number that you entered and the number of seconds that you measured match each other.

The Time Mode

If you choose the Time mode, you will find settings that should look familiar. The Time mode in the Loop block looks and functions exactly as its counterpart in the Wait block. With this mode, you can set the Loop block to repeat the code that is inside for a period of time. You can determine how much time by entering a number in its Seconds input. Note that the Loop block will finish running its contents before exiting. Let's say you tell the Loop block to repeat the code inside for 5 seconds. If you have a motor move for 10 seconds within the loop, the program will still do the 10 seconds of motor movement. Then the program will evaluate that it is past 5 seconds and exit out of the loop.

The Brick Button Mode

The Brick Button mode in the Loop block is similar to the Compare – Brick Buttons mode in the Wait block. The repetition continues until one of the selected brick buttons are activated by one of these actions: released (0), pressed (1), or bumped (2). Let's change the Loop program to look like Figure 6-18. To change the mode in the Loop block, click the mode selector and choose the Brick Button mode. Then, select 4 and 5 for the Brick Button ID input and 2 for the State input.

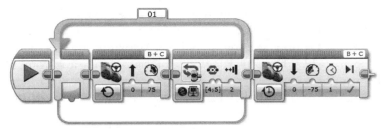

Figure 6-18: The Brick Button mode in the Loop block

When you run this program, the Auto-Driver will go forward until the top or bottom brick button is bumped. Then, it will move backward for 1 second. Test out this program with your robot and see whether I'm right.

TRY IT: AUTO-DRIVER, BEEP EVERY SECOND WHEN YOU DRIVE FORWARD!

Let's see if the Auto-Driver can report its movements to you by making a beeping sound every second when it moves forward. First of all, you'll want to program the Auto-Driver to go forward for a second using the Move Steering block. Then, you'll want to add the Sound block that makes a beeping noise. I found that the Overpower sound in the System folder sounds like a beeping noise. Then, you can put these two blocks in a Loop block with the Unlimited mode. As long as the program is running, the Auto-Driver will move forward beeping every second!

Demonstrate multiple Loop blocks with different modes. Also, try the Display and Sound blocks in the Loop block in addition to the Motor blocks.

The Loop Interrupt Block

Some things in this world can make people stop in their tracks. They drop what they are doing and begin a new activity that is altogether different from what they were doing just a second before. Take, for example, a man who is walking down Wall Street. He is wearing a nice suit, which he likes to wear on Mondays to remind the people who work for him that he's done well in his job and deserves respect. His knuckles are scarred from years of boxing while he was in the Marine Corps as a youth. This man is walking briskly down the sidewalk to a meeting in a building on Broad Street when he passes a child with a puppy on a leash. Instantly, the man kneels down and asks the child if he can pet the puppy. The man fondly thinks back to when he was a young boy in Bay Ridge and his mother surprised him with a beagle mutt. He named the dog Wally.

Wherever that man was going and whatever he was planning to say when he got there didn't matter as soon as he saw the puppy. The sight of the little dog ended his task. Ladies and gentlemen, I present to you the Loop Interrupt block! This block stops what a loop is doing, regardless of where the loop is in its cycle. Check out Figure 6-19. It has only the Loop Interrupt mode and comes with a text box in the top-right corner. When you click it, you will get the pop-up list that shows all the names of the Loop blocks that you have in that program. Then, you can pick the Loop block that you want to interrupt.

The program escapes the Loop block and jumps to the next block as soon as it meets the corresponding Loop Interrupt block. Even though the Loop block has an Unlimited mode, the Loop Interrupt block will break the infinite loop. It can be placed in a different sequence of the code apart from the one that contains the loop that it is interrupting, or even within the interrupted loop.

Figure 6-19: The Loop Interrupt block

Let's take a look at the example in Figure 6-20 and see how the Loop Interrupt mode can be used in a program.

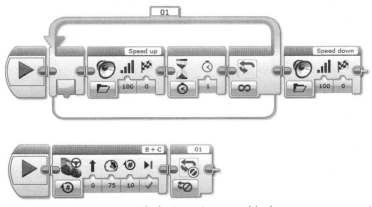

Figure 6-20: A program with the Loop Interrupt block

What will happen when we run this program with the Auto-Driver? The Auto-Driver will move forward (bottom line of the code), and at the same time, it will repeat the Speed up sound in intervals of 1 second (the code inside of the loop on the top line of the code). After that, the Auto-Driver's motors will make 10 rotations and the program will meet the Loop Interrupt block, which will stop the Loop block that was repeating the Speed up sound. The Auto-Driver will then play the Speed down sound. Create a new program called **Loop Interrupt** and make it look like Figure 6-20. Download the program to the Auto-Driver and see if it performs the way that I described to you!

The Switch Block

Life is all about making decisions. How many times did you have to choose one thing over the other today? Based on your situation, you will often ask yourself a question to evaluate the options of that choice, and depending on the answer your choice will be different. For example, you have $10 that you can spend for your lunch. Before you sit down at the restaurant, you will look at the menu and ask yourself a question: Is there any dish that is under $10? If the answer is yes, you will walk in. If the answer is no, you will look for another restaurant.

You can program your robot to choose between two options based on the answer of the yes or no question that you set ahead of time. The question for your robot can be something like this. Is the center button pressed? If the answer is yes, then say "Hello," but if the answer is no, then say "Good bye". The programming block that allows this is the Switch block. This block will "test" a question and depending on the answer, it will lead the program to follow one case of code or the other. Figure 6-21 shows what this looks like.

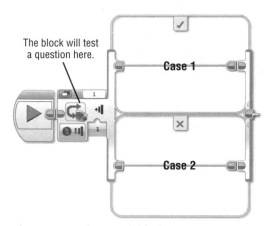

The block will test a question here.

Figure 6-21: The Switch block

As with the Wait or Loop blocks, you can choose different sensors in the mode selector, and depending on what sensor you choose, you can design the test questions differently. Again, you will have many chances to use the sensors with the Switch block after we learn about them in Chapter 8. In this section we will focus more on how the Switch block is structured and how it affects a program's flow. Also, we will see how the Compare and Measure mode work in the Switch block.

The Compare Mode in the Switch Block

In the mode selector, all the sensors have the Compare mode except the Text, Logic, and Numeric options. With the Compare mode, potential questions can be something like this: Is brick button 3 pressed? Is the color that the color sensor is reading red?

You will design a yes or no question with different types of inputs. If the answer is yes, the program will run the code that is in the top section of the Switch block, where the check mark is, and if the answer is no, it will execute the code that is in the bottom section, where the X mark is. Here, the check mark means true, and the X means false (see Figure 6-22).

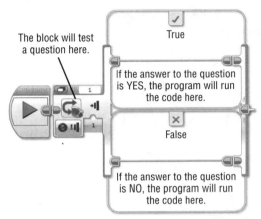

Figure 6-22: The true and false cases in the Switch block

Let's see the example with the Compare mode and the brick buttons. Once you choose this mode, you will find that the beginning of the block will change like in Figure 6-23. Wait, doesn't this look familiar? This mode is just like the Compare mode in the Wait block. You select one or more numbers in a range of 0 to 5 for the Brick Button ID input, and choose the button's status of released (0), pressed (1), or bumped (2) for the State input.

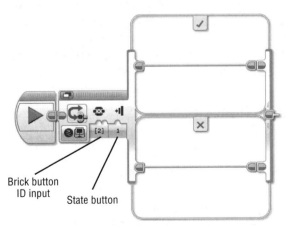

Figure 6-23: The Brick Buttons – Compare mode

Based on the inputs that you use, the test question will change. For example, if you select 1 and/or 3 for the Brick Button ID input and 1 for the State input, the test question for the program will be this: "Is one of brick buttons 1 and/or 3 pressed?" If you write the code for the Auto-Driver to go forward for 5 seconds for the true case and move backward for 5 seconds for the false case, the Auto-Driver will move forward for 5 seconds when the brick button 1 and/or 3 is pressed, and it will go backward for 5 seconds in any other cases. Figure 6-24 shows this example. Create a program called **Switch** and make it look like Figure 6-24.

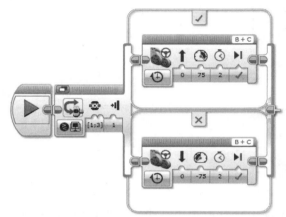

Figure 6-24: A program with the Switch block with the Brick Buttons mode

As soon as you run this program, the program will ask the question immediately and, unless you hold down the button 1 and/or 3 when the program begins, the program will go directly to the false case. Then the program will end. What if you want your program to ask this question over and over again? Bingo! You may then use the Loop block. If you put the Switch block in the Loop block as Figure 6-25 shows, the program will come back to the beginning, ask the question again, perform either the true or false cases depending on the answer to the question, and this procedure will be repeated over and over again.

The Measure Mode in the Switch Block

When you choose Brick Buttons, Color Sensor, and Infrared Sensor, you will find another mode: Measure mode. In this mode, you can program the Switch block to ask the program a different type of question. It is not a yes or no question but rather a multiple-choice question to specify multiple sensor values. In this case, the Switch block can have more than two cases with codes. As a default, the structure of the Switch block appears to be the same as when it has true or false cases, but it is actually slightly different (see Figure 6-26).

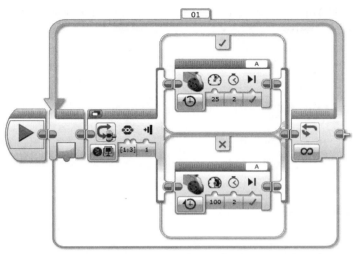

Figure 6-25: The Switch block with the Brick Buttons mode in the Loop block

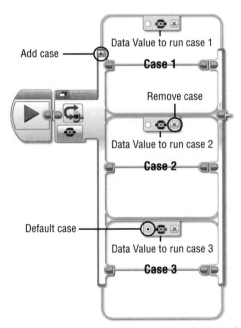

Figure 6-26: The Measure mode in the Switch block

NOTE If the incoming value doesn't meet any of the values in any case, the program will run the case that is marked as a default case.

Let's come back to the example with the Brick Buttons mode and choose the Measure mode. With this mode, the Switch block asks this question: "Which brick button is pressed?" You can design different cases for each answer. See the example in Figure 6-27.

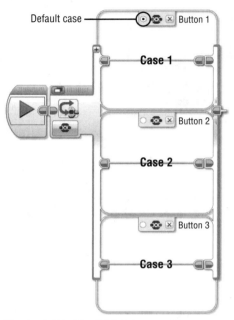

Figure 6-27: The Brick Buttons – Measure mode

When the program sees the Switch block, it asks which brick button is pressed. If it runs an examination with the incoming values and button 1 is pressed, it will run the program in case 1. If button 2 is pressed, the program in case 2 will be executed. If button 3 is pressed, the program in case 3 will be run. What if no button is pressed? In that case, the program runs the code in the case marked as the default (in this example, case 1).

Using a Value from a Data Wire

Three options do not have either the Compare or Measure modes: the Text, Logic, and Numeric modes. Their questions for the program are completed by the value that they get from other blocks though a data wire. The values can be text, numbers, or the true/false conditions. You get to use these modes after learning a bit about data wiring in Chapter 11.

FLAT VIEW VS. TABBED VIEW

There are two options for viewing the Switch block. The default option is the flat view, which shows all the cases in a row. You can toggle to the flat view by clicking the button in the top-left corner. The tabbed view displays one case at a time, with other cases shown as tabs on the top of the switch border (see Figure 6-28).

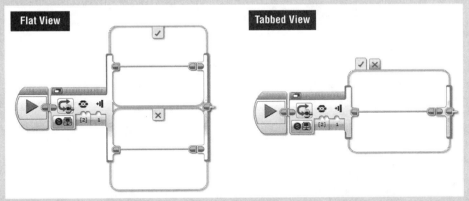

Figure 6-28: Flat view and Tabbed view in the Switch block

In either view option, you can still resize the Switch block as you did with the Loop block. Click any part of the Switch block and you will get the points around the border of the block. By dragging them in and out, you can adjust the size of the block. In the tabbed view, you can even set the height of each case.

Summary

In this chapter, you learned about the following:

- How the Flow blocks work
- How to program the robot with the Wait block
- How to repeat a line of code with the Loop block
- How to use the Loop Interrupt block
- How to set up different conditions that the robot can choose between based on incoming values with the Switch block

Building the Spy Rabbit: A Robot That Can React to Its Surroundings

So far, you have used the Auto-Driver to test new programming skills that you have learned. Now, though, it is time to explore a different robot. In this chapter, you build the robot called Spy Rabbit (which you also use in Chapter 8, "Sensing the Environments: Using the Infrared, Touch, and Color Sensors," and Chapter 9, "Using the Timer and the Rotation Sensor"). This robot requires more advanced building skills than the Auto-Driver, and you will use new pieces to put it together. Shh! Here comes the Spy Rabbit.

Understanding the Spy Rabbit

The Spy Rabbit is a robot that has two faces, and it transforms its body from one shape that shows one face to the other shape to present another face. The first is a rabbit face that you can see in the left photo in Figure 7-1. The other one is a humanoid robot like the photo on the right.

You will use this robot as you learn about sensor programming in Chapters 8 and 9. The robot's original design comes with the infrared sensor, but you will get to add more sensors later on.

Figure 7-1: The two faces of Spy Rabbit

The Spy Rabbit's Personality

If you see a rabbit that doesn't hop but rolls around, watch out. It might be a Spy Rabbit! The Spy Rabbit looks like a cute and dorky rabbit most of the time, but once in a while, especially when your attention is somewhere else, its rabbit face rears back to expose a different robot. When it opens up, it uses its face (which is the infrared sensor) to spy around. We will add more sensors, such as the touch and color sensor, in the following chapter, and you will get to add more personality to it. But for now, let's get started building the Spy Rabbit.

Assembling the Spy Rabbit

Organize the parts shown in Figures 7-2 and 7-3, and then follow the step-by-step building instructions (shown Figures 7-2 through 7-36) to build the Spy Rabbit.

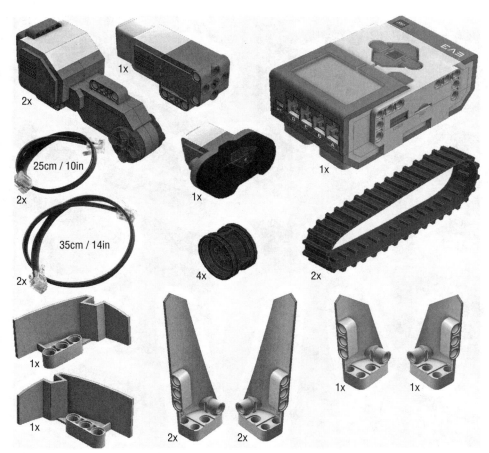

Figure 7-2: The parts for building Spy Rabbit – 1

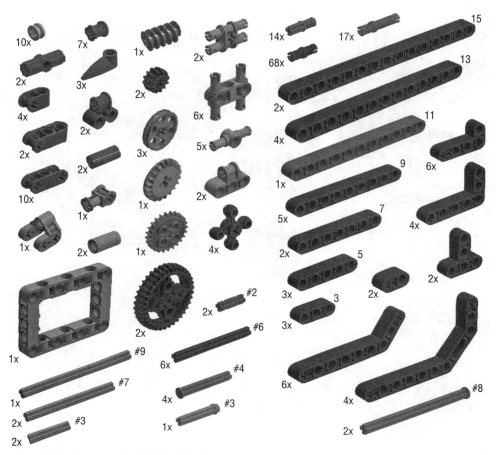

Figure 7-3: The parts for building Spy Rabbit – 2

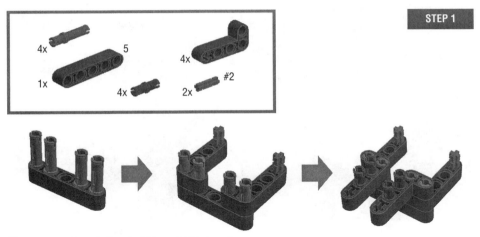

Figure 7-4: Step 1: Starting the rabbit's head

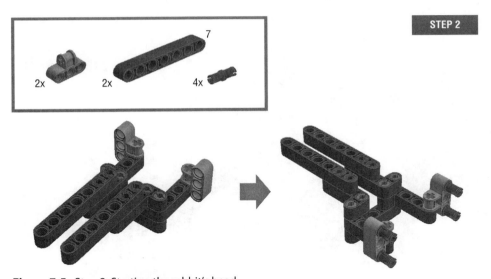

Figure 7-5: Step 2: Starting the rabbit's head

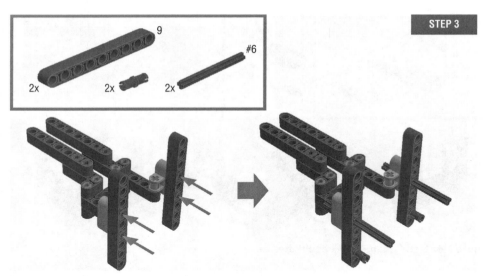

Figure 7-6: Step 3: Starting the rabbit's head

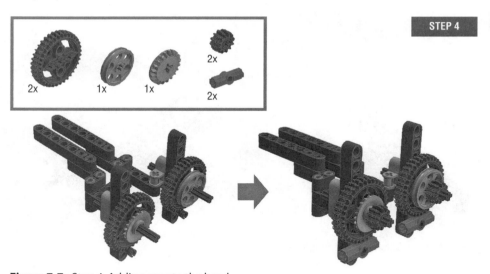

Figure 7-7: Step 4: Adding eyes to the head

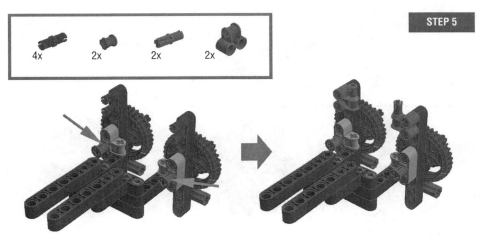

Figure 7-8: Step 5: Adjusting the eyes on the head

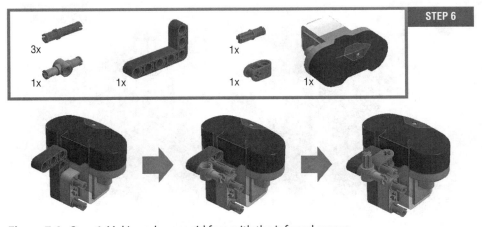

Figure 7-9: Step 6: Making a humanoid face with the infrared sensor

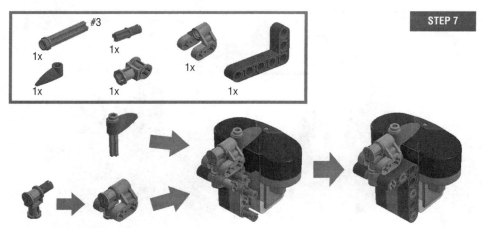

Figure 7-10: Step 7: Finishing up the face

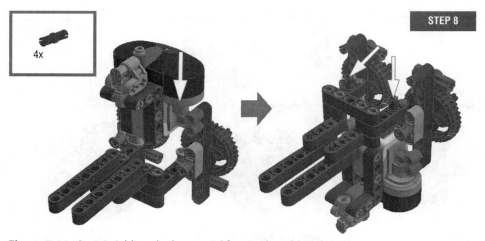

Figure 7-11: Step 8: Adding the humanoid face to the rabbit's head

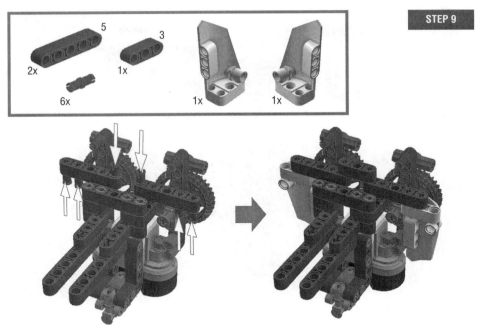

Figure 7-12: Step 9: Finishing up the rabbit's head

Figure 7-13: Step 10: Adding ears to the rabbit's head

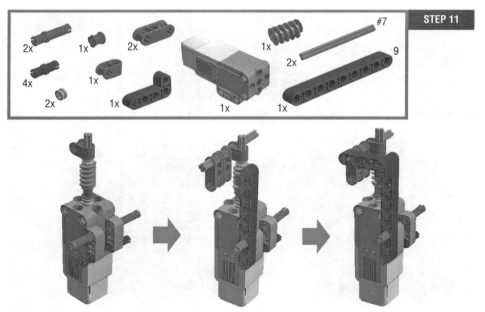

Figure 7-14: Step 11: Assembling pieces around the medium motor

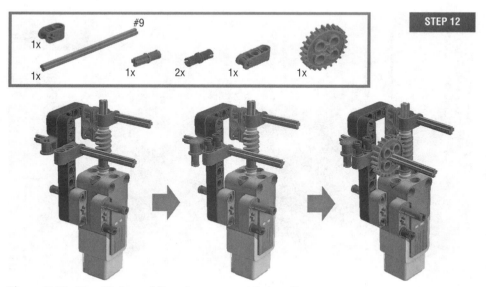

Figure 7-15: Step 12: Assembling pieces around the medium motor

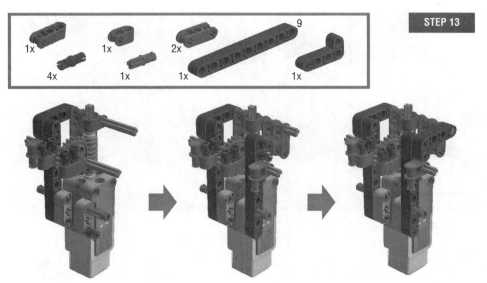

Figure 7-16: Step 13: Assembling pieces around the medium motor

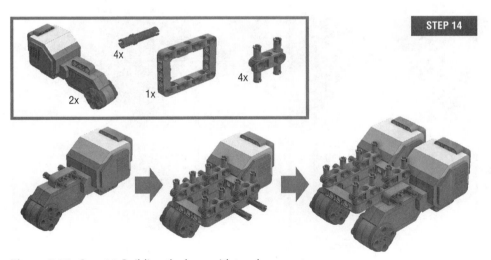

Figure 7-17: Step 14: Building the base with two large motors

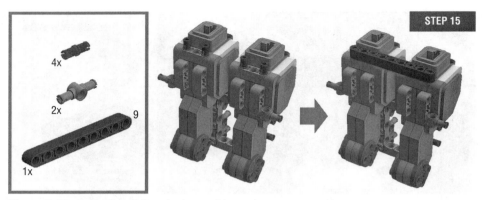

Figure 7-18: Step 15: Building the base with two large motors

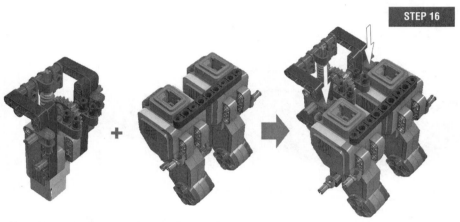

Figure 7-19: Step 16: Combining the part from step 13 with the base

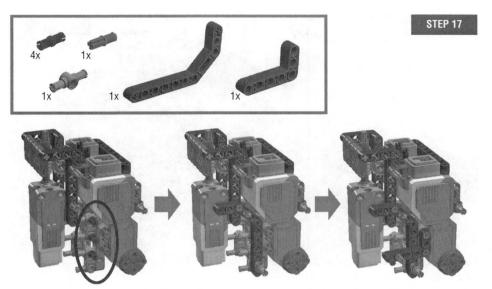

Figure 7-20: Step 17: Firmly affixing the medium motor to the base along with supporter pieces

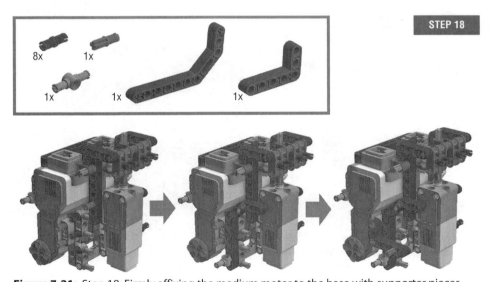

Figure 7-21: Step 18: Firmly affixing the medium motor to the base with supporter pieces

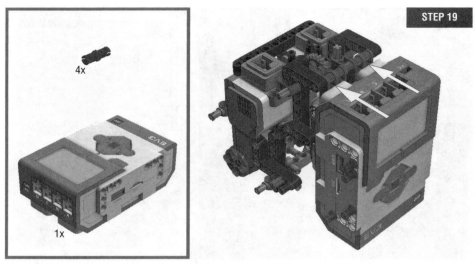

Figure 7-22: Step 19: Adding the EV3 brick

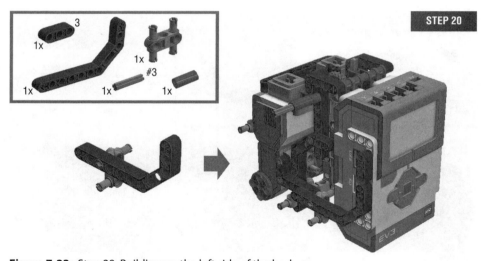

Figure 7-23: Step 20: Building up the left side of the body

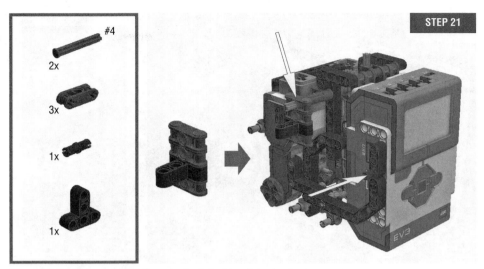

Figure 7-24: Step 21: Building up the left side of the body

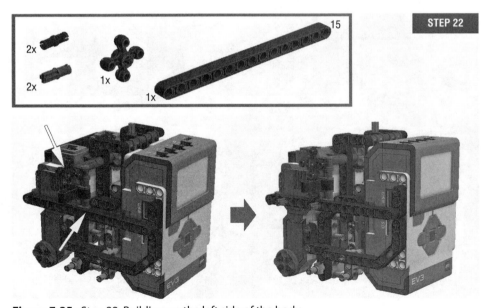

Figure 7-25: Step 22: Building up the left side of the body

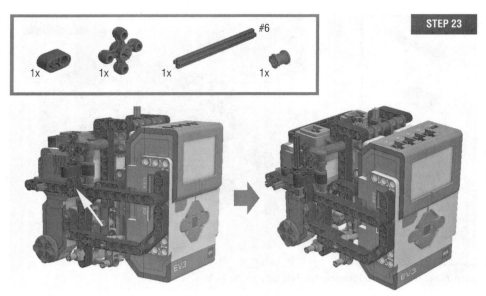

Figure 7-26: Step 23: Building up the left side of the body

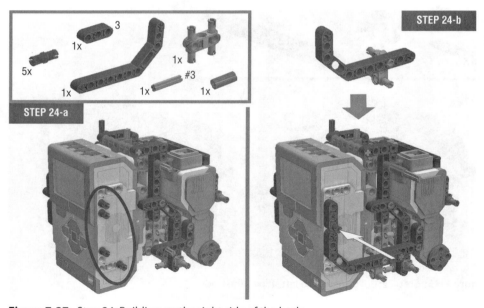

Figure 7-27: Step 24: Building up the right side of the body

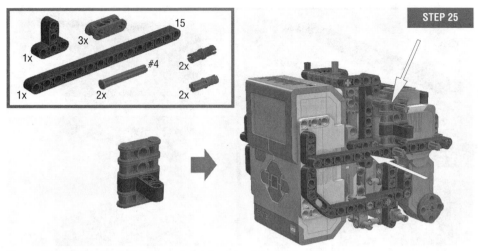

Figure 7-28: Step 25: Building up the right side of the body

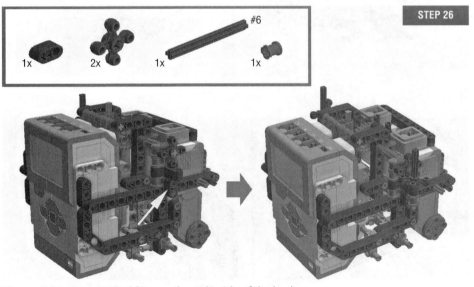

Figure 7-29: Step 26: Building up the right side of the body

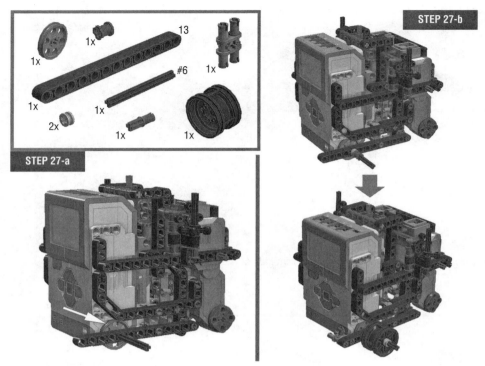

Figure 7-30: Step 27: Adding a hub

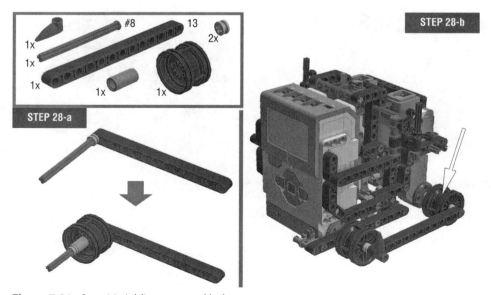

Figure 7-31: Step 28: Adding a second hub

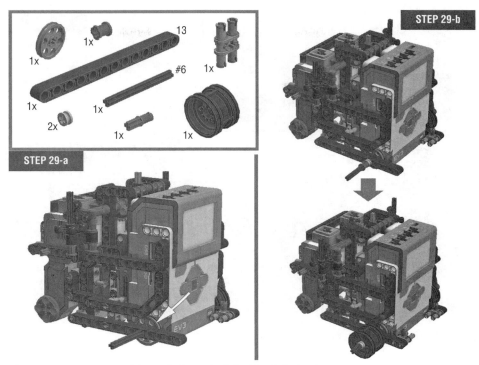

Figure 7-32: Step 29: Adding a hub on the left side of the body

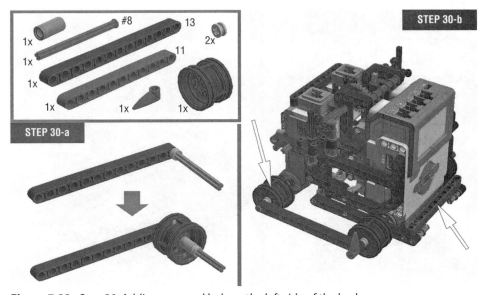

Figure 7-33: Step 30: Adding a second hub on the left side of the body

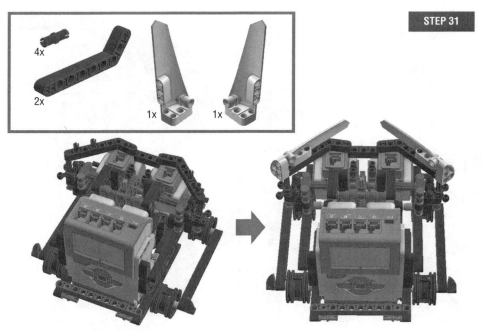

Figure 7-34: Step 31: Attaching the arms to the body

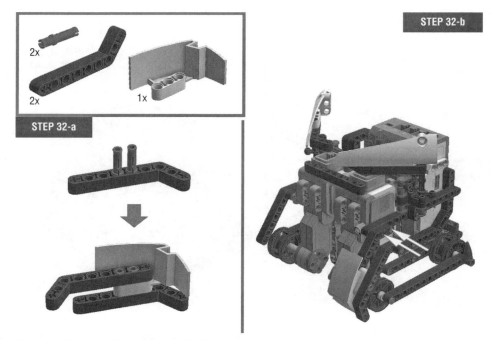

Figure 7-35: Step 32: Adding a rabbit's foot

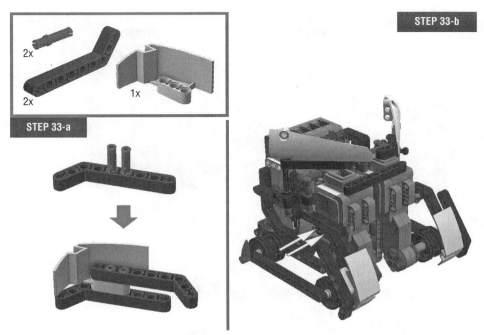

Figure 7-36: Step 33: Adding a rabbit's foot

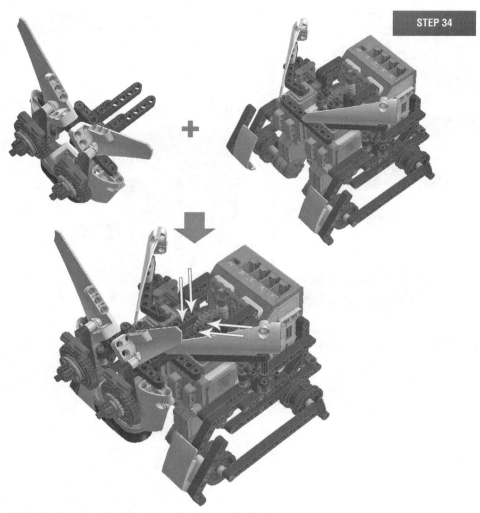

STEP 34

Figure 7-37: Step 34: Combining the head with the body

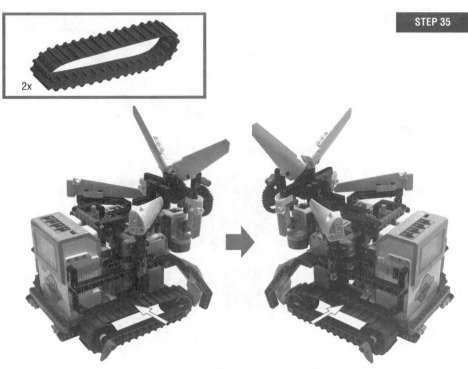

Figure 7-38: Step 35: Adding treads to the hubs

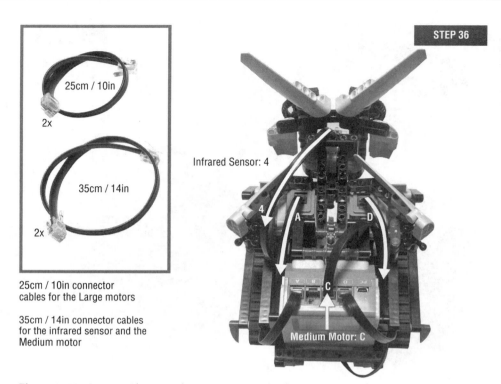

Figure 7-39: Step 36: Plugging the connector cables from the infrared sensor and the motors to the EV3 brick

Now that you have finished assembling your Spy Rabbit, it is time to test it.

Testing the Moving Parts of the Spy Rabbit

Congratulations! You have finished building the Spy Rabbit. Again, you will use this robot to learn about programming sensors in the following chapters. Before we jump into those chapters, though, let's see how the robot moves around and transforms.

Create a new program named **Spy Rabbit-test**, and make it look like Figure 7-40. Double-check to make sure that you have all the motors in, as directed in the instructions, and make sure that you set up all the corresponding ports for the motors with the programming blocks in the program.

Figure 7-40: Program to test the Spy Rabbit's movements

When you run this program, the Spy Rabbit will go forward for a second, open its rabbit head, turn around, and then move forward again. Then, it will close its head. Because of the position of the large motors, you need to set up their power with a negative number to make them move forward.

NOTE A quick reminder: The power level is the number when you ignore the plus or minus signs. This number represents the speed and power of the motor. The plus and minus signs change the direction of the motor. These rules apply in the same way when you program the medium motor.

With this program, the head of the Spy Rabbit should stop when it is all the way up and all the way down. If, for some reason, the robot doesn't perform like this, you may want to tweak different numbers for the motor degrees on the medium block. If you leave the medium motor set to keep going up or down, you may hear something get stuck, and it may loosen some other part of your robot. I know that you don't want to decapitate your robot, so watch out when you program the head of the Spy Rabbit.

Summary

In this chapter, you learned about the following:

- What the Spy Rabbit does and what its personality is like
- How to build the Spy Rabbit
- The program that shows the Spy Rabbit's transformation

CHAPTER 8

Sensing the Environments: Using the Infrared, Touch, and Color Sensors

So far, you have learned how to program the Spy Rabbit robot's actions, particularly its physical movements. In your program, you set up the values for moving the motors, displaying images, and playing sounds. The robot then applies them as its actions. Your robot, however, can do more than just process preset values. You can program your robot to collect information from its surroundings and then use that information to determine its behaviors. For example, you can program your robot to look around to see if there are any objects within a range of 5 inches. You may then choose to make the robot play a sound when it does find an object within that range. Sensors are the devices that allow your robot to do just that. This chapter covers the EV3 sensors and how to write programs for your robot to read and use the information from the sensors.

In this chapter you will get to add more sensors to the Spy Rabbit that you created in Chapter 7, "Building the Spy Rabbit: A Robot That Can React to Its Surroundings," and program the robot to do just that! Get ready to make the Spy Rabbit act smarter.

Understanding Sensors

Wait a minute, what are the sensors? A sensor, usually as a part of a robot or a machine, is a device that responds to an outside stimulus, converts information about the stimulus into a form that the robot can understand, and sends the information to the main computer of the robot to which it belongs. The main computer then processes this information as it relates to its program and decides the robot's next action.

Let's think for a second about an automatic door. When a motion sensor at the top of the door detects movement in front of the door, it sends a message to the main computer to which the sensor is connected. Then, the main computer engages the motor to open the door. "Sensing movement" is the role of the motion sensor and "opening the door" is how the main computer is programmed to react when the sensor's input value changes. You might also say "play music" instead of "open the door" or even "play music and open the door." The idea that I am trying to relate is that when you use sensors, they report only the results of sensing. It is up to you to decide how your robot is to react to the sensors.

Programming a sensor is a doorway to opening interactions between your robot and its environment. You can enrich your robot's behavior by adding interactions to what it senses. Let's see what we can do with EV3's sensors.

Intro to the EV3 Sensors

As discussed in Chapter 1, "Introducing LEGO MINDSTORMS EV3," the EV3 set comes with the infrared, touch, and color sensors, in addition to the remote infrared beacon (IR beacon), shown in Figure 8-1.

Figure 8-1: The EV3 sensors (from left): infrared, touch, color sensors and remote infrared beacon

Each sensor collects different types of data from the outside world:

- The **infrared sensor** can tell us how far an object is in front of it, or it can communicate with the remote infrared beacon.

- The **touch sensor** is a clickable button, and it reports back whether that button is pressed, released, or bumped.

- The **color sensor** can identify seven different colors. Alternatively, the color sensor can be used to measure the brightness of light that is reflected from a surface or just ambient light.

To use these sensors on your robot, you need to plug them into one of the ports on the EV3 brick with the connector wire. As a default, port 1 is for the touch sensor, port 3 is for the color sensor, and port 4 is for the infrared sensor. They are all interchangeable, but I recommend following the default ports whenever possible; doing so will help you remember which sensor is plugged into which port.

After you decide what sensor you want to use on your robot and you connect it to the EV3 brick, you are ready to add it into your program. Various programming blocks work with the sensors, but in this chapter, we mostly explore sensor programming with the Wait, Loop, and Switch blocks. Let's get started.

SENSOR BLOCKS IN PROGRAMMING

In this chapter and the one that follows, we test the sensors and use their values along with the Wait, Loop, and Switch blocks. However, you will also see the "sensor blocks" in the yellow tab of the programming block.

Sensor blocks differ from the Wait, Loop, or Switch blocks because they do not have any action command, such as "wait" or "repeat." Instead, they only collect sensor values and send them to other blocks through data wires. For example, you can use the value from the infrared sensor (for instance, a reported value of 50) to set how many degrees the motor should turn (50 degrees). You will use these blocks extensively when you learn to use data wiring in your programs in Chapter 11, "Programming with Data Wires and Using My Block."

Using the Infrared Sensor and Remote Infrared Beacon

Let's first take a look at the infrared sensor. The Spy Rabbit has one of these sensors as part of its design. It works like the robot's eyes for "seeing" objects in front of it, or receiving the signal from the remote infrared beacon. You can work with this sensor in three different ways: Remote mode, Beacon mode, and Proximity mode. In the Remote and Beacon modes, the sensor should work very closely with the remote infrared beacon, which is a great new feature of the EV3 set. Let's see how it works before jumping into the three modes.

Remote Infrared Beacon

The remote infrared beacon, also called the IR beacon, enables you to control your robot without having to touch it. To use the IR beacon, your robot must have the infrared sensor installed because it works as a receiver for the signal from the IR beacon. Let's take a closer look.

NOTE   Before you use this remote control-like device, make sure that it has two AAA batteries, which you can install or change by unscrewing the two screws on the back.

As Figure 8-2 shows, the IR beacon has five gray buttons. The biggest button is for turning the device on and off. When it's on, you will see a green light.

	Button ID
No Button	0
Button 1	1
Button 2	2
Button 3	3
Button 4	4
Button 1 & 3	5
Button 1 & 4	6
Button 2 & 3	7
Button 2 & 4	8
Button 9	9
Button 1 & 2	10
Button 3 & 4	11

Figure 8-2: Button ID numbers for the five buttons (left) and button combinations on the IR beacon

You can use these buttons individually or in two-button combinations. Each button or combination of buttons has its own button ID. For example, the largest gray button's ID is 9, and a combination of buttons 2 and 3 has a button ID of 7. When you send a signal from the IR beacon by pressing its button(s), the infrared sensor receives the button ID number that was sent. The table on the right side of Figure 8-3 shows the button IDs that correspond with each button or button combination.

Apart from these buttons, you will find a red circle with a number (the number on the red circle is small, so look closely) and a red sliding switch in the middle of the IR beacon (see Figure 8-3). This switch is a channel selector, and the number on the red circle shows the current channel number. If you slide the channel selector up and down, you will see the numbers change from 1 to 4.

Channels are like roads for the signals. In real life, each road may have a different destination, just as each channel will lead the signal to its own destination. For example, pressing button 1 in channel 1 and pressing button 1 in channel 2 can deliver different outcomes. When you write your code, the programming block needs to know what type of signal is coming from which channel number. You will get used to this requirement as you work with the three modes with the infrared sensor in the following sections.

Remote Mode

This first mode deals with the use of the IR beacon as a control device of sorts. With this mode, the IR beacon works just like a regular remote control, sending a signal to an infrared sensor. Each button or combinations of buttons can initiate different commands. For example, you can program the robot to stop both the A and C motors when button 1 on the IR beacon in channel 1 is pressed.

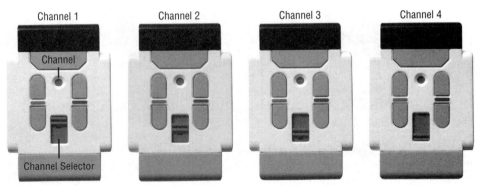

Figure 8-3: Channels and channel selector

BRICK APPS: IR CONTROL

Good news! If you want to try the IR beacon as your robot's remote controller without much effort, there is a quick way to control the motors without programming. As Figure 8-4 shows, if you go to the Brick Apps on the EV3 brick, you will be able to choose the IR control. Note that the infrared sensor has to be plugged in port 4 to use this app.

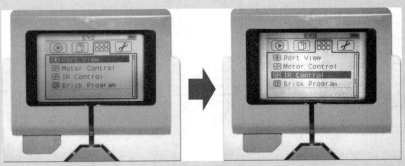

Figure 8-4: Go to the Brick Apps and choose the IR control.

Then you will have the screens resembling those in Figure 8-5, and you can toggle these two screens by pressing the middle brick button.

Continues

continued

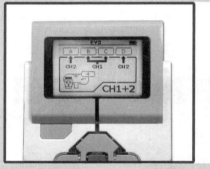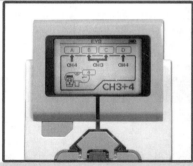

Figure 8-5: The control screens of the IR control app

When the screen says CH1+2, you can control motor B and C (or A and D) with the four buttons on the IR beacon in channel 1 and control motor A and D in channel 2. The set of buttons on the left can tell motor B to go forward (top button) or backward (bottom button). The set of buttons on the right controls motor C in the same way. If you toggle the screen to the other screen, which says CH3+4, you can control motor B and C in channel 3 and A and D in channel 4. In the Spy Rabbit, motor C controls his head, so try to use the IR beacon to open and close his head. You can choose either CH1 or 3, and then control motor C with the set of buttons on the right (see Figure 8-6).

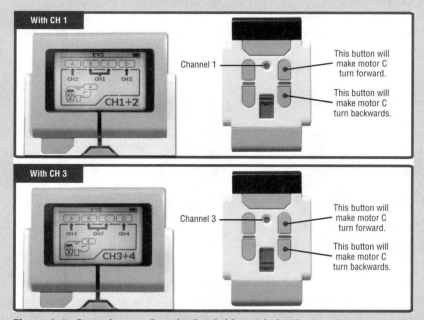

Figure 8-6: Control motor C on the Spy Rabbit with the IR control app.

Then, what does this mode look like as a string of programming blocks? When you use this mode with the infrared sensor, you will always see the Channel or Button ID inputs or both on the block. Figure 8-7 shows an example of the Wait block with this mode. Sometimes they are shown as an output of the block.

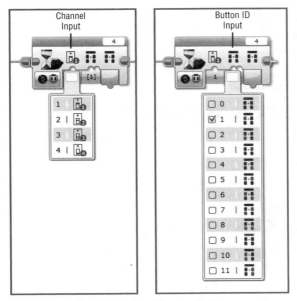

Figure 8-7: The Channel and Button ID inputs

You will find three different flavors of Remote mode in the programming blocks:

- **Compare – Remote**: In Compare – Remote mode, you set up the button ID and the channel in a block, and the program will compare this with the button ID that the sensor receives in the same channel.

- **Change – Remote**: In Change – Remote mode, the program checks whether a current value that the sensor is getting has been changed. For example, suppose that the sensor is detecting no button ID coming from channel 1. If any button is pressed on the IR beacon in channel 1, the program block with this mode will sense a change.

- **Measure – Remote**: In Measure – Remote mode, you set the channel, and the program block will directly report which button(s) is pressed on the IR beacon in the same channel. You will see this mode in the Switch block, and depending on which button ID the sensor is getting, you can have up to 12 cases of a code.

Figure 8-8 shows how these modes will appear in the Wait, Switch, and Loop blocks.

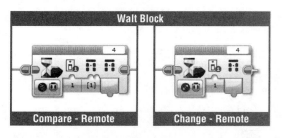

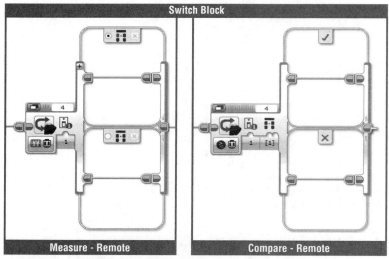

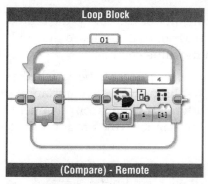

Figure 8-8: The Compare – Remote, Change – Remote, and Measure – Remote modes in the Wait, Switch, and Loop blocks

Beacon Mode

With the Beacon mode, the infrared sensor also gets signals from the IR beacon, but it will be a different type of data than with the Remote mode. Instead of sensing which button(s) is/are pressed, the sensor can actually detect which direction (the heading of the signal) the signal is coming from and how far away the signal's origin (proximity) is. Thus, the sensor can estimate the location of the IR beacon.

The sensor can search for the IR beacon for an approximate distance of 79 inches/ 200 centimeters (represented as values between 0 and 100) and in a little bit larger than half-circle search range from the direction the sensor is facing. When the signal is directly in front of the sensor, the heading value is 0. When the sensor detects the signal from its left, the value is a negative number and goes down to –25, and if the signal is from its right, the value is a positive number and goes up to 25 (see Figure 8-9).

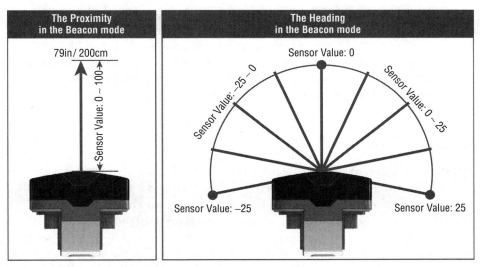

Figure 8-9: The proximity and heading in the Beacon mode

Keep in mind that it is also important to set up the correct channel when you program with the IR beacon. If your program tells the infrared sensor to search for a signal on channel 3 of the IR beacon, it won't find it when its channel is actually set to 1, 2, or 4.

Let's see what this mode looks like in programming blocks. Because the infrared sensor technically gets two different types of data in this mode, the proximity and heading of the IR beacon often show as two modes in the programming blocks. The former is referred to as beacon proximity and the latter is called beacon heading.

These modes will appear as follows:

- Compare – Beacon Proximity
- Compare – Beacon Heading
- Change – Beacon Proximity
- Change – Beacon Heading

In the Compare modes, the program shows how the incoming beacon proximity or heading values from the IR beacon differ from the threshold input value that you set up on the block. In the Change modes, the block checks whether the incoming beacon proximity or heading values change from a number that you specify beforehand. Figure 8-10 shows how these modes will be shown in the Wait, Switch, and Loop blocks.

WARNING   When the infrared sensor is searching for the heading of the IR beacon, make sure that the IR beacon is in the infrared sensor's searching area. The right side of Figure 8-9 shows the range that the infrared sensor can search. If the IR beacon is out of this range, the infrared sensor may give you some unexpected values. So, keep this in mind when you use the Beacon mode.

Proximity Mode

The last infrared sensor mode that is covered here—Proximity mode—is used to determine approximate distance between the robot and another object. Unlike the other two modes, you can use this mode without the IR beacon. If you choose this mode, the infrared sensor emits infrared light, which is invisible to the naked eye. The sensor can then sense when the infrared light reflects off of a nearby object. In this way, the sensor can recognize how far away that object sits from the robot.

The infrared sensor can detect from a distance of up to 27 inches/70 centimeters. The sensor reports back the distance on a scale of 0 to 100 that shows in a relative way how "far" the object is from the sensor. Just like any of the other values from the infrared sensor, these values don't have a specific unit (see Figure 8-11).

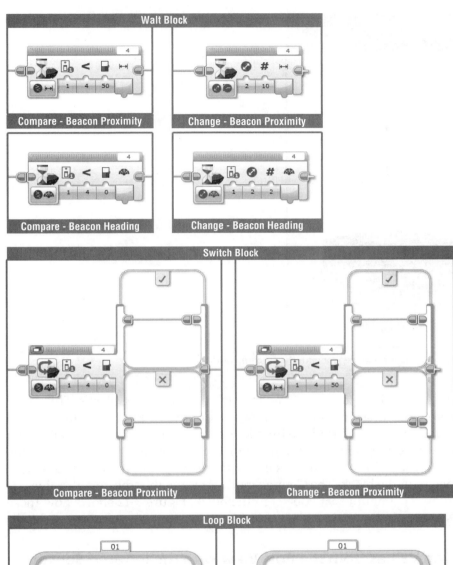

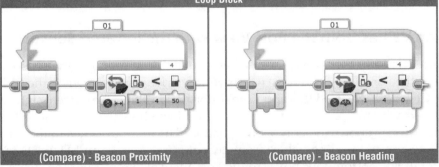

Figure 8-10: Compare – Beacon Proximity, Compare – Beacon Heading, Change – Beacon Proximity, and Change – Beacon Heading modes in the Wait, Switch, and Loop blocks

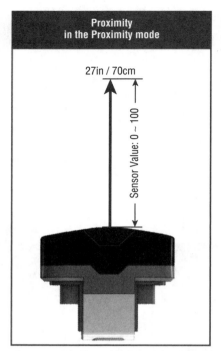

Figure 8-11: The infrared sensor with the Proximity mode

Let's consider how to use this mode in the programming blocks. This mode in the programming blocks will be shown as Compare – Proximity and Change – Proximity. You should find the functions of these modes familiar. Remember that with the Compare mode, the program looks at the difference between the proximity value that the sensor is currently reading and the input value that you specify in the block. The Change mode sees whether the default value has shifted by the amount that you set in the block. Figure 8-12 shows how these modes appear in the Wait, Switch, and Loop blocks.

Reading Values from the Port View with the Infrared Sensor

There is a Brick app that you can use when you are programming the sensors; it is called the Port View. When we went over the Brick Apps screen on the EV3 brick in Chapter 2, we used this app to get information about the current state of the Auto-Driver's motors. Figure 8-15 will remind you how to find this app; the right-most image shows the Port View in action. The top four boxes in the Port View show current reading values from output ports A, B, C, and D (ports for the motors). The bottom four boxes in the Port View also represent the current reading values, but from input ports 1, 2, 3, and 4 (ports used for sensors). As you select each box, you will see more information about the device that is plugged into that port. The right image of Figure 8-13 is the Port View of the Spy Rabbit, and it shows that there are three motors and one sensor plugged into the Brick.

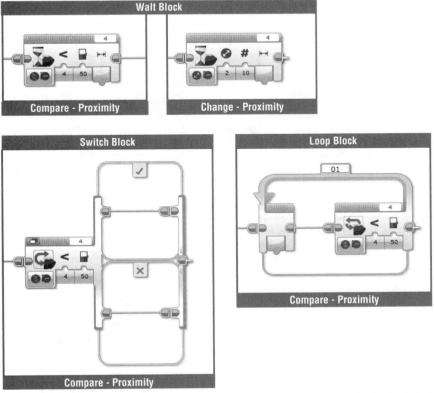

Figure 8-12: The Compare – Proximity and Change – Proximity modes in the Wait, Switch, and Loop blocks

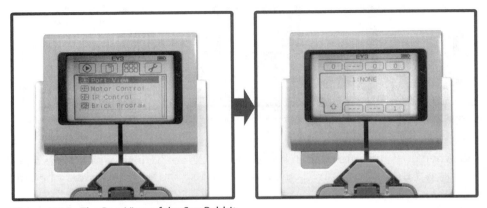

Figure 8-13: The Port View of the Spy Rabbit

On the Port View, select the port that has the infrared sensor, which is the bottom box on the far right. You will get a screen like the image on the left in Figure 8-14. If you click it again, you get the list of the infrared sensor modes, as shown in the image on the right of Figure 8-14.

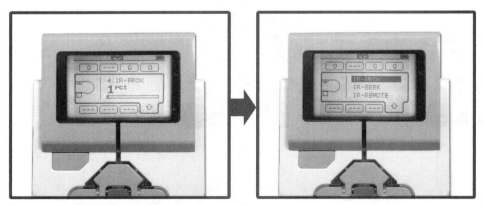

Figure 8-14: The infrared sensors on the Port View.

The IR-PROX mode works the same as the Proximity mode, which means that the output value represents the distance of an object from the sensor.

In the IR-SEEK mode, the sensor detects the heading of the signal from the IR beacon. The IR-REMOTE mode shows the status of the IR beacon's buttons (pressed, released, bumped). You can use both IR-SEEK and IR-Remote to see whether the IR beacon and the infrared sensor are communicating well (see Figure 8-15).

Figure 8-15: Three modes with the infrared sensor on the Port View

So, when does this information prove useful? As you've just learned, the values that you get from the infrared sensors do not use the familiar units. The Port

View can prove useful to see how the sensor values relate with the actual units of measurement that we rely on in real life. If you want to program your robot to make a sound when it sees something closer than 10 inches, you must note what value the infrared sensor gets when it sees something 10 inches away by using the Port View. You can use this value in your code, when you program the infrared sensor. You can do the same thing when you program the infrared sensor with the IR beacon. Open the Port View and choose the IR-SEEK. You can then move the IR beacon from side to side in front of the infrared sensor and estimate how the position of the IR beacon relates to the heading value.

Programming with the Infrared Sensor and Remote Infrared

Now it's time to program the infrared sensor. Have the Spy Rabbit and the IR beacon ready. Begin by creating a project called **Spy Rabbit – Infrared Sensor**.

Exercise 1: Spy Rabbit, Will You Be My Pet?

Spy Rabbit can be an obedient pet. Let's tell him to run away and come back to you. To begin, create a program called **Remote Control**. In this program, you create the code that allows you to train the Spy Rabbit with the IR beacon. Check out the plan for this action in Figure 8-16.

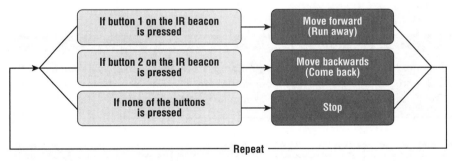

Figure 8-16: Programming plan for the Remote Control program

To implement this plan, you can create a program like that in Figure 8-17. After you download this program, you can have the Spy Rabbit run away from you by pressing button 1 on the IR beacon using channel 1 and have him come back to you by pressing button 2. When none of the buttons are pressed, he will stop. As long as the program is running, he will repeat this action of running away and coming back.

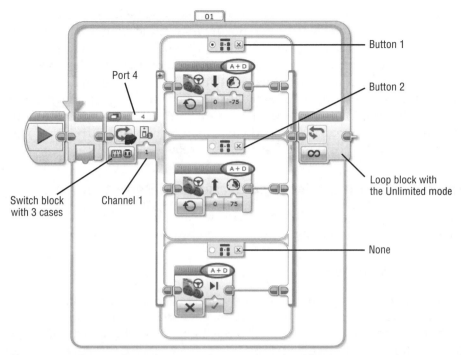

Port 4

Button 1

Button 2

Switch block with 3 cases

Channel 1

Loop block with the Unlimited mode

None

Figure 8-17: Remote Control program: Programming the IR beacon to control motor A and D on the Spy Rabbit

---

TRY IT: SPY RABBIT MAKES SOUNDS

Add the sound blocks to the Remote Control program and make the Spy Rabbit a bit livelier. Try programming him to say "something" (your choice) when he is running away from you and say "something else" when he is coming back.

TRY IT: SPY RABBIT GETS EXCITED

At the end of the day, even the Spy Rabbit is a rabbit. When you feed him, he will get excited. Let's create a program for the Spy Rabbit to show his excitement: He will wait for you to put a carrot near his mouth, which is under the infrared sensor. When the sensor "sees" the carrot, your robot will show his excitement by opening up and spinning around. Use the programming chart in Figure 8-18 as a reference.

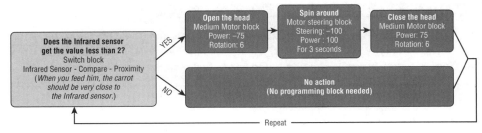

Figure 8-18: Programming chart for showing excitement

TIP Depending on the last action of the program, sometimes the head of the Spy Rabbit is left up. If you want to put the head back down before you run any other program, you can use one of the Brick Apps in the EV3 brick called Motor Control. With this app, you can readjust the position of the Spy Rabbit's head. (Remember, motor C controls the head.)

Exercise 2: Mission's On: Find the IR Beacon

As a spy, our rabbit friend will have to go on search missions. As practice, we will train him to find the position of the IR beacon. We will program the Spy Rabbit to open up his head first and wait until the IR beacon comes close. Then, we will have him search what direction the signal comes from and change the direction of his movement toward the IR beacon. We will also use the Loop block for the Spy Rabbit to repeat this searching action until the IR beacon is out of sight.

Create a program called **Finding – IR Beacon** and follow the program shown in Figure 8-19. See whether your Spy Rabbit has what it takes.

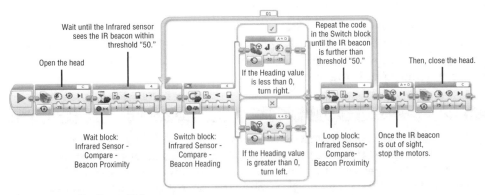

Figure 8-19: Finding – IR Beacon program

TRY IT: SPY RABBIT RUNS AWAY

Let's try to have the Spy Rabbit move away from the IR beacon. To do that, you still want to program the Spy Rabbit to find the IR beacon (reference the Finding – IR Beacon program), but have him turn to the opposite direction from the IR beacon.

Exercise 3: Watch Out for Obstacles

We want the Spy Rabbit to maneuver well, and he can do that by using his infrared sensor. We will create a program to have the Spy Rabbit change his direction of movement when he sees something within 6 inches. Before you put programming blocks together, use the Port View to measure what value the infrared sensor reports back when it sees an object that is 6 inches away (see Figure 8-20).

Figure 8-20: Measuring the distance between the infrared sensor and an object and getting a reading value from the sensor using the Port View

Programming blocks should be ordered like the top chart in Figure 8-21, and the program will look like the code on the bottom of Figure 8-21. Create a program called **Avoiding** and test it.

TRY IT: SPY RABBIT DISPLAYS WARNING SIGNS ON THE SCREEN

The Spy Rabbit can tell you when something is coming closer to him. Maybe it's a spy from the other side? Using the Port View, measure the infrared sensor values when an object is 12 inches away, 8 inches away, and 3 inches away. (Hint: Use the IR-PROX mode in the Port View.) Then, program the Spy Rabbit to display warning signs at each stage. When the object is far, the warning should be mild; when it is close, though, the warning should be severe.

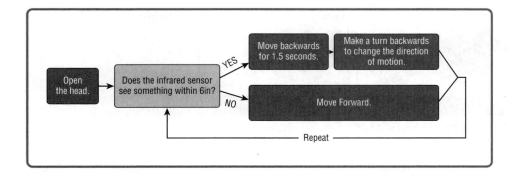

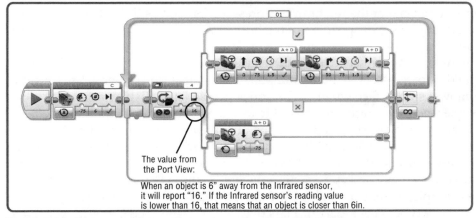

The value from the Port View:

When an object is 6" away from the Infrared sensor, it will report "16." If the Infrared sensor's reading value is lower than 16, that means that an object is closer than 6in.

Figure 8-21: The programming chart and actual code for the Avoiding program

How did you enjoy using the infrared sensor? As we just discovered, by programming the infrared sensor on your robot, you can make your robot react to objects around it as well as the signal from the IR beacon. You may already think that your robot is already amazing with just an infrared sensor, but this is just the beginning! We have another sensor coming up, which reacts to a different type input. I present to you, the touch sensor!

Using the Touch Sensor

The touch sensor works in a familiar way when compared with the other EV3 sensors. It has a red button and detects its three different conditions: pressed, released, and bumped (see Figure 8-22).

Figure 8-22: The touch sensor's three conditions

The pressed condition of the button means the condition of the button is "pushed in." You can program to move the motor forward whenever the touch sensor detects that the red button is pressed. As soon as the button is released, the motor stops. This position of the button is referred to as State: 1 in the programming blocks.

To have the touch sensor detect the released condition of the button, the button should be pressed before that command. For example, you can program the robot to show a smiley face when the button is pressed and display a sad face when it's released. This status is referred to as State: 0 in the programming blocks.

When you say the button is bumped, that means it was pressed and immediately released. Bumping is like the action of typing with a keyboard. Each key on a keyboard is an individual button, and you tap the keys to type. The keys that you used as you type a sentence were "bumped" (pressed and released). For example, if you want to type the letter E you tap the E key once. If you press this key, it types eeeeee... until it is released. The bumped status is referred to as State: 2 in the programming blocks.

When you use the Wait block with the touch sensor, you will have Compare – State or Change – State modes. With the Compare mode, the programming block has the program wait until a user-specified button state occurs. Change mode has the program wait until a current button state changes to another. In the Switch block, you simply choose one of the three button states. If the state choice requirement that you set is satisfied, the code on the top of the switch happens, and if not, the bottom code runs. In the Loop block, the touch sensor setup is similar to the Switch block. You will choose which button states will stop repeating the loop code. When the program gets to the end of the loop and before it repeats the code inside of the loop, it will check the button state.

When that button state occurs, the program gets out of the loop and moves to the next block (see Figure 8-23).

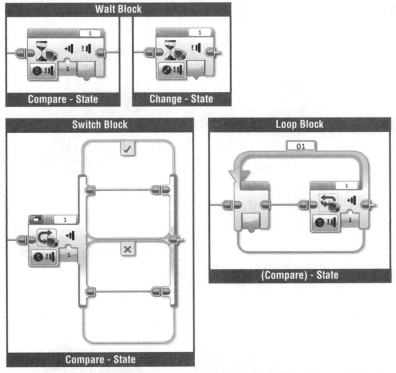

Figure 8-23: The Touch Sensor mode in the Wait, Switch, and Loop blocks

Adding the Touch Sensor to the Spy Rabbit

The Spy Rabbit is missing an important part. What is it that makes a rabbit cuter? Did you say the tail? Yes, it is his tail. We are going to give the Spy Rabbit a tail that is made out of a touch sensor. The tail on the back will help the Spy Rabbit to maneuver around better by sensing objects that blocks his way when he moves backward. We will program the Spy Rabbit to change direction when the tail touches something behind it. Follow these instructions shown in Figures 8-24 to 8-27 and complete the Spy Rabbit's missing tail.

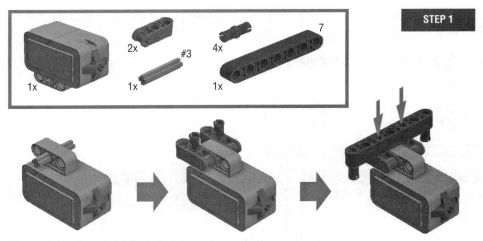

Figure 8-24: Step 1: Adding supporter pieces on the touch sensor

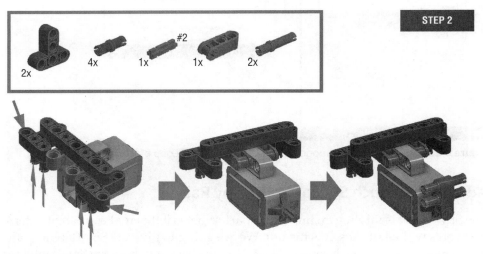

Figure 8-25: Step 2: Adding supporter pieces on the touch sensor

Reading Values from the Port View with the Touch Sensor

As you saw with the infrared sensor, you can also use the Port View to read the status of the touch sensor's red button. If you choose the port into which the touch sensor is plugged, you will find a 0 value on the screen when the button is not in a pressed state and 1 value when the button is released (see Figure 8-28). Then what about the bumped state? If you bump the button, you will see the value change between 0 and 1.

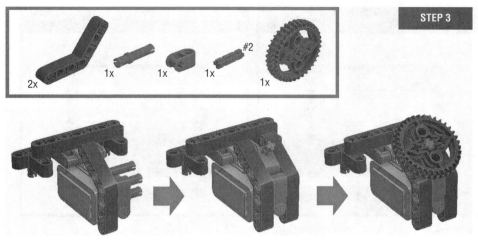

Figure 8-26: Step 3: Finishing up the tail bumper

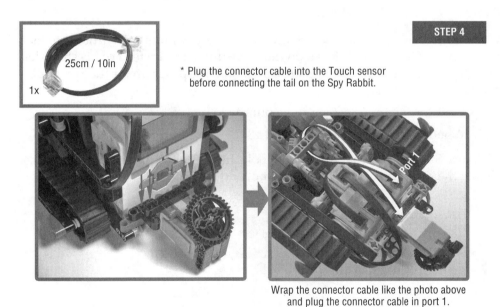

Figure 8-27: Step 4: Adding the tail on the Spy Rabbit

Programming with the Touch Sensor

Well, before programming the tail to be used as the Spy Rabbit's back bumper, we should use it to practice some touch sensor programming. To begin, create a project with the name of **Spy Rabbit – Touch**.

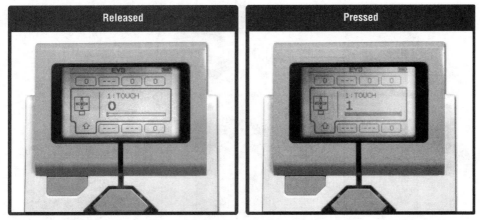

Figure 8-28: The touch sensor on the Port View

Exercise 1: Who's Behind Me?

When someone taps your shoulder, you naturally want to turn around to face that person. The Spy Rabbit can do the same thing, but instead of his shoulder, you should tap his tail. To complete this action, the program for the Spy Rabbit should look like this:

1. Wait for the touch sensor to be bumped.

2. When it is bumped, turn around 180°.

Figure 8-29 shows what this action looks like with the programming blocks. Create the program called **Turn Around**, and let's try it.

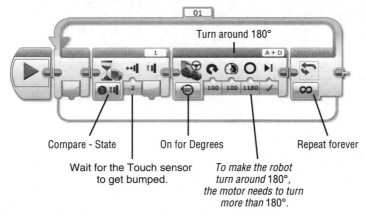

Figure 8-29: Turn Around program

If someone keeps tapping your shoulder for no reason and making you turn around a thousand times, you will start to get annoyed, even if you are a nice person. The Spy Rabbit is a nice rabbit, but his patience will run out after a while. He will run away from you if you tap his tail five times. To add this behavior to your current code, you need to do only a little bit of tweaking. Instead of having a Loop block set with the Unlimited mode, you can choose the Count mode. Use 5 for the counting number. After the Loop block, add the Move steering blocks to have the Spy Rabbit move away from you (see Figure 8-30).

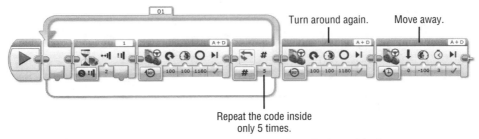

Figure 8-30: Turn Around program with the Count mode in the Loop block

---

TRY IT: THE SECRET FUNCTION OF THE SPY RABBIT'S TAIL

I know the tail is adorable as it is, but let's give the tail another job to initiate a cute action. We will use the tail to make the Spy Rabbit move his head up and down just like he is nodding. Program the touch sensor on the tail to move the medium motor forward for 0.5 seconds and backward for another 0.5 seconds when it is bumped. And if you want to keep this function, and have this reaction whenever you bump the touch sensor, you can put all of the program blocks in a loop.

Exercise 2: A Tail Bumper

The tail can also help the Spy Rabbit navigate uncertain terrain. Because he doesn't have an "eye" in the back of his head, we can make the touch sensor tail act like one. Let's grab the Avoiding code that we used for programming the infrared sensor. In that code, the Spy Rabbit backed up when it saw an object and pivoted to change his direction of motion. What if there is another object behind him when he is backing up? Right here, the touch sensor tail will be useful. Once an object triggers the touch sensor, it tells the Spy Rabbit to change his direction again. See Figure 8-31 to check what you need to add.

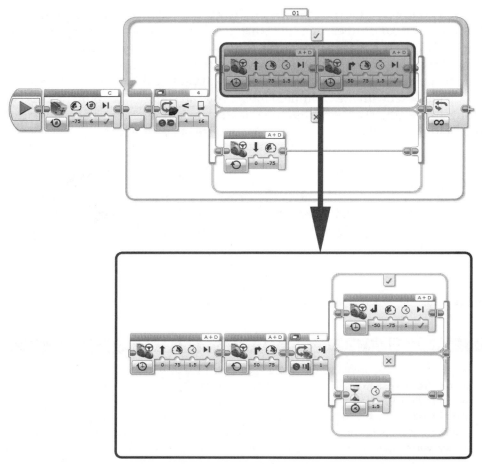

Figure 8-31: Adding the bumper program to the Avoiding code

Programming the touch sensor is a lot of fun, isn't it? We used the touch sensor as a bumper with the Spy Rabbit, but take a second to brainstorm other ways to use the touch sensor in other robots. Maybe it can be in the shape of a pair of lips on the red button, and the robot activates when someone gives it a smooch (the touch sensor will be pressed). What about making it into an electronic drum so that whenever it is bumped, it can generate a sound? There are so many cool things that you can do with sensors. Here comes another sensor that will make your robot even more awesome. Meet the color sensor.

Using the Color Sensor

The final sensor covered in this chapter is the color sensor. It is shaped like the touch sensor, but in place of a red button, it has LED lights. As its name suggests, this sensor can identify seven different colors, can detect the intensity of the reflected light from a surface, and can measure the amount of ambient light in a space. EV3 programming distinguishes these features with three modes: Color, Reflected Light Intensity, and Ambient Light Intensity modes.

Color Mode

The Color mode allows the sensor to recognize seven colors: black, blue, green, yellow, red, white, and brown. If the sensor "sees" a color that doesn't match with any of these seven colors, it will detect "No Color" or a similar color. When you are programming, each color is represented with its own number, and you need to use these numbers instead of their names. Here is how the matching works:

No Color=0
Black=1
Blue=2
Green=3
Yellow=4
Red=5
White=6
Brown=7

Note that the color sensor is tuned to the LEGO color palette, which means that it only reads a particular shade of a certain color as that color. For example, it doesn't read every shade of green as green. The color sensor will only identify a particular green to be the color green. For this reason, I would suggest for you to check the colors that you want to use with the color sensor before you use them with the Port View. If you want to use a certain red, show it the color sensor first. Let's say that the sensor shows the reading value on the Port view as a "5." That red is an acceptable shade of red for the sensor to recognize. However, if it shows a different number, the sensor doesn't read that red as red, and you should try a different shade. Annoying, yes. The end of the world, no.

When programming blocks, you will find this mode appears like this: Compare – Color, Change – Color, and Measure – Color. In Compare mode, the programming block initiates the code based on the comparison of the reading color value and the value that you set up in the block. In Change mode, the programming block executes the code if the color that the color sensor is reading changes. In Measure mode, the color sensor directly reports the color value that is currently being read to the block (see Figure 8-32).

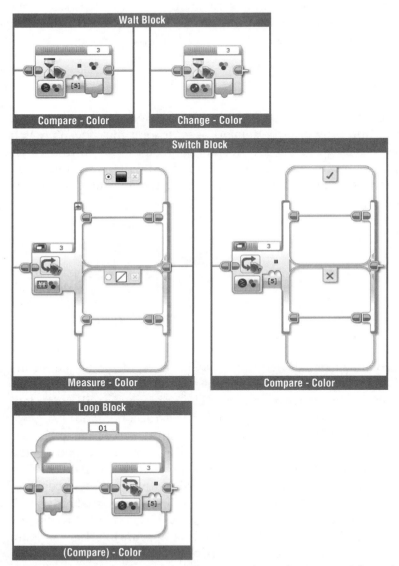

Figure 8-32: The Compare – Color, Change – Color, and Measure – Color in the Wait, Switch, and Loop blocks

WARNING   For a more accurate measurement when you use the color sensor with the Color mode or the Reflected Light Intensity mode, the sensor should be very close and parallel to the object or surface that it's examining. If the color sensor is set at an angle to a surface or too far from a surface that it is intended to read, the result will not be very accurate.

When using these modes, consider this factor when you add the color sensor to your robot. The position and angle of the sensor are very important, and if you want to program your robot to distinguish colors on the floor, the sensor should point directly down to the floor, and its placement should be as low as possible.

Reflected Light Intensity Mode

This mode works like the Color mode, but it detects the degree of the brightness of an object or a surface. When this mode is active, the sensor emits a red light. This light is used to make a reflection on a surface, and the color sensor evaluates the intensity of the reflected light that comes back. Here is a question: Which surface tone reflects light more intensely, a dark one or a light one? The answer is a bright surface. Imagine a sunny day after snow has fallen. Your experience was probably that it was very bright out. That is because the white of snow reflects a great deal of light. In contrast, black absorbs light, which means that it is less reflective (see Figure 8-33).

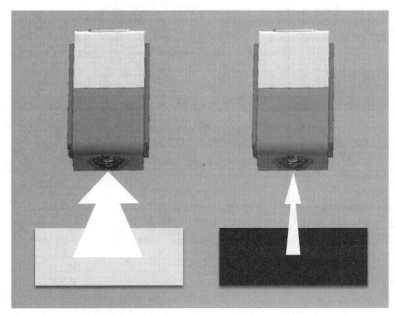

Figure 8-33: The brightness of a surface and Reflected Light Intensity

The value that the color sensor reports back to you will be a number that spans from 0 (weak intensity of reflected light, usually meaning there is a very dark surface) to 100 (a strong intensity of reflected light, meaning a very bright surface). In the Wait, Switch, and Loop blocks, this mode is shown either as Compare – Reflected Light Intensity or Change – Reflected Light Intensity. In Compare mode, the block makes a decision based on the difference between the current reading values and the threshold value that you put in the block. In Change mode, the programming block runs the code if the incoming value changes by a user-specified amount. See these modes in the Wait, Switch, and Loop blocks in Figure 8-34.

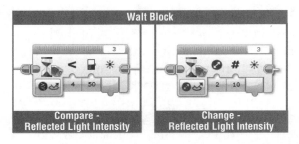

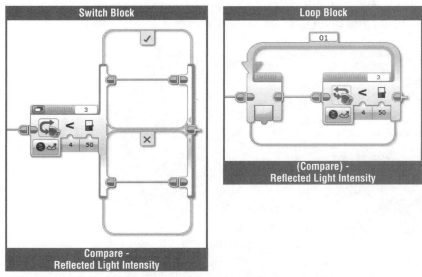

Figure 8-34: The Compare – Reflected Light Intensity or Change – Reflected Light Intensity in the Wait, Switch, and Loop blocks

Ambient Light Intensity Mode

The last mode with the color sensor is the Ambient Light Intensity mode. With this mode, the sensor measures the brightness of the room or space where it is placed. Whereas the sensor detects the reflected light from a surface with the Reflected Light Intensity mode, the color sensor with the Ambient Light Intensity mode absorbs the light that is coming from its surroundings and calculates its intensity. The intensity of the light is marked as percentages from 0 (very dark) to 100 (very bright). This mode is shown as either Compare – Ambient Light Intensity or Change – Ambient Light Intensity in the Wait, Switch, and Loop blocks. They work in exactly the same manner as in the Reflected Light Intensity mode, but only with the intensity value of the ambient light (see Figure 8-35).

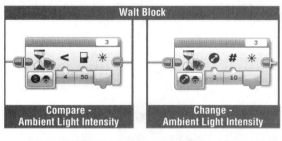

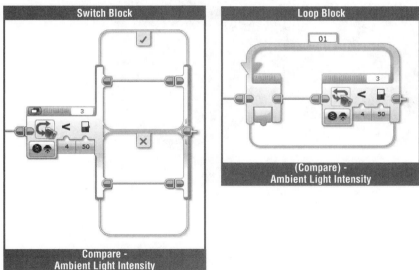

Figure 8-35: The Compare – Ambient Light Intensity or Change – Ambient Light Intensity in the Wait, Switch, and Loop blocks

THE LED LIGHTS ON THE COLOR SENSOR

The LED lights on the color sensor emit a different color of light depending on what mode is active. In Color mode, red, green, and blue are on; in Reflected Light Intensity mode, only red is on; and in the Ambient Light Intensity mode, only blue is on. By checking the color of the LED light that the sensor is emitting, you can quickly tell what mode is being used.

Adding the Color Sensor to the Spy Rabbit

Since the Spy Rabbit's "birth," he has grown to be a fairly complex organism. But now that he has a color sensor, he will finally live up to his nature as a rabbit as well as a spy. As a spy, he will be able to detect more accurate information with three sensors. As a rabbit, he can finally find some grass and feed himself. Follow the instructions in Figures 8-36 to 8-40 to add the last sensor to the Spy Rabbit.

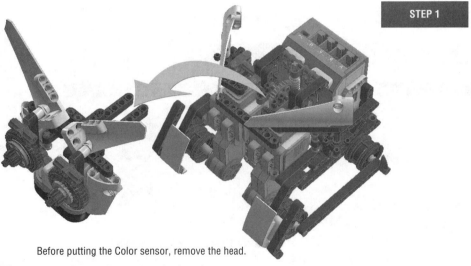

Before putting the Color sensor, remove the head.

Figure 8-36: Step 1: Removing the head

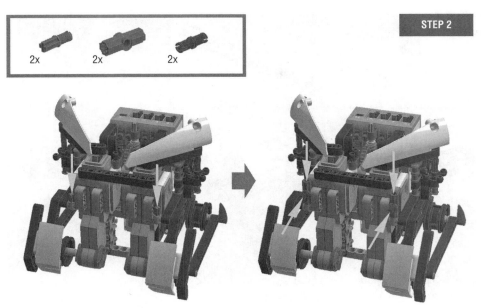

Figure 8-37: Step 2: Adding pieces on the body of the Spy Rabbit

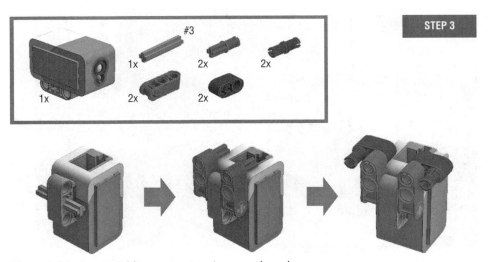

Figure 8-38: Step 3: Adding supporter pieces on the color sensor

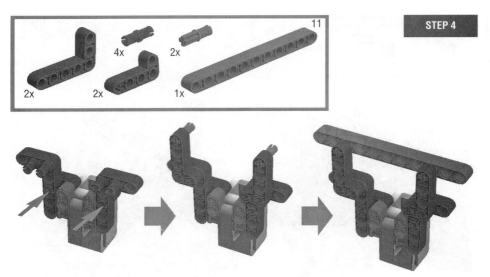

Figure 8-39: Step 4: Adding supporter pieces on the color sensor

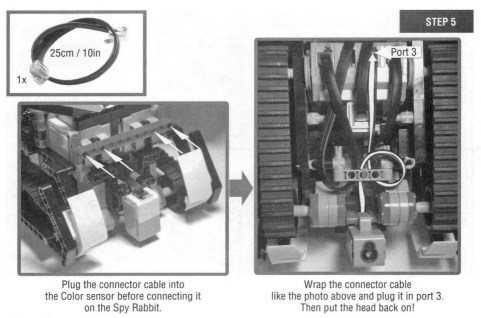

Plug the connector cable into the Color sensor before connecting it on the Spy Rabbit.

Wrap the connector cable like the photo above and plug it in port 3. Then put the head back on!

Figure 8-40: Step 5: Attach the color sensor on the body of the Spy Rabbit then put the head back on.

Reading Values from the Port View with the Color Sensor

In addition to displaying the infrared and touch sensors' current values, the Port View also shows the color sensor's current values. It reports the values in all three modes. If you select the port that has the color sensor plugged in and then click the center brick button again, you will see the lists of the modes: COL – REFLECT, COL – AMBIENT, and COL – COLOR. The first two modes show the intensity of reflected light or ambient light in a range of 0 (very dark) to 100 (very bright). The Color mode reports the color with its own number (see Figure 8-41).

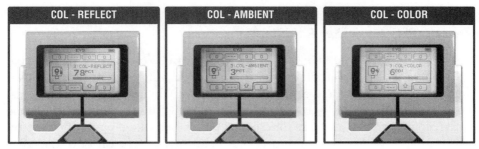

Figure 8-41: The color sensor on the Port View

Programming with the Color Sensor

Now it's time to program the color sensor. Create a project called **Spy Rabbit – Color**, and follow along with the following exercises to see how the Color sensor can make the Spy Rabbit even more unique.

Exercise 1: Lunch Time—Find Some Grass

Prior to this exercise, you fed Spy Rabbit carrots—see the sidebar "Try It: Spy Rabbit Gets Excited" earlier in this chapter—but with the color sensor, he can find grass on his own. When he finds grass, he will open his head and say, "Bravo." Then he will spin around to express his excitement. His final action will be to put his head down so that he can eat.

First, we will need to find the right shade of green for the sensor. As I mentioned before, the color sensor doesn't read every shade of green as "green." To find the right shade, you can use the Port View and test different greens to see which one the color sensor will read as green. Once you find the right one, place a piece of paper or tape with that green on the floor, and then program the Spy Rabbit to move toward it. In this case, you will have the Spy Rabbit go in a straight line, and you will place some green in his path. Create a program called **Find Grass**, and write code like that shown in Figure 8-42.

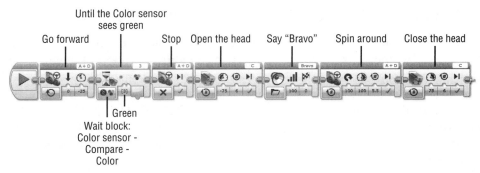

Figure 8-42: Find Grass program

Exercise 2: Play Music, Spy Rabbit

Not every spy has a cold heart. The Spy Rabbit can be creative in un-spy-like ways. That is to say, he can play music for you. You can program him to play a particular note when he sees a particular color. You can have up to seven notes.

Let's try with three colors: red, yellow, and blue. Before creating the code, use crayons, color pencils, markers, or colored paper to make a band of colors on a piece of paper with red, yellow, and blue color blocks. The order of the color doesn't really matter. Eventually, you will have the Spy Rabbit run over the colors and read them with the sensor.

Next, create the new program called **Play Music** and write a code with the Switch block with three cases for each color and one case for default. In each case, place the Sound block that plays a specified note. For instance, if the color sensor sees red, play note C until it detects a different color; if it sees yellow, play note D until it sees a different color; and if it sees blue, play note E until it finds a different color. If it sees none of these colors, stop playing. Put this Switch block in the Loop block. The last step is adding another line in your program to have the Spy Rabbit go straight. The program you will get looks like the code in Figure 8-43.

Place the Spy Rabbit at the beginning of the line and run the program to see what he plays. If the color of the line turns red, then blue, and then green, he will play the notes C, D, and E. Make sure that the Spy Rabbit's color sensor is pointed at the colored line when he moves.

TRY IT: ARE YOU A SPY OR A MUSICIAN?

So far, you've tried to make three colors play three notes. Can you try to use seven colors so that the Spy Rabbit can play seven different notes? You'll need to add more cases in the Switch block to the program that you used for Exercise 2. Then, create another colored paper line with a more varied combination of colors (maybe you can get notes from an actual song, like "Mary Had A Little Lamb," and transfer each note to an assigned color on the paper line) and see whether the Spy Rabbit can play it.

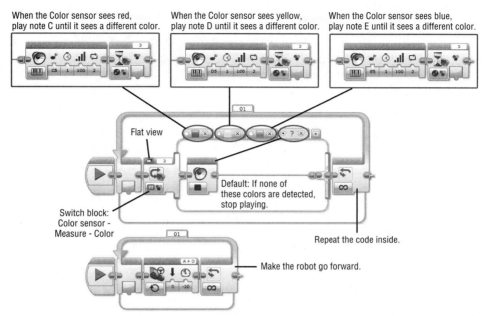

Figure 8-43: Play Music program

Summary

In this chapter, you learned about the following:

- How to program the infrared sensor and IR beacon
- How to program the touch sensor
- How to program the color sensor
- How to use the Port View to see the current values that are being reported by the infrared sensor, touch sensor, and color sensor
- How to add the touch sensor and color sensor to the Spy Rabbit

CHAPTER 9

Using the Timer and the Rotation Sensor

At the rate that you've been learning new concepts and skills, you must feel like a sprinter in the 400-meter dash. From the beginning of the book up to Chapter 8, "Sensing the Environments: Using the Infrared, Touch, and Color Sensors," you've been learning nonstop. Now, you are close to mastering the fundamentals of EV3 programming and moving on to more advanced programming and more robots. In this chapter, you learn how to use the timer and the rotation sensor. More fun activities are also in store as you make the Spy Rabbit better and better. For example, you can make the Spy Rabbit measure how much time passes after he starts driving forward and until his tail bumper is pressed. Also, the Spy Rabbit will be able to know exactly how many degrees his motor has turned in a second.

Understanding the Timer

The timer is built in to the EV3 brick, so you don't need to connect anything to it to use this sensor. There are a total of eight timers in all, and you can use them in the same program to time up to eight different things. You will get to choose which timer you will use in a programming block. The timer will allow you to time many different things. For example, as you can use a stopwatch to see how fast you can finish a 100–meter dash in real life; with the EV3 timer, you can also measure the time that a robot takes to drive a certain distance. Or you can see how much time passes between a robot's actions.

To understand how the timer works, imagine how one uses a stopwatch. A stopwatch measures time from the moment that the start button is pressed until the button is pressed a second time to stop the counting. Like a stopwatch, the EV3 timer measures elapsed time, starting at 0.0 seconds.

Note, however, that the timer always starts when the program begins. Regardless, if you use the timer in your program, the built-in timer will be running. So, it is important to reset your timer to 0.0 seconds when you want to start timing an event in your program. You can reset the timer at any point in your program, and it will start timing anew from that point. If the timer is never reset, it simply measures the time that has elapsed since you started the program (see Figure 9-1).

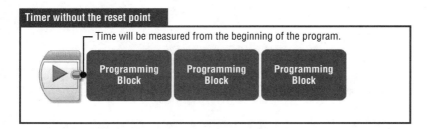

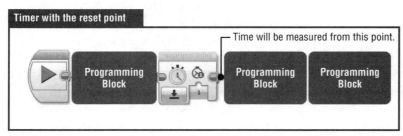

Figure 9-1: Timer with/without the reset point

To reset the timer, you need to use the Timer block, which is under the yellow tab in the programming palette. Just like any other sensor blocks, you can send out the data that you get from the Timer block to other blocks via data wires. But also it has a Reset mode, shown in Figure 9-2.

Figure 9-2: The Reset mode in the Timer block

Again, you can use the Timer block with the Reset mode anywhere in your program. When the program recognizes the Reset mode, the specified timer in the block resets to 0.0 seconds and starts measuring elapsed time from that point on.

Working with the Timer in Programming Blocks

You will see the Timer mode used in several programming blocks. This section explains how to use it in the Wait, Switch, and Loop blocks.

The Timer in the Wait Block

As in most of the other modes in the programming blocks, in the Wait block the Timer mode will appear as either:

- Timer – Compare – Time
- Timer – Change – Time

The Compare – Timer mode checks whether the timer meets a certain threshold value. This value can be a whole number; you can also include tenths of a second (or one place past the decimal point; for example, 2.5 seconds). When a program meets the Wait block with this mode, it will command, "Wait until the measured time from the timer satisfies the condition in the Wait block." With the Change – Timer mode, the Wait block makes the program wait until the timer's value changes by a certain threshold.

As Figure 9-3 shows, the timer in the Wait block measures the time interval between the point where the timer reads 0.0 (either the moment when the program started or when the timer was reset) and where the program meets this block. If the measurement meets the threshold, the Wait block allows the program to advance to the next block. If not, the Wait block holds up the program until the threshold number of seconds has been reached.

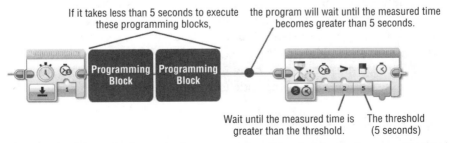

Figure 9-3: If the action between the reset point and threshold value (in seconds) takes less time than what the timer says, the program waits until it meets that time.

Well, then, what is the difference between using the Timer and Time modes? Using the Wait block with the Timer mode, the program checks the status of a timer that has already been ticking toward the threshold value. In the Timer mode, time has been measured before a program gets to the Wait block. On the other hand, when the program gets to the Wait block with Time mode, the program will start a new timer, and the measurement of time begins at that moment (see Figure 9-4).

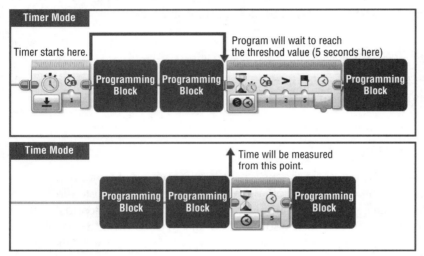

Figure 9-4: Timer mode versus Time mode

The Timer in the Switch Block

In the Switch block, you will find the Timer – Compare – Time mode. When the program reaches the Switch block with this mode, the timer first measures the number of seconds that have elapsed since the timer was last reset. Then, to verify a statement, the Switch block compares the measured time with the threshold that you entered. Examples of statements that the Switch block could test include "The value of the measured time is greater than 4 seconds" and "The value of the measured time is less than 3 seconds." If the statement is true, the program executes the top line of the code in the Switch block. If the statement is false, it runs the bottom line of the code (see Figure 9-5).

The Timer in the Loop Block

In the Loop block, the Timer mode appears the same way as in the Switch block, with Timer – Compare – Time mode. You get to set up the compare type and the threshold in the Loop block with this mode. When the program reaches the end of the code inside of the Loop block, the timer measures the elapsed time from the reset point. Then, the program compares the measured time and the threshold value in the block to determine whether the measured time has met the threshold. The program repeats the code inside of the Loop block until the comparison is right. Figure 9-6 shows an example of this process.

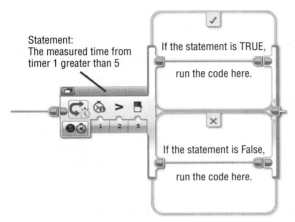

Figure 9-5: The Wait block with the Timer mode

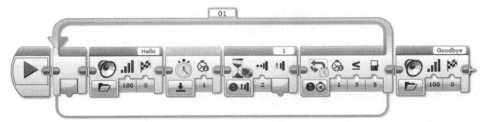

Figure 9-6: The Loop block with the Timer mode

When you start this program, you will hear the robot say, "Hello." After "hello," if you press the touch sensor within 5 seconds, the comparison in the Loop block will be true, and the program will exit out of the loop and say, "Good-bye." However, if you wait for more than 5 seconds after hearing "hello" to press the touch sensor, the program goes back to the beginning of the code inside of the loop and will play "hello" again. Note that the loop condition with the Timer mode will be evaluated only when the code inside is completed. If the code inside is not finished, a program will stay in the loop, waiting to complete the code inside, and won't get to evaluate the timer condition on the loop block. In our case, if the touch sensor is never bumped, the program won't get a chance to escape from the loop. As a result, you won't get to hear "Good-bye."

Programming with the Timer

Now it's time to insert the Timer mode into your robot. Have the Spy Rabbit ready and create the project called **Spy Rabbit – Timer**.

Exercise 1: Secret Code Is Activated

One of the skills that you need to learn as a spy is how to understand secret code. In this section, you train the Spy Rabbit to understand the secret code that you create. If the Spy Rabbit gets the right code, he will open his head, but if the code is wrong, he will generate an error alarm. If you hear this alarm, that means someone who doesn't know the code is trying to use the Spy Rabbit.

So, here is the "code" that you will assemble (starting with a simple code). You want to have the Spy Rabbit open his head when the tail bumper is pressed for more than 3 seconds. If his tail is bumped or pressed for less than 3 seconds, the alarm will go off. To do this, you need to measure how long the tail is pressed.

Start the program with the Wait block with the touch sensor saying, "Wait for the touch sensor to be pressed." As soon as it is pressed, you want to start measuring how long it takes until the touch sensor is released. To do this, place a Timer block to reset the ticking timer to zero, and then add a Wait block that says, "Wait for the touch sensor to be released." When the touch sensor is released, the program knows how long it took.

Then, you want to check a statement in the Switch block: The timer ran for more than 3 seconds. If the statement is true, the Spy Rabbit opens his head. If the statement is false, the alarm starts. Figure 9-7 shows how it looks as code. Create the program called **Secret Code** and try these blocks. Does the Spy Rabbit understand your signal?

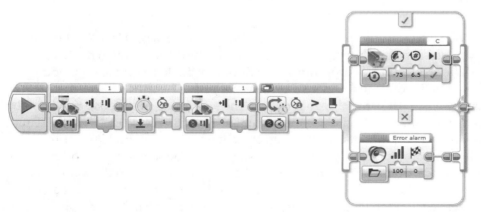

Figure 9-7: The program for the secret code: "Is the tail bumper pressed longer than 3 seconds?"

TRY IT: MAKE THE SECRET CODE MORE SECURE

The secret code from exercise 1 can be pretty easy to break. Can you try to add another layer of difficulty to your secret code? You can modify the program you used in exercise 1 by adding more programming blocks.

What about trying this:

1. Duplicate the entire program (except the Start block) that you used in exercise 1 and put the blocks in the top container of the Switch block.
2. Delete the Medium Motor block that is in the top container of the first Switch block.
3. Change the threshold value in the second Switch block to 1.5 seconds and change the compare type to Less Than.

With this code, to have the Spy Rabbit open his head, you need to press the touch sensor for more than 3 seconds and release it, and then press it again for less than 1.5 seconds and release it. What do you think? Now the code is more difficult to crack.

Try more creative secret codes by changing time threshold values in the Switch block's comparison signs. You can have more intense alarms or actions when someone puts in the wrong secret code.

Exercise 2: Wake Up

The Spy Rabbit will do whatever you tell him to do, even though you ask him to do something silly because it is *your* robot. (Remember, robots only do things according to how they are programmed.) Forget about the missions for a moment; instead, let's do something silly. We are going to have the Spy Rabbit be reborn as the Snooze Rabbit. He will say, "Morning," every 5 seconds over and over again until his tail is bumped. Once his tail is bumped, he will stop saying "morning" and will play "fanfare" instead. Figure 9-8 shows the code that makes it happen.

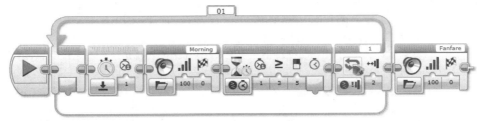

Figure 9-8: The code for the Snooze Rabbit

In this code, you will see the Loop block with the Touch Sensor mode that says, "Repeat the code inside of the Loop block until the touch sensor is bumped." The code inside of the Loop block makes the Snooze Rabbit say "morning" every 5 seconds. As you can see, whenever the program repeats the code inside of the Loop block, the timer resets so that it can start timing from 0.0 seconds again.

If you don't reset the timer, the time will add up whenever the program repeats the code. The interval time between the Timer block and the Wait block is 5 seconds, and as soon as the timer starts timing, the robot will say, "Morning." The timer will still be going until it reaches 5 seconds. The programming block that comes after is to make the robot play "fanfare" if the touch sensor is bumped. Remember, when you bump the touch sensor, if the timer hasn't reached 5 seconds yet, the program will wait until it gets to 5 seconds first and then play "fanfare."

Create the program called **Snooze** and follow the code in Figure 9-8. Do you know anyone who struggles to wake up in the morning? Then, it's time to put the Snooze Rabbit to work.

TRY IT: MOVE AROUND, SNOOZE RABBIT

So far, the Snooze Rabbit is being nice by staying still while it tries to wake people up. If you really want him to be effective at waking people up, you can make him a bit meaner. Rather than just saying "morning," what if you made him move around a little so that it's hard to predict where his tail is pointing? You can have him turn in a big circle whenever he says "morning," and you can add the Move steering block that makes him turn a little bit after the first Sound block. If he keeps driving around, it will be harder to shut him up.

Understanding the Motor Rotation Sensor

So far, you used the motors as the main device that moves the parts of the robot and programmed them with the Action blocks. However, both the large and medium EV3 motors have a built-in rotation sensor. As you learned, sensors report data to the EV3 brick, and the program uses them to take certain actions. The data that the motor rotation sensor sends to the EV3 brick is how far it has turned as well as its current power level.

The current power level will be measured between –100 (when the motor is moving backward with full power) and 100 (when the motor is moving forward with full power).

When the motor rotation sensor measures how far it moved, the turning amount is represented in two ways: in degrees and rotations. A rotation here means a motor's full turn, which is 360°. So, one rotation is 360°, two rotations are 720°, and so on. Also it can be a decimal number, like 0.5 rotations (180°), 1.8 rotations (648°), and so on.

Wait, but doesn't the motor turn in two ways, forward and backward? Don't worry; the rotation sensor detects the direction of the turn. If the motor rotation sensor is turning forward, the measuring value is a positive number. If it is turning backward, the measuring value is a negative number. Figure 9-9 shows the forward and backward turning movements on the motor.

Figure 9-9: Motor turning directions

NOTE Unlike other sensors, when you use the rotation sensor it won't work if it is connected to ports 1, 2, 3. or 4. It is still used like a motor, so you must plug it into ports A, B, C, or D. Make sure to specify in the programming block the motor from which you want to get the rotation values.

Using the Motor Rotation Sensor in Programming Blocks

Similar to the timer, the motor rotation sensor measures the rotation of the motor as long as the motor is turning. If your robot is running in a circle for 2 seconds from the beginning of the code, then if you try to measure the motor's rotation values, the motor rotation sensor reports the value that it detected for 2 seconds. Is there any way that you can measure the rotation values in a certain range of the code? Yes.

As you might have already guessed, you can reset the motor rotation sensor at any point in your program. Therefore, you can make the motor rotation sensor restart the measurement of the motor's rotation values from zero again. To do this, you must use the Reset mode in the Motor Rotation block. Just like the Timer block, you can find the Motor Rotation block under the yellow tab in programming palette (see Figure 9-10).

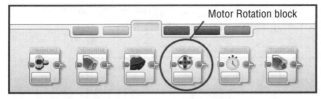

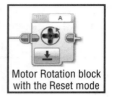

Motor Rotation block with the Reset mode

Figure 9-10: The Reset mode in the Motor Rotation block

If you use the motor rotation sensor without resetting it at any point in your program, it will give you the number of rotations that have occurred since the beginning of the program. If you get some ridiculous values when you use the motor rotation sensor, you probably forgot to reset the motor rotation sensor.

The Motor Rotation in the Wait Block

In the Wait block, you will find the following modes:

- Motor Rotation – Compare – Degrees, Rotations, or Current Power
- Motor Rotation – Change – Degrees, Rotations, or Current Power

With the Motor Rotation – Compare mode, the program waits to get certain data (in degrees, rotations, or its current power) that satisfies the comparison in the Wait block. Figure 9-11 shows, for example, that if the Wait block says, "Wait until the motor rotation value from port C is greater than 6," the program will wait until the motor plugged into port C turns enough so that the motor rotation sensor reports back a value that is greater than 6.

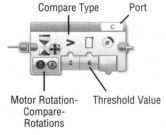

Figure 9-11: The Motor Rotation – Compare – Rotations mode in the Wait block

In the Motor Rotation – Change mode, the Wait block still detects the same types of data (motor degrees, rotations, or its current power), but instead of comparing the reading value with the threshold value, it checks whether that value has been changed by a certain amount (see Figure 9-12). If you run this code, motor B and C will go on until the rotation sensor in motor C sees the motor's rotation change by 5 in either direction.

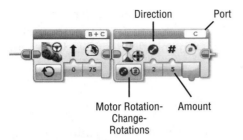

Figure 9-12: The Motor Rotation – Change – Rotations mode in the Wait block

Just as a reminder, when you set the direction in this mode, 0 (represented by the arrow that points up) means increase, which makes the program check whether the amount of change has been added up. 1 (represented by the arrow that points down) means decrease, which tells the program to check whether the amount of change has been subtracted. 2 (represented by the arrows on each end) means either direction, and the program will accept the change that happened with both scenarios.

The Motor Rotation in the Switch Block

In the Switch block, you can choose the Motor Rotation – Compare – Degrees, Rotations, or Current Power modes. With these modes, the program asks, "Does the reading value from the motor rotation sensor meet the comparison condition?" If the answer is true (yes), the line of the code on top is run. If the answer is false (no), the other line of the code is executed. See the example in Figure 9-13.

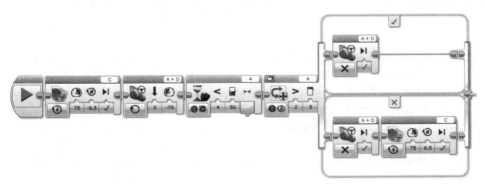

Figure 9-13: Example of using the Switch block with the Motor Rotation – Compare – Rotation mode

If you run this program with the Spy Rabbit, he will open up his head and start moving forward until the infrared sensor sees an object within a distance threshold value 50. If the infrared sensor sees something, and if the motor rotation sensor in port A detects that more than five rotations have been made, the Spy Rabbit will stop (top line of the code). If the rotation value that the motor rotation sensor reported is less than 5, he will stop and close his head (bottom line of the code).

The Motor Rotation in the Loop Block

You can also use the values from the motor rotation sensor to determine whether the program should stay in the loop and repeat the code inside or escape from the loop and stop repeating the code. There are Motor Rotation – Compare – Degrees, Rotations, or Current Power modes. You can set up a comparison condition in the Loop block, and the program will check whether the value from the motor rotation sensor satisfies the condition. Depending on what mode you choose, the motor degrees, rotations, or current power will be used for the comparison. The program repeats the code inside of the Loop block until the incoming value fulfills the comparison condition. Take a look at the chunk of code in Figure 9-14.

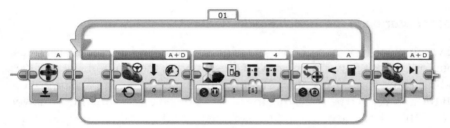

Figure 9-14: Example of using the Loop block with the Motor Rotation – Compare – Rotation mode

Once the program reaches the Motor Rotation block, it resets the motor rotation sensor in port A to zero. Then, the program starts the code inside of the Loop block, which makes motors A and D go forward until the infrared sensor gets the signal from the IR beacon. If the motor A turns more than three rotations when the infrared sensor detected the signal from the IR beacon, it will repeat the code in the loop. To stop the robot, or in other words to escape the loop, you should send the IR beacon signal before motor A makes three rotations.

Programming with the Motor Rotation Sensor

Now it's time to implement the Motor Rotation mode in your program. Using the rotation sensor, you will make your program more complex. Have the Spy Rabbit ready and create the project called **Spy Rabbit – Motor Rotation**.

Exercise 1: Warming Up

Sometimes, before a big mission, the Spy Rabbit takes some time to do a warm up. What he usually does to check his system is open his head bit by bit every 2 seconds until it is open up all the way. Create a program called **Warming up** and replicate the code in Figure 9-15.

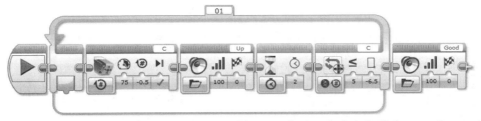

Figure 9-15: The program to make the Spy Rabbit open his head a little by little every 2 seconds

Can you see what's happening in this code? In the loop, we told the program to turn the medium motor in –0.5 rotations, which makes the Spy Rabbit open up his head a little bit, say, "Up," and then wait for 2 seconds.

You might be wondering why the number of the rotations is negative. A negative or positive number corresponds with the direction of the motor. To open the Spy Rabbit's head, the medium motor should turn backward, which is the reason why it says –0.5 in the Medium Motor block. The Spy Rabbit repeats this action until the medium motor makes –6.5 rotations. Whenever it repeats the code inside of the loop, the number of rotations will add up like (–0.5) + (–0.5)…+ (–0.5); because the number of rotations is a negative number, the sum number will be smaller and smaller.

When the number of rotations gets smaller than –6.5, the program escapes the loop, and Spy Rabbit says, "Good." Now we know the Spy Rabbit is ready to work. Why don't we add more code for more actions? Maybe we can grab some parts of the code that you used in the Avoiding program in Chapter 8?

TRY IT: SYSTEM OFF

When the Spy Rabbit was warming up the system, he opened his head. You can use this Warming up program at the beginning of any program for the Spy Rabbit. Then what about creating a code that we can use at the end of the code? Can you modify the Warming up program to make him close his head at a rate of 1.5 rotations per second?

Exercise 2: Wind Up the Spy Rabbit

Being a spy can be very tiring. For this reason, sometimes our robo-rabbit can be very difficult to work with. When he is not in a working mood, there is only one way to make him move: You have to wind him up.

Turn his motor A for three rotations in any direction, and he will move on his own for three rotations. Figure 9-16 shows the code for this action.

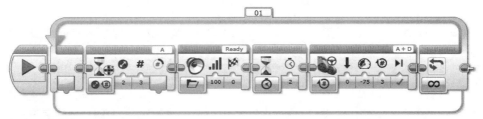

Figure 9-16: Wind up the Spy Rabbit's motor for three rotations to make him move himself for three rotations.

When you run this program in the Spy Rabbit, he just waits until his motor A turns three rotations in any direction, which means you can turn his motor A either backward or forward. Because the Spy Rabbit has treads connected to its motor, it will seem like it's not easy to manually turn his motor. However, if you use the red piece attached on the back hub, you'll find it easier to move the tread to turn motor A. Once you turn motor A, the Spy Rabbit will say, "Ready," and wait for 2 seconds for you to put him down to the floor. Then he will go forward for three rotations. Because all the blocks are in the Loop block with the Unlimited mode, you will have as long as you want to make him move. Create the program called **Wind up** and see whether this program works for the Spy Rabbit.

TRY IT: MORE EXERCISE FOR YOU, SPY RABBIT

From exercise 2, you finally made the Spy Rabbit move forward a little bit, but he needs to move around some more. Maybe you can make him go backward, as well? Let's have him move backward when we wind up his motor D so that we can make him do more exercises. Hint: Start from the Wind up program. Copy and paste the whole line of the code, including the Start block. Then, change the port for the motor and make the Spy Rabbit go backward.

ON BRICK PROGRAMMING: USING THE BRICK PROGRAM APP

So far, we have learned how to use the fundamental programming blocks with the software to control the motors, use data from sensors, display images, and so on. But what if a computer or the software is not available? Luckily, the EV3 brick comes with an app that allows you to do programming that is similar to the software. You may find it to be a bit limiting, but it is very useful when the software is not available or you want to test some tasks quickly. You can find this app on the Brick Apps screen, which appears when you select the third icon from the left on the top of the EV3 main screen. Once you click Brick Program, you will get the Start and Loop blocks on the screen with a broken line and a pointing-up arrow in the middle (see Figure 9-17).

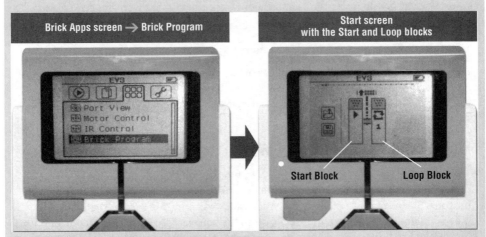

Figure 9-17: Open the Brick Program app and see the start screen.

Adding a New Programming Block

The broken line and the arrow mean that you can add a programming block in that place. You can navigate the blocks on your program by using the left and right buttons and, when navigating, you will see the broken line and the arrow between the blocks. When you see them on your program, if you press the up button, you will get the Block palette. There will be two types of blocks: action and wait. All the Action blocks have a small arrow at the top right corner, and icons on the block represent what they do. All the Wait blocks have an hourglass at the top right corner and sensor icons that indicate which sensor will control the wait. You can tell which icon refers to which sensor, but you may also find some icons that you have never seen; these are sensors that don't come with this particular set. You can navigate the Block palette with the up, down, left, and right buttons and choose the block that you want to use by pressing the center button (see Figure 9-18).

Continues

continued

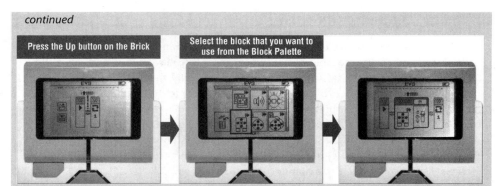

Figure 9-18: Open the Block palette and choose the block that you want to use.

Deleting or Replacing Existing Programming Blocks

If there is a block that you want to delete or replace, you can navigate to that block and press the up button. Then, you will see the Block palette again. You can select the trashcan icon to delete the block or choose another block that you want to replace it with.

Modifying Programming Block Settings

To change the settings of the programming blocks, you need to select the block by pressing the center button, then change the parameters by using the up and down buttons. Be aware that each programming block has only one setting that you can play with, unlike the programming blocks in the software. For example, in the Medium Motor block in the Brick Program, you can only change the power level; and in the Move Steering block, you will have the only option to modify the direction of steering. Keep in mind that you need to use the preassigned ports that are shown on the programming block, and you won't be able to change them. For example, to program the Medium motor, the motor needs to be plugged in port A, and to program the infrared sensor you need to use port 4.

Running a Program

Once you are done with your program, you can navigate to the Start button and press the center button. Note that you can also set up how many times you want to repeat the code by adjusting the Loop block's setting. You can select a number between 1 and 10 to specify how many times you want the code to repeat. After 10, you will find the infinity option, and the code will repeat forever until you press the back button.

Saving and Opening a Program

If you navigate your code to the Start block, you will see the save and open icons on the left side of the Start block. If you click the save icon, the EV3 brick will let you save the code in the `BrkProg_SAVE` folder that you can find on the File Navigation screen—you can find this screen by clicking the second icon from the left on the top of the EV3 main screen. If you click the open icon, you will be able to open saved programs that you created with the Brick Program.

Summary

In this chapter, you learned about the following:

- How the timer works in EV3 programming
- How to use the timer in the Wait, Switch, and Loop blocks
- How the rotation sensor works
- How to use the motor rotations in the Wait, Switch, and Loop blocks
- How to program the motor rotation sensor
- How to do on brick programming by using the Brick Program app on the EV3 brick

CHAPTER 10

Building Mr. Turto:
A Sea Turtle Robot

You had a great time with the Spy Rabbit, didn't you? While you were learning what he could do, you also learned a couple more programming tricks. After working with the Spy Rabbit for three chapters, it is time to build another friend. In this chapter, you get to meet a new robot named Mr. Turto, who will help you explore additional programming techniques.

Understanding Mr. Turto

So far in this book, you have learned to build robots that drive around, like a vehicle or a tank. Remember, though, that you do not want to limit yourself to just one method of moving your robot. Mr. Turto introduces a new moving mechanism: the crawl.

As you might guess from his name, Mr. Turto is a turtle-like robot that crawls on a flat, smooth surface, just like a sea turtle crawls across the beach (see Figure 10-1). Although graceful in the water, leatherback sea turtles move slowly on land. When it comes time for female sea turtles to lay their eggs, they must lumber across the sand, using their front flippers to drag themselves forward. Before starting to put him together and testing his motions, take a look at how Mr. Turto's body is structured and how it works.

Figure 10-1: The Mr. Turto robot

The Structure of Mr. Turto's Body

A sea turtle has a big and heavy shell on its back, which really slows it down on land. Mr. Turto's body is structured to replicate these characteristics. How, then, does the crawling motion work? Imagine that you are on a skateboard, lying on your belly. To move forward, you could stretch your arms out in front of you and then push your body forward by sweeping your arms to the side of your body. like the second movement of a jumping jack. Mr. Turto's front flippers work like your arms would in that example (see Figure 10-2). A tire on each flipper creates friction, yet it allows his flippers to pivot and push his entire body forward (or backward). The wheels under his body allow it to slide smoothly when it gets pushed.

For Mr. Turto's flippers to sweep and pull his body forward more than once, the flippers should freely move back into a position so that they can pull the robot forward another time. But what is going to happen if the tires on the flippers are still touching the ground? The flippers will push the body backward when they return to the front. If that is the case, Mr. Turto will just go forward and backward and not make any forward progress.

To prevent this from happening, I added a medium motor to Mr. Turto's torso that allows him to lift up his body. When his body is raised up slightly, he can swing his flippers back and forth without them making contact with the ground. So, if you want to program Mr. Turto to go forward, you need your program to say, "Lift up the body, move the flippers to the front, lower the body down, and then move the flippers to the sides of the body." Mr. Turto's front flippers can also be controlled individually to make Mr. Turto turn right or left. Let's build him and see how he moves.

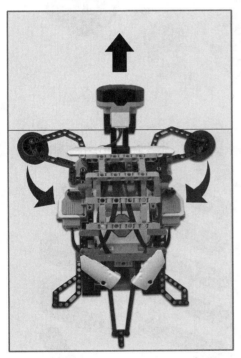
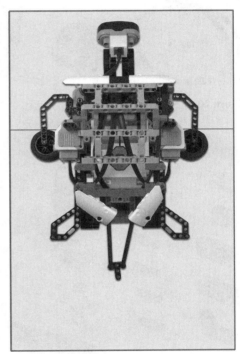

Figure 10-2: Mr. Turto's moving mechanism

Assembling Mr. Turto

Collect the parts shown in Figures 10-3 and 10-4, and then follow the step-by-step building instruction in Figures 10-5 to 10-39 to put Mr. Turto together.

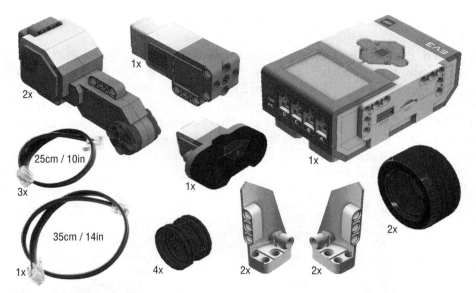

Figure 10-3: Parts for Mr. Turto: 1

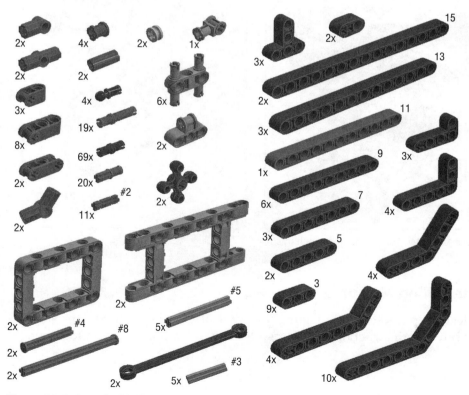

Figure 10-4: Parts for Mr. Turto: 2

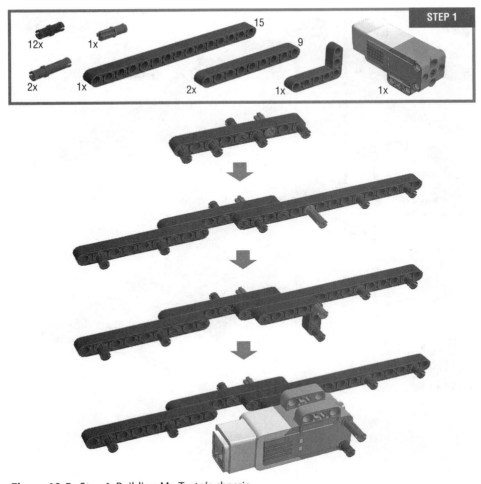

Figure 10-5: Step 1: Building Mr. Turto's chassis

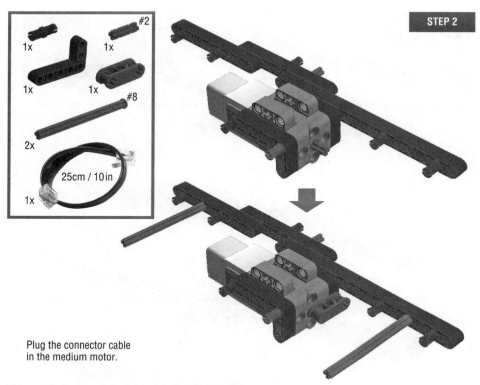

STEP 2

Plug the connector cable
in the medium motor.

Figure 10-6: Step 2: Building Mr. Turto's chassis

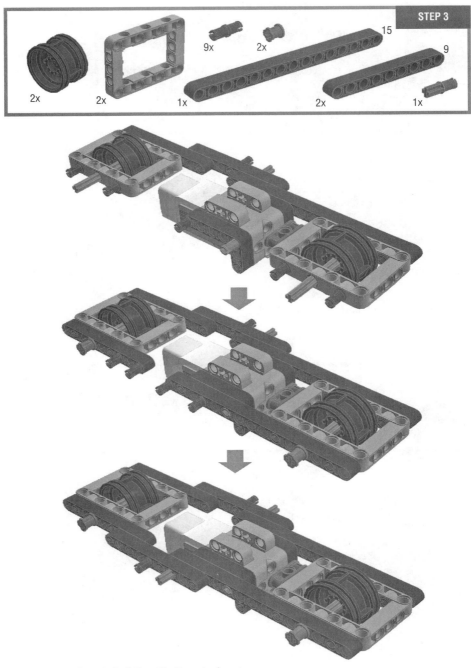

Figure 10-7: Step 3: Building Mr. Turto's chassis

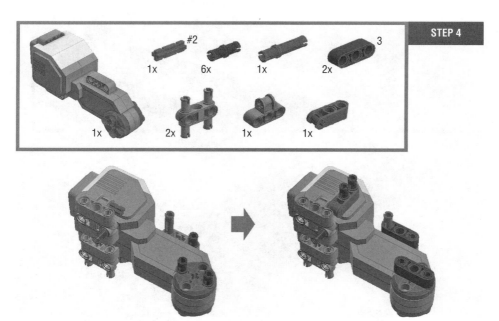

Figure 10-8: Step 4: Building the front left flipper

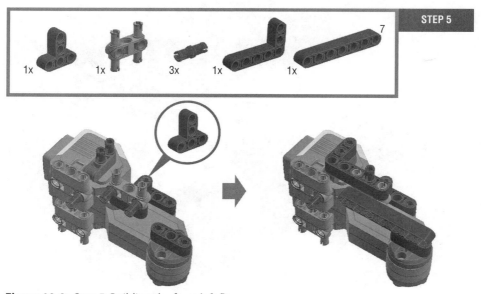

Figure 10-9: Step 5: Building the front left flipper

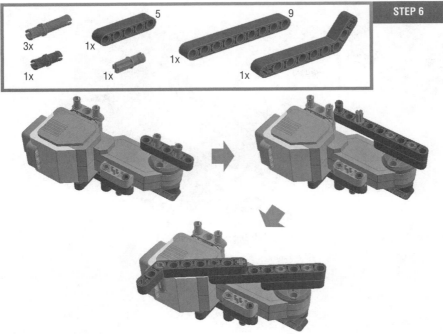

Figure 10-10: Step 6: Building the front left flipper

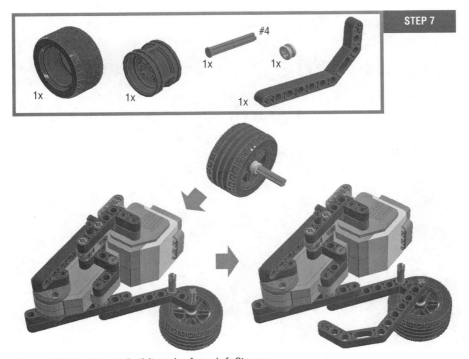

Figure 10-11: Step 7: Building the front left flipper

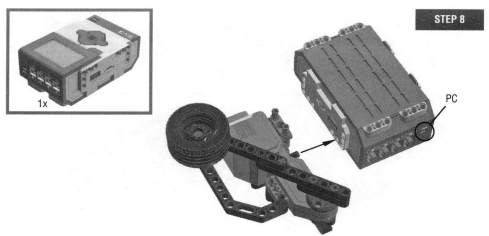

Figure 10-12: Step 8: Connecting the front left flipper to the EV3 brick

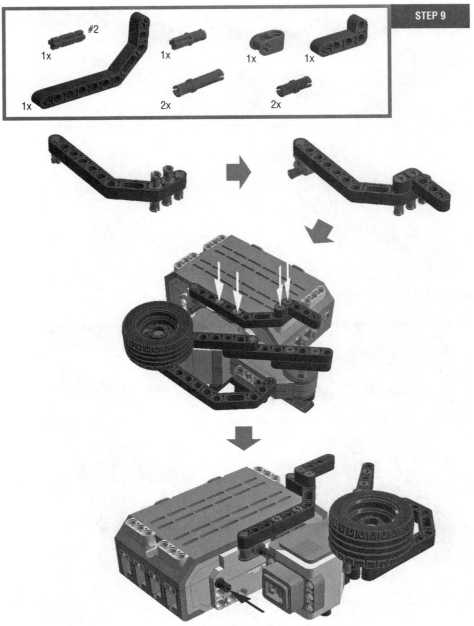

Figure 10-13: Step 9: Connecting the front left flipper to the EV3 brick

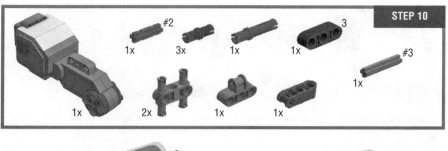

Figure 10-14: Step 10: Building the front right flipper

Figure 10-15: Step 11: Building the front right flipper

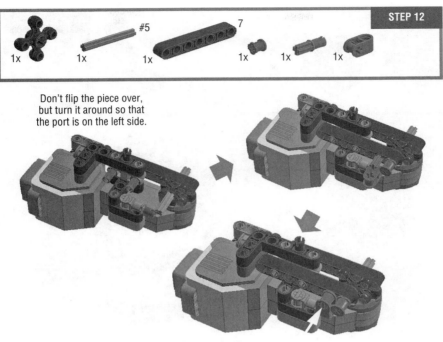

Figure 10-16: Step 12: Building the front right flipper

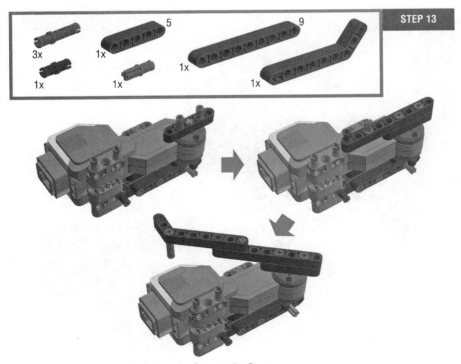

Figure 10-17: Step 13: Building the front right flipper

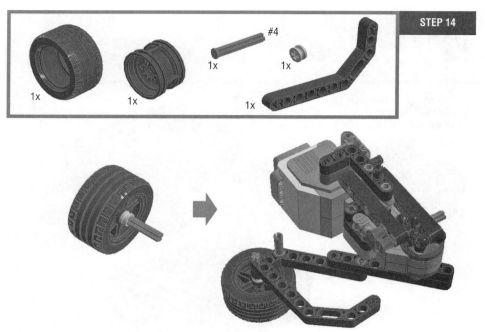

Figure 10-18: Step 14: Building the front right flipper

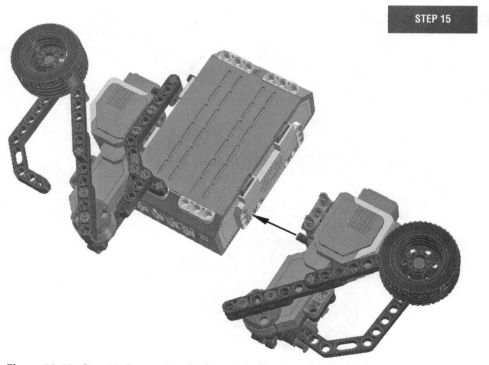

Figure 10-19: Step 15: Connecting the front right flipper to the EV3 brick

STEP 16

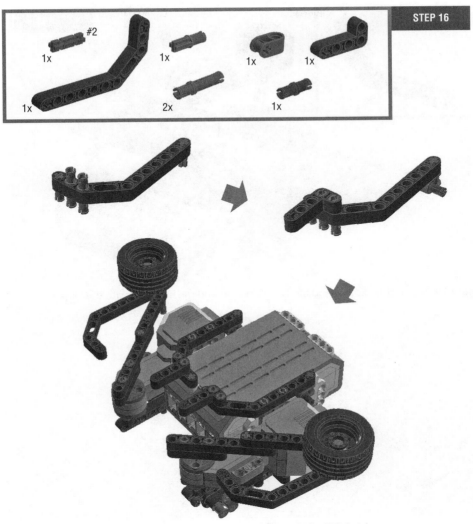

Figure 10-20: Step 16: Connecting the front right flipper to the EV3 brick

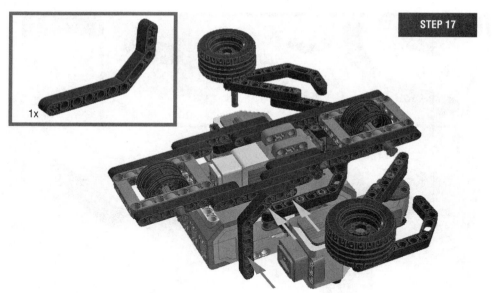

Figure 10-21: Step 17: Combining Mr. Turto's chassis and the EV3 brick with the flippers

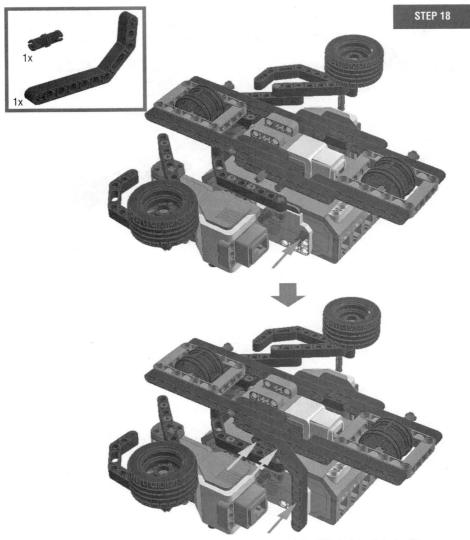

Figure 10-22: Step 18: Combining Mr. Turto's chassis and the EV3 brick with the flippers

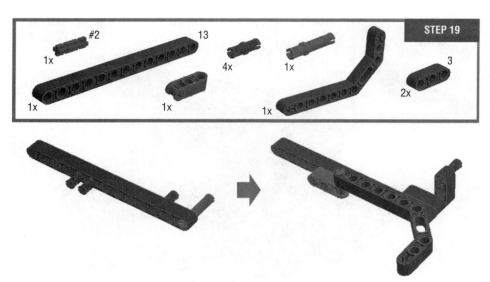

Figure 10-23: Step 19: Building the back right flipper

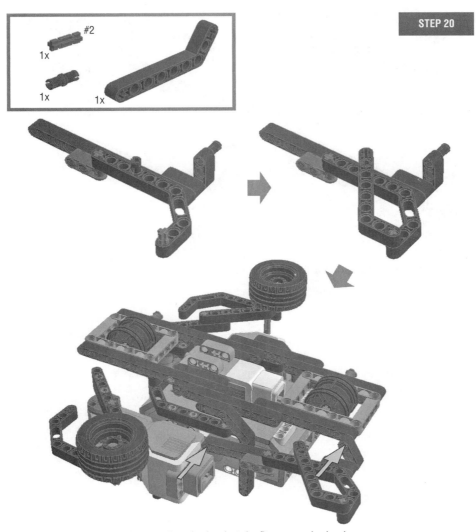

Figure 10-24: Step 20: Connecting the back right flipper to the body

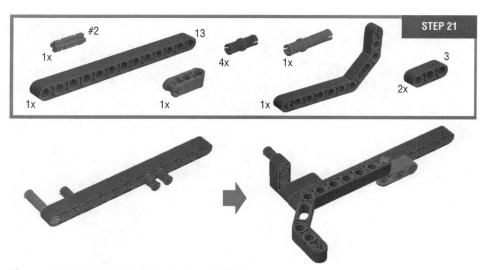

Figure 10-25: Step 21: Building the back left flipper

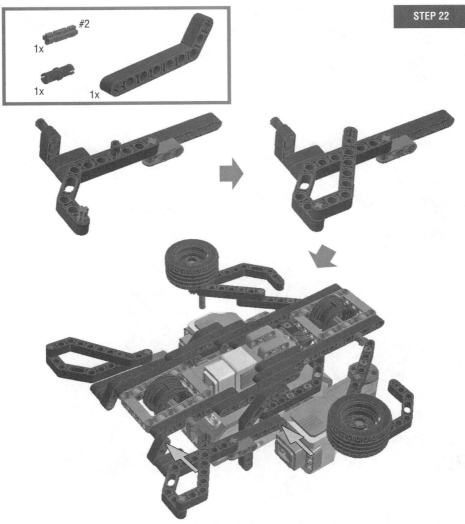

Figure 10-26: Step 22: Connecting the back left flipper to the body

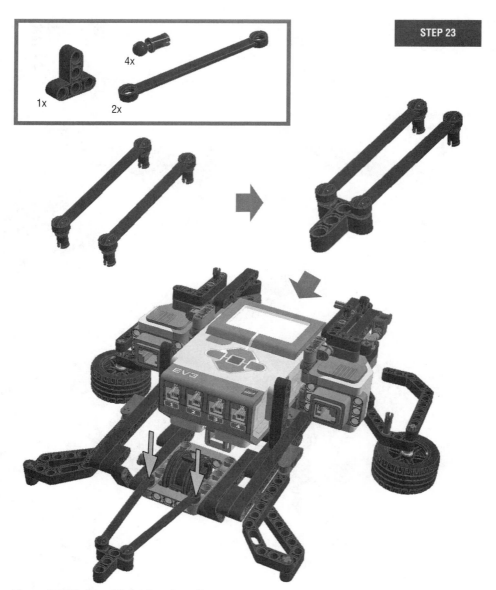

Figure 10-27: Step 23: Adding the tail

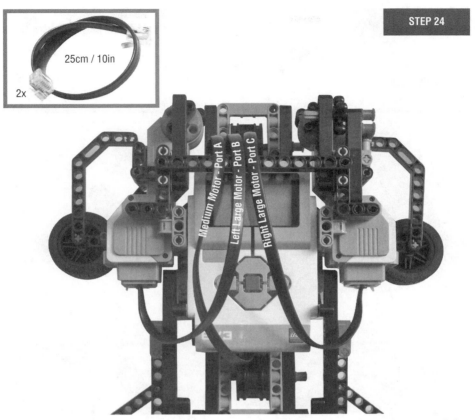

Figure 10-28: Step 24: Plugging the connector cables: port A = medium motor; port B = left large motor; and port C = right large motor

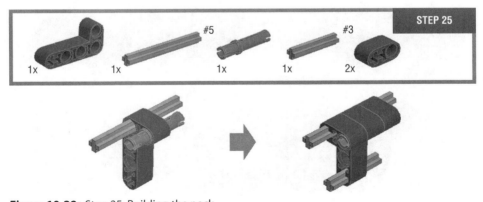

Figure 10-29: Step 25: Building the neck

STEP 26

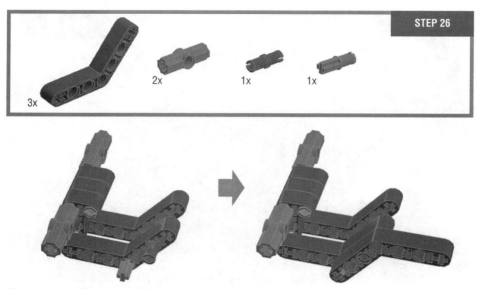

Figure 10-30: Step 26: Building the neck

STEP 27

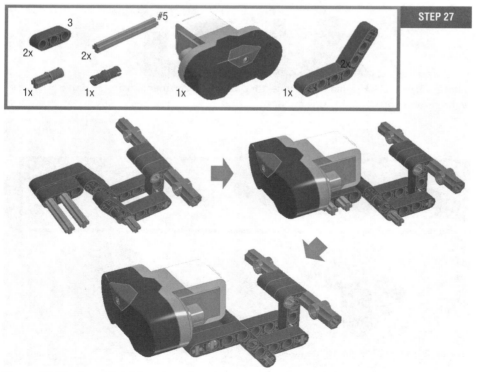

Figure 10-31: Step 27: Adding the infrared sensor to the neck (the head of Mr. Turto)

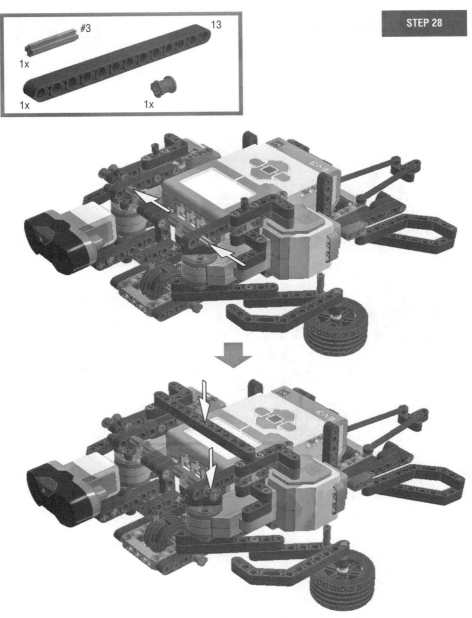

Figure 10-32: Step 28: Connecting the head to the body

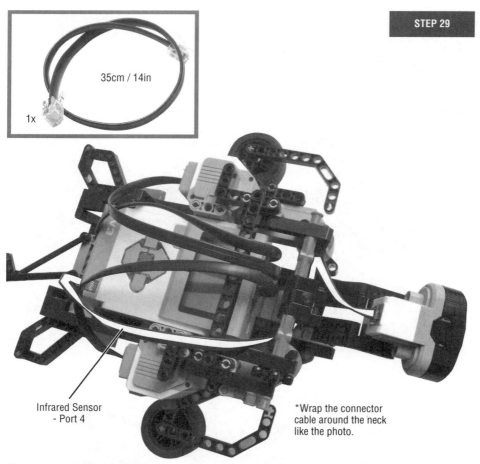

35cm / 14in

1x

Infrared Sensor
- Port 4

*Wrap the connector
cable around the neck
like the photo.

Figure 10-33: Step 29: Plugging in the connector cable: port 4 = Infrared Sensor

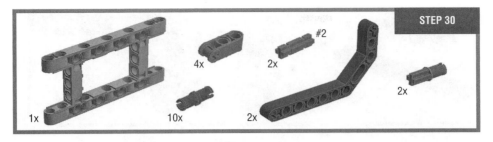

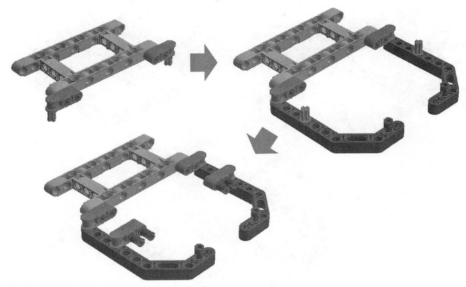

Figure 10-34: Step 30: Building the shell

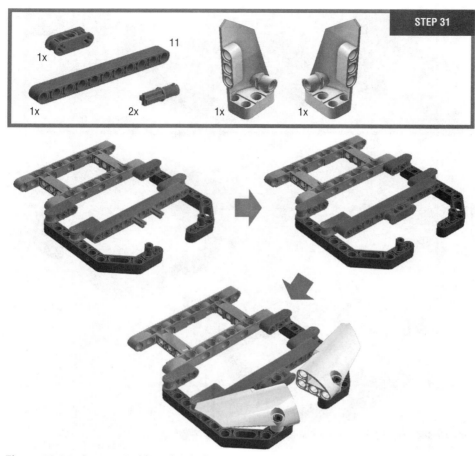

Figure 10-35: Step 31: Building the shell

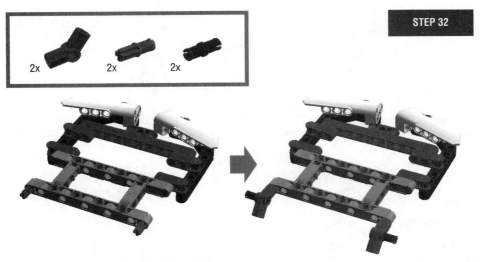

Figure 10-36: Step 32: Building the shell

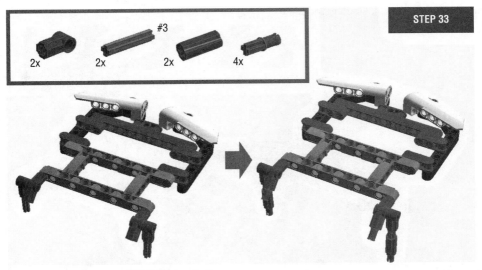

Figure 10-37: Step 33: Building the shell

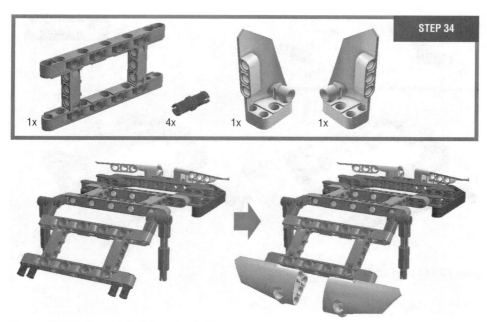

Figure 10-38: Step 34: Building the shell

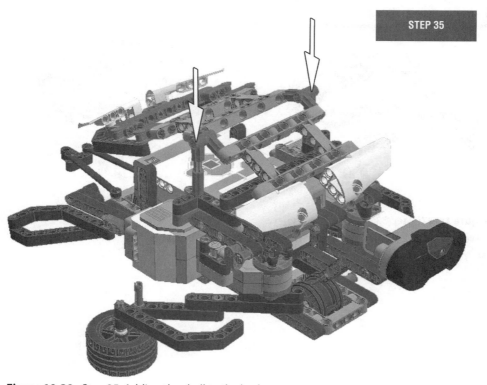

Figure 10-39: Step 35: Adding the shell to the body

Testing Mr. Turto's Movements

Now that you have Mr. Turto assembled, let's put him into action. Note that he will best perform on a hard, smooth surface like a hardwood floor or a table. (Don't let him fall!) In this section, you just test his movement to see whether everything is in the right place. You will do more programming with sensors in the next chapter.

Make sure that the large motors for the flippers are plugged into ports B and C and that the medium motor is connected to port A. Next, lift up the front part of the body and check to determine whether the red piece on the medium motor is positioned like it is in Figure 10-40.

Figure 10-40: Make sure that the red piece on the medium motor is placed like it is in the photo.

Create a project called **Mr – Turto** and make a new program called **Mr – Turto – test**. When you are ready, write code that looks like Figure 10-41. The two front flippers should be position to rest against the side of Mr. Turto's body before you run the program.

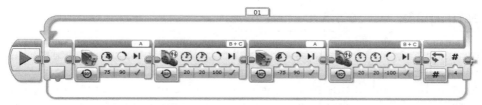

Figure 10-41: Program to test Mr. Turto's movements

When you run this program, Mr. Turto will lift up his torso (first Medium Motor block) and sweep his two front flippers forward (first Move Tank block), without them touching the ground. While his flippers swing forward, you will see Mr. Turto lift up his head. (The same motor powers his right flipper and his head, so when the flipper swings forward, the head moves up, and when the flipper sweeps backward, the head goes down.) Once the flippers are in their forward position, his torso lowers back down (second Medium Motor block), and Mr. Turto will drag his body forward by swinging his flippers back against his torso (second Move Tank block). He will repeat this action four times (Loop block with the Count mode). Note that he performs better when the large motor's power is set to low. It will be slower, but more predictable, just like a real sea turtle.

Summary

In this chapter, you learned about the following:

- How Mr. Turto is structured and how he moves
- How to build Mr. Turto
- How to program Mr. Turto to move like a real sea turtle

Programming with Data Wires and Using My Blocks

You may recall that previous chapters alluded to "programming with data wires" but delayed the lesson by saying that it will be covered in Chapter 11. Well, here we are, Chapter 11 at last. Up to this point, we've used the principle method of EV3 programming, which is connecting programming blocks to each other in a row. This chapter, however, teaches you a new technique that allows the programming blocks to exchange data between one another via data wires. For example, you can use the reading value from the infrared sensor as the input value that controls the volume of the sound on the sound block. In addition, you will learn how to design your own programming block. Mr. Turto will be your partner throughout the chapter, so have him ready.

What Is a Data Wire?

Programming blocks can be "data wired" to one another. A data wire is a virtual pipeline for moving data. When a data wire connects one programming block to the other, the value that one block collects is sent to the other block to be used as its input value. For example, the value that you get from the infrared sensor can be sent to the Sound block to be used to control the sound volume. So, if the value from the infrared sensor was 65, then the sound's volume will be set to 65 correspondingly. The output value from the Infrared Sensor block is used as an input value for the Sound block.

Confused? Think of it like this: Programming blocks work like train stations. Data that a block sends out or takes in represents the trains, and data wires are the tracks (see Figure 11-1). Like train stations have switches to reroute the trains, programming blocks have hubs that send out or accept data. These hubs are called block outputs and block inputs. You can wire one block's block output to another block's block input, and the data moves around within your program.

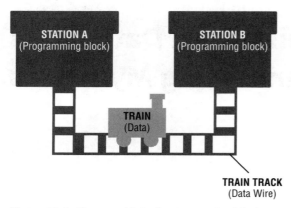

Figure 11-1: You can think of programming blocks as train stations, data as trains, and data wires as train tracks.

You will be the one laying down the train tracks (the data wires) for the data that travels throughout your program. By mastering this skill, you will allow yourself more flexibility in programming your robot by removing the need to decide on block settings beforehand.

How Do Data Wires Work?

Now that you know what a data wire is, you want to learn how to put it into your code. This section uses a simple example to demonstrate how data wires work, and then introduces you to some techniques for managing them. Also, you will learn to choose between different types of data wires. So, get ready for some data wiring activities.

Getting Started with Data Wire Programming

Before beginning an example, let's connect the touch sensor to Mr. Turto. Plug the sensor into port 1 with a connector cable. Don't worry about how you attach the cable to his body. It can just hang there like a leash for now.

Make a new program called **Mr-Turto-Touch** in the project Mr. Turto from Chapter 10, "Building Mr. Turto: A Sea Turtle Robot." Then follow the instructions in Figure 11-2 and Figure 11-3 to write the example code.

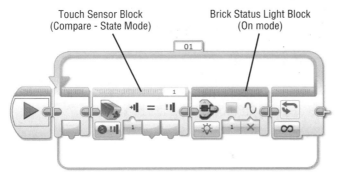

Figure 11-2: Creating a line of code with the Touch Sensor block and Brick Status Light block

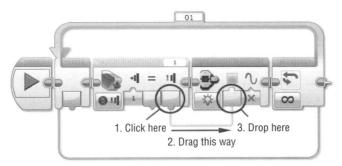

Figure 11-3: Connecting the block output in the Touch Sensor block to the block input in the Brick Status Light block

Download this program to the EV3 brick and see what happens when you run it. The brick status light will be green when you start the program, and if you press the button the light will turn orange. Because the line of code is in the loop, the light will go back and forth between green and orange as long as you press and release the button.

Let's take a closer look at the program and see what each block did. What happened to the Touch Sensor block? As you learned before, the touch sensor button has three states: released, represented by the number 0; pressed, represented by the number 1; and bumped, represented by the number 2. When you make any of these three actions, the Touch Sensor block receives its corresponding number as a reading value. Then, this measured value is the output value of the Touch Sensor block and ready to be sent out.

What about the Brick Status Light block? Like the touch sensor's states, each color of the brick status light also has a corresponding number: 0 means green, 1 means orange, and 2 means red. The Brick Status block needs one of these numbers as its input value so that it may determine what color of light should turn on.

So, here we are with two blocks, one has the value that will be sent out and the other block is waiting to receive a value. We connected these two blocks with a data wire so that the output value from the Touch Sensor block can be the input value for the Brick Status Light block (see Figure 11-4).

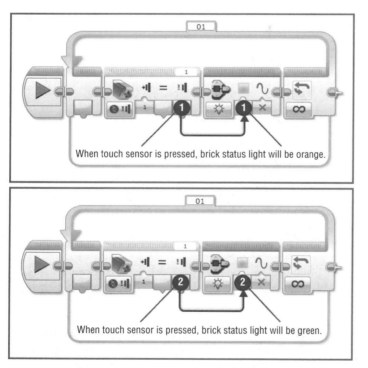

Figure 11-4: A summary of the program Mr-Turto-Touch that directs the touch sensor state to determine the color of the brick status light

However, you'll find that even though you bump the touch sensor button, which should give you a value of 2, you never get to see the red light turn on as a result. This is because the bumping action is actually the combination of two actions, pressing and releasing. So, when you bump the touch sensor, the data wire quickly carries the values of 1 (pressed) and 0 (released) from the Touch Sensor block to the Brick Status block. The Brick Status block will never receive the value of 2 from the touch sensor.

Using Block Input and Output

To use the data wire, you need to pull out the data wire from one block and plug it into another block, just like you did in the example program. How do you know where on a programming block you can pull out or plug in the data wire? Recall the train analogy: A programming block has gates for data to come in or go out like the train station has gates for trains that are arriving or departing. There are two types of gates: one for receiving the data, which is called the block input; and another for sending the data out, which is called the block output. Luckily, they appear differently on a programming block, as shown in Figure 11-5. The block input has a bump that sticks out from the top, and the block output has a small bump pointing down. These small parts basically represent which direction the data will travel (into the block or out of the block).

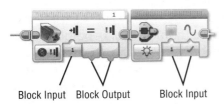

Block Input   Block Output   Block Input

Figure 11-5: Block input and block output in a programming block

Then, how do you delete a data wire that has already been connected? You'll want to click the block input where the wire ends and drag it out, as shown in Figure 11-6. When you click as directed, the data wire will disappear.

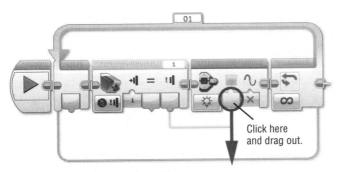

Click here and drag out.

Figure 11-6: Deleting a data wire

Note that you can pull out multiple data wires from a block output, which means that you can use the same data for more than one block. A block input, however, can only have one value coming in. For example, when you use the infrared sensor, you can have two wires coming out from its block and connect them to the Sound and Large Motor block's block inputs to control the volume of the sound and the power of the large motor. However, the block input for controlling the volume of the sound in the Sound block cannot have two different output values coming in.

Understanding Data Types and Data Wire Types

You have learned how to construct the data wires, so let's see what kind of values that they can carry. Data wires can transfer five types of information between blocks: numeric, text, logic, numeric array, and logic array. This chapter covers only the first three. The remaining two data types will be covered in Chapter 12, "Using Data Operations Blocks," when we learn about arrays. This section discusses the kind of information each data type delivers and how they are used in programs, but first you need to see how they appear in a program.

If you take a look at block input and output closely, you will see the sticking parts have different shapes: half-circle shape (numeric data), pointy shape (logic data), square (text data), and so on. The shapes indicate the data type. Just as there are different lines of trains, there are different types of data. And just like a gate at a train station only lets an assigned train come in or out, each block input/output in a programming block is designed to allow only a specific type of data. The shape of a block input/output tells you what type of information it can carry. For example, we used the block input and output that have half-circle shaped sticking parts in the program that we made in Figure 11-2 and 11-3, which can transfer numeric data (numbers).

The data type that a block output carries determines the data wire type. They are distinguished by color and thickness. For example, the numeric data wire is a thin yellow line, and the logic data wire is a thin green line. Each data type has a corresponding data wire. Figure 11-7 shows the summary of the block input and output of each data type and corresponding data wires.

Let's go over each data type and see how the different types of data will be and how they can be used in the program.

- **Numeric data type**: This data type is composed of numbers. These numbers can be positive (greater than zero), negative numbers (less than zero) or zero. They also can have decimal values such as 2.8, 10.234, –4.56, and so on. Figure 11-8 shows an example of using this value type with the data wire. The value that the Timer block gets, which is a numeric value, can be wired to control the power of the motor. The Timer block will send out the amount of time that it measures, which increases as time goes by, to the

Power input of the Move Steering block. Because this sequence of the blocks is in a loop, the program repeats the code within and as a result, motors B and C will accelerate until their power value settings hit 100.

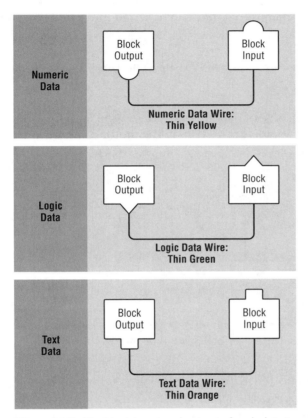

Figure 11-7: The block input and output of each data type and corresponding data wires

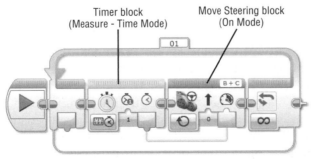

Figure 11-8: A program where the timer controls the power of motors B and C

■ **Text data type**: Do you want to display your robot's name on the EV3 screen? If so, you need to use this type of data. Text data appears as lines of text, which can be a word (boy, girl), a sentence (I am a boy, you are a girl.) or a sequence of any supported text. Note that numeric values can be read as text, which means that they can be wired into a text block input on a programming block.

NOTE To see the EV3 supported text, go to EV3 help on the Lobby area - General - Supported Text.

Let's take a look at an example of using the text data type with the data wire. The example that Figure 11-9 shows is to display the motor rotation value from motor B on the EV3 screen.

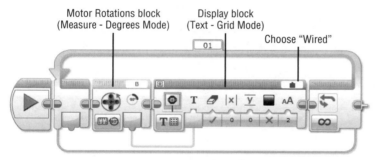

Figure 11-9: A program to print out motor B's rotation value on the EV3 screen

If you run this program with Mr. Turto, whenever you manually swing his flipper that is connected to port B, the screen will show the reading values. (Take off Mr. Turto's shell to have a clearer view of the screen, if you want.) You will find that the data wire that connects the Motor Rotation block output and the Display block input is a numeric data type wire, not a text data type. It's because the type of data wire is determined by the value type that the block output sends out, which in this case is a numeric type of value. Note that you should choose Wired in the Block Text field in the Display block when you program it to show the text from a data wire.

■ **Logic data type**: The logic data type has one of two potential values: true or false. This data type can be used for values that can have two conditions like a compare result so that you can find the Compare mode in a programming block. For example, you can set up the Touch Sensor block to compare whether the touch sensor is being pressed or not being pressed. Then, the block can send out the true or false result of this statement via a logic data wire. Also, the brick status light's pulse status can have a true or false value. When it gets the true input, the light will be blinking. We can use these two blocks together and use the touch sensor's compare result (pressed: true, released: false) as an input for the brick status light's pulse status. If the touch sensor is pressed, the brick status light will be blinking. This true or false logic values also can be read as a numeric value. When it's true, it has a numeric value 1, and when it's false, it has 0. Therefore, you can use the logic value to control the value that can have 0 or 1 as its input such as the color of the brick status light. See the two examples in Figure 11-10.

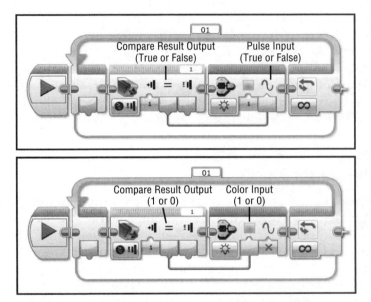

Figure 11-10: Using the logic value from the Touch Sensor block to control the brick status light's pulse status (top) or the color of the light (bottom)

Just like the U.S. Postal Service needs to collect mail so that it may deliver it, a programming block should first collect its data before in order to send them out to another block. In EV3, we collect data by using sensors. Each sensor has its own programming block, which allows collected data to be sent out to other blocks. In the following section, we will learn how they work and how to use these blocks with data wires.

Sensor Blocks and Data Wires

At the beginning of the book, we first started programming with EV3 by learning Action blocks such as the Motor Steering block, Motor Tank block, Display block, and so on. These blocks are mostly for executing a robot's actions, which is the outcome of the program. How then did we configure these blocks to make the robot perform those specific actions? We set up the input values for each parameter by manually typing in the values. Now that you are learning data wiring, you will find that you can pull a value from another block with a data wire and plug it into where you usually type in.

Just as there are programming blocks that wait to get the input values to produce outcomes (Action blocks), there are also blocks whose job is to collect the information from the robot's surroundings and export the data to other blocks. As you might've guessed, I'm talking about the sensor blocks.

Sensor blocks don't really do anything by themselves in a program, but you can use them to collect data to configure the other blocks. For example, if the program has the Infrared Sensor block alone, it will still get the reading values from the sensor but won't make any changes to a robot's performance. However, if you add a Large Motor block to the project and pull the reading value from the infrared sensor to control the level of the large motor, the results could be very useful for future robot designs. Let's see what the settings of the sensor block look like.

Setting Up the Sensor Blocks

You'll find six sensor blocks under the yellow tab in the programming palette: Brick Buttons, Color Sensor, Infrared Sensor, Motor Rotations Sensor, Timer, and Touch Sensor blocks. They all have two modes between which you can choose: Measure and Compare.

When you choose the Measure mode in the sensor blocks, they will simply read the incoming values that come from the sensor. For example, if you choose the Measure – Beacon mode in the Infrared Sensor block, the measured values will be the beacon heading (numeric value), beacon proximity (numeric value), and beacon detected status (logic value; true or false).

The Compare mode presents an additional setting. You can set up the comparison statement, such as "Is the motor rotation sensor turned greater than 90°?" Then the outputs are going to be the compare result, yes or no (true or false; logic value) and the actual measured value. See this example in a programming block in Figure 11-11. When you use the Infrared Sensor, Color Sensor (Reflected Light Intensity and Ambient Light Intensity modes), and Timer blocks with the Compare mode, you will see the similar format on the block.

Some blocks' comparison statements will differ from the example in Figure 11-11. If the sensor tends to detect the state of stimulus, there won't be the compare type input or threshold value. The comparison statement will be more like asking whether a specific event happened or not, such as "Is the touch sensor pressed?" or "Is the color sensor reading red?" The outputs of these blocks will be the compare result and the actual measured value. Figure 11-12 shows what they'll look like in a program.

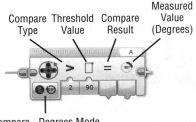

Figure 11-11: The Motor Rotation block with the Compare mode

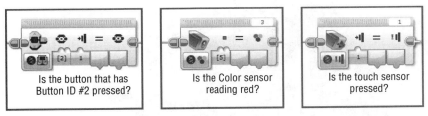

Figure 11-12: The Brick Buttons, Color Sensor, and Touch Sensor blocks with the Compare mode

Now let's use some sensor blocks in your programs. Mr. Turto will volunteer as our testing robot for the following exercises. If you still have the touch sensor attached, take it off for the time being. Instead, mount the color sensor onto his shell (see Figure 11-13).

Let's find and open the program that we made in Chapter 10, "Building Mr. Turto: A Sea Turtle Robot," which is called Mr-Turto-Test. This is the program that makes Mr. Turto move forward. Note that the position of the red piece on the medium motor should point to your left and the flippers should be next to his torso when you use the Mr-Turto-Test program.

Exercise 1: Yay! I Found Something

When Mr. Turto gets excited, he moves his flippers back and forth and lifts his torso up and down. So, what makes him act this way? As a lonely turtle robot,

Mr. Turto gets excited when he finds someone very close to him. Unfortunately, he can't tell the difference between living beings and objects (yet), so he will get excited when he finds a random object in front him.

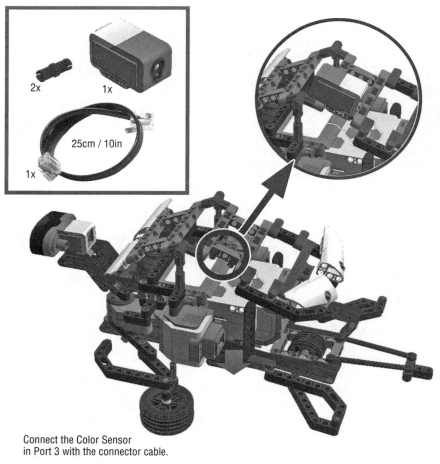

Connect the Color Sensor
in Port 3 with the connector cable.

Figure 11-13: Adding the color sensor on Mr. Turto's shell

To give Mr. Turto this personality trait, you must program him to use his infrared sensor to detect how close he is to an object and change his movement accordingly. You can control his flipper movements in two ways. First, you can change it by altering the power of the motor (affecting the speed of the flipper's movement), or second, you can change it by altering the number of degrees that the motor turns (affecting the flipper's turning radius). Here, we modify the motor's rotation, in degrees. Just like the code that we used in the program Mr-Turto-Test, the motor that controls the flipper can move in 100° maximum, which makes Mr. Turto move his flipper in about a quarter of the radius of a circle. So, if we have a smaller value than 100 for motor degrees, the flipper's moving radius will be smaller as well. In this case, because it will take less time to make a smaller radius the flippers are moving back and forth at a faster rate than when the motors turn 100°. Because the infrared sensor gets smaller values when an object is closer, we can use these values to control the motor degrees so that when Mr. Turto finds something close by, his flippers will move back and forth more quickly.

Let's write this program together. Make a program called **Mr – Turto – IR sensor – Degrees**, and then connect the Loop block to the Start Block. Inside of the loop, put in an Infrared Sensor block with the Measure – Proximity mode. Then, go to the Mr-Turto-Test program and copy the code inside of the loop (copy: select the blocks that you want, and then press Cmd+C [OS X] / Ctrl+C [PC]) and bring them to the current program (paste: Cmd+V [OS X] / Ctrl+V [PC]).

Now it's data wiring time. Pull out the data wire from the Infrared Sensor block and connect it to the motor degrees input in the first Move Tank block. Then, pull out another data wire and connect it to the same input in the second Move Tank block. Wait, there is one more thing that requires our attention before we run the program! On the code that we initially copied from the Mr – Turto – Test program, we had –100° as the degree input value for the second Move Tank block because we needed to move the motors backward to have the flippers come back to the sides of the torso. Now that the second Move Tank block gets its degree input value from the infrared sensor's reading, the degree value will always be a positive number. As a solution, we'll need to change the direction of the motors. You can change the power levels to be negative, which means on the code, the power levels on the second Move Tank block should be changed from 20 to –20. The program should look like the one in Figure 11-14.

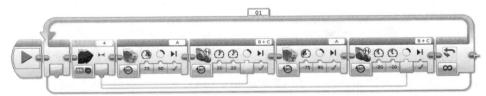

Figure 11-14: Program where the infrared sensor value controls the degrees of motors B and C

Run the program and have him come toward you. Can you tell how happy Mr. Turto is to see you?

Exercise 2: Can You Hear Me?

Poor Mr. Turto is a lonely robot, and he is always looking for someone to listen to him. He will keep moving forward and shouting to get anybody's attention. When everything is far away, his infrared sensor reading value will be 100.

When he gets closer to someone or something, his voice will become softer and softer. When he is really close to that object, (his infrared sensor reads the value that is smaller than 10), he will stop and gently say "Hi."

To get this behavior, you need to use the Switch block along with an infrared sensor that is set to Compare – Proximity mode. Then, complete the compare statement in this way: Is the reading value smaller than 10? If the answer is true, meaning that Mr. Turto found something close by, you want to program him to stop (Move Tank block with the Off mode) and say "Hi" (Sound block). If the answer is false, which means things are still not close enough, you want to program him to move forward (you will use the line of the code that was inside of the loop in the Mr-Turto-Test program) and shout (the Sound block again).

You also want to control the volume of his voice to be softer as he approaches an object, which means that the volume control value should be getting smaller as the infrared sensor reading value diminishes. The data wire will prove useful right here. You can add in the Infrared Sensor block with the Measure – Proximity mode after the code that makes Mr. Turto move. Use its output value as the input value for the volume in the Sound block. See the program in Figure 11-15. Does it all make sense? You will find that I put the Switch block in the Loop block and added the Loop Interrupt block at the end of the top line of the code. With these blocks, the program will get to repeat only the bottom line of the code in the Switch block because once it runs the top line of the code, the program will exit from the loop.

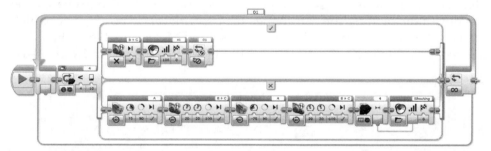

Figure 11-15: Program that controls the volume of Mr. Turto's voice, which is controlled by the distance between him and the object

Create a program called **Mr – Turto – IR sensor – Volume** and follow the program shown in Figure 11-15. When you run the program, is Mr. Turto desperately shouting?

Exercise 3: Bright Light Makes Mr. Turto Awake

Before you start this exercise, have a flashlight handy. Why? A flashlight is important because Mr. Turto can change his behavior by reacting to the amount of light that his color sensor picks up. When Mr. Turto's color sensor senses a great deal of light, he will move his flippers faster back and forth, but when the sensor gets only a small amount of light, he will move very slowly. You can adjust the amount of light that the flashlight shines into the sensor by moving it closer or farther away.

In this scenario, the speed of Mr. Turto's flippers changes depending on the amount of light that the color sensor gets. Can you see how we can use the data wire here? Let's make a program called **Mr – Turto – Light** and copy and paste the code from the Mr-Turto-Test program.

First, change the Loop block mode to Unlimited. Second, let's put the Color Sensor block between the first Medium Motor block and the first Move Tank block, and set it to the Measure – Ambient Light Intensity mode. Finally, connect the output values from the color sensor to both of the motor Power inputs on both of the Move Tank blocks. We are using one output value for four inputs, meaning that you have four data wires coming out from the color sensor.

There is one more block that you want to add to this program to make it work better. Because the range of the value that the color sensor can measure (with the Measure – Ambient Light Intensity mode) spans from 0 to 100, there is a chance that the motor power can be set to 0 through its connection with the data wire. If this happens, the Move Tank block won't be able to finish its task, which is to turn the motor 100°, because its power level is set to 0. In that case, the program would be stuck there, and Mr. Turto would stop moving. To avoid this situation, it is important to add the Wait block with the Compare – Ambient Light Intensity mode right before the Color Sensor block. Set up the compare type input to 2 and the threshold value to 5 (if the motors receive a value that is lower than 5 for their power value, they won't have enough torque to move the flippers). With this block, the color sensor will wait until it receives a value greater than 5. As a result, the Move Tank blocks won't get the number less than 5 for their power value. Figure 11-16 shows the final program.

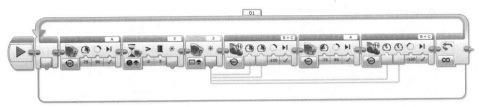

Figure 11-16: The amount of light from the color sensor controls the speed of the movement of Mr. Turto's flippers.

Download this program and run it on Mr. Turto. Point the flashlight at his color sensor and see how he reacts.

Introducing My Blocks

Knowing how to make a program with data wires is a big step forward. You may realize that the line of program blocks is getting longer as it becomes more complicated. This section introduces a tool that is very useful for simplifying your program by making a line of code that does a task. For example, the entire Mr-Turto-Test program can be loaded into a single new programming block. Basically, you can make your own customized block, and you can use it in your program over and over again like with any other programming block. In EV3 programming, we call this type of block a My block. Not only can a My block store a line of code, but it can also have parameters that will be inputs or outputs of the block. You will get to choose parameters for your My block when you build one. You can export your My block and save it on your computer so that you can share the My block with other people or use the block in other programs as well by importing. Let's try it out.

Using the My Block Builder

We'll use the Mr-Turto-Test program as an example. After you make this line of code as a My block, there will be no need to copy and paste the whole program. Instead, you will have a single block to do the same job. How convenient is that?

Open the Mr-Turto-Test program and select all the blocks except the Start block. Go to the Tools menu at the top of the screen and choose My Block Builder. You can follow the instruction in Figure 11-17. A My Block Builder window will pop up.

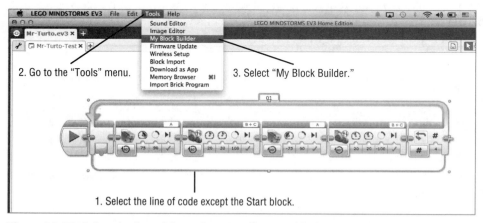

Figure 11-17: Select the line of the code except the Start block and then go to the Tools menu and select My Block Builder.

Once you get the My Block Builder window open (see Figure 11-18), name the block (I named this block Move_Forward) and write a short description about what it does. Note that you can only use lower/uppercase letters and underscores for the name. You can also choose the icon for your block from the My block icons palette at the bottom.

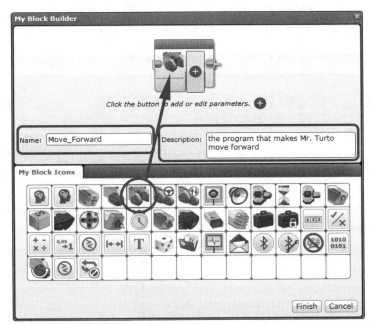

Figure 11-18: In the My Block Builder window, name the My block, put in a short description about the block, and choose the block icon.

We will add two parameters to the Move_Forward block: one for controlling the input value for the motor power and the other for setting up the Loop block's count number. You can add a parameter by clicking the + icon on the block. You will then see a new blank parameter on the block, as shown in Figure 11-19. In addition, two more tabs will show up next to the My Block Icon tab.

The new tabs that you made, Parameter Setup and Parameter Icons, are for setting up parameter features. If you click the Parameter Setup tab, you can define parameter type, parameter data type, default value, and parameter style. As you can see in Figure 11-20, I named the parameter Motor Power and set it up to be an input value (parameter type) for the motor power. The data type should be a number, and I set its default value to be equal to 20. For its style, I chose the vertical slider and set its minimum value to 5 (the minimum power level that the motors can have to produce enough torque to move the flippers) and its maximum value to 100.

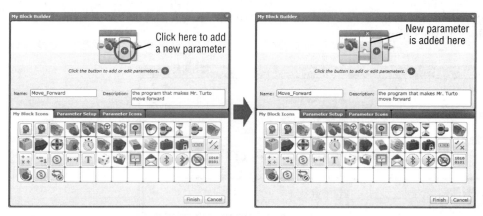

Figure 11-19: Adding a parameter to your My block

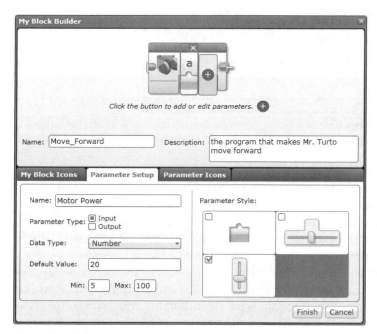

Figure 11-20: Setting up parameter features

If you click the Parameter Icons tab, you will see a number of icons that you can choose between to customize your parameter. When you select one, it will be shown in the block (see Figure 11-21).

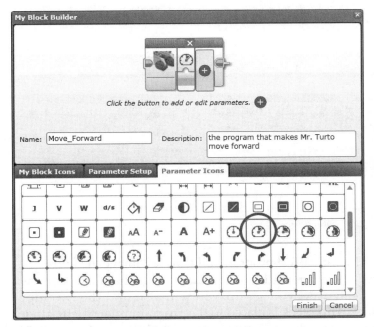

Figure 11-21: Selecting an icon for your parameter

As mentioned previously, you want to have a total of two parameters, one for the motor power and another one for the Loop block's count number. Add another parameter in the same way that you did the first one and set up its configuration like in Figure 11-22.

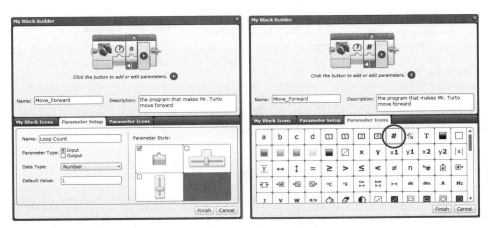

Figure 11-22: Adding another parameter for controlling the loop count

Click Finish, and the code of the Move_Forward block will be shown in another program window as a gray parameter block. You can then wire parameters to the motor Power inputs and the count input of the Loop block, as shown in Figure 11-23.

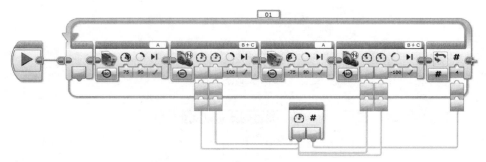

Figure 11-23: Data wiring the parameters

Then go back to the Mr-Turto-Test program. Like the left image in Figure 11-24 shows, instead of the whole line of the code, you will see the Move_Forward block that you just created. As you set up, you will also find the two input parameters on the block. This block is placed in the programming palette, under the My blocks tab (turquoise tab), as shown in the right image in Figure 11-24.

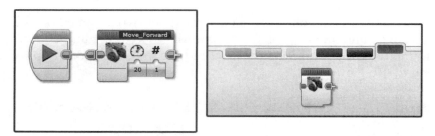

Figure 11-24: The Move_Forward block shown in the program (left) and the programming palette (right)

If you edit your My block, you can double-click it to open the program window. Congratulations. You've just made your first My block.

Exporting and Importing My Blocks

Once you build the My block, it will be listed on the My blocks tab in the project properties, as shown in Figure 11-25.

Here, you can export any My blocks that you made for saving to your computer. If you click the name of the block on the window, you will see the Export button at the bottom become activated. Click it. The Save window then pops up, and you get to choose where your computer will keep the file. If you go to the folder where you saved it, you will find the file with a .ev3s extension. With the block that we just created, it will be Move_Forward.ev3s. Why is it useful to save My blocks on the computer? It is useful because you can then import these block files for use in other projects as well as share them with other people.

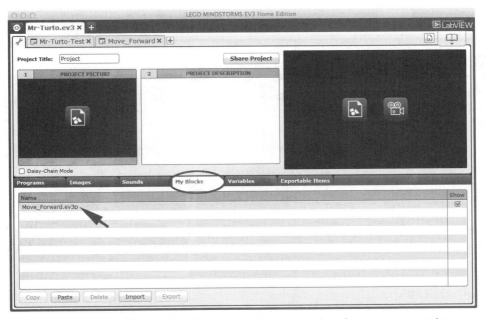

Figure 11-25: The My blocks will be listed on the My blocks tab in the project properties.

Importing a My block is similar to exporting it. You'll find an Import button next to the Export button. If you click it, the Open window pops up, and you can find the My block that you want to import. Figure 11-26 shows how to export and import a My block.

You have learned a lot of new skills in this chapter. Programming with data wires is a great way to actively use data across different blocks, and it enables you to give many more personalities to your robot. While your program is becoming richer and more advanced with new loops and data wires, My blocks will help you to simplify you program so that it is neater and more organized.

Exporting a My Block

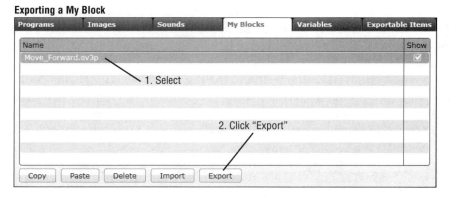

Importing a My Block

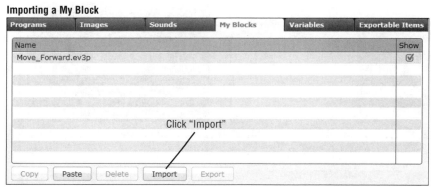

Figure 11-26: Exporting and importing a My block

Summary

In this chapter, you learned about the following:

- What data wires are and how they work
- Data types and data wire types
- How to use data wires in your program
- How to configure the sensor blocks
- How to build a My block

CHAPTER 12

Using Data Operations Blocks

If you have been following along to this point, you have already learned a great deal about EV3 programming. You've learned many techniques that have helped to expand your programming skills, but there is one more advanced EV3 programming technique that this book has yet to cover. Let's begin.

Using data wires, from the previous chapter, you were able to move data from one programming block to another. The values that you used were "raw." In other words, when we wired together the two programming blocks, one block's output data went directly to the other block's input without any processing in between. In this chapter, you learn how to process these raw values so that they become more useful within your program.

Suppose, for instance, that you want to use the values from the infrared sensor to control the power of the large motor to have it go backward until the touch sensor is pressed. To move the motor backward, you need a negative power value, but the value from the infrared sensor will range only from 0 to 100. The programming blocks that you learn about in this chapter can change this value to a negative number. In addition to simple data operations, you will also learn how to store a value in the EV3 brick memory. Once it's there, you can use it later or have a different program update it so that it can be used as another block's input value. The programming blocks that enable these functions are in the data operations palette, which appears as a red tab. Now let's find out what each block does and how we can use it in one of our programs.

The Variable Block

The first block that you will see in the data operations palette is the Variable block. Simply speaking, unlike all the other blocks that you have learned about so far, the value that this block carries can be changeable or updatable, meaning that a program can process and update the block's value while the program is running. For example, if the infrared sensor gets a reading of 57, the value will stay as it is until the outside conditions change, or until that which it is measuring changes. The program itself cannot change this value; instead, it can only use it.

Suppose, however, that the Variable block has 57 as its initial value. You can program the initial value to update itself by increasing the value by 10, which gives you a progression of 67, 77, 87, and so on. This progression of climbing values all happens while the program is running. At the end of the program, it will still be the same block, but with a different value. I know it can be a little bit confusing, but once you understand what a variable is, this will all become much clearer.

What Is a Variable?

Let's imagine that computer memory is a big shelf that has multiple racks and that thousands of briefcases are packed onto each of those racks. Those briefcases break down the big storage area into smaller units so that all the data can be stored within the computer memory in a more organized way. You can add a new briefcase or delete an old one. Each briefcase can carry a different type of data and may have different levels of security that limit what you can do with what's inside. For example, if the briefcase has a Read Only setting, then when a program is running, it can only read the data in this briefcase. The program will not be able to alter (or "write") new data.

A variable is another type of briefcase in your computer's memory. Its security setting lets a program read the existing data or write over the old data with new data. In other words, the data contained within a variable can be both readable and updatable. The data inside the briefcase can vary—thus it is *variable*.

With the Variable block, you can create a variable in the memory of the EV3 brick. Once the variable stores a value (you can set up the initial value or it can be wired with another block's output), that value stays in memory so that when a program is running, it can access the stored value over and over again, wherever it is in the program. The Variable block has two modes that represent the two paths in which you might use a variable. The first is used to read existing data (Read mode), and the other writes new data (Write mode). Let's see how you can employ the Variable block in a program.

Setting Up the Variable Block

When you place a new Variable block, you must define three things: the new variable's name, data-accessing mode (Read or Write), and the data type that it will carry. This section covers each step, and as you progress, you will get used to the block's interface.

Adding a New Variable

To use a variable in the EV3 brick's memory, you need to add one in there. Again, think of the brick's memory as a big shelf; you need to add a briefcase there to store something. If you click the text field in the upper-right corner of the block, an Add Variable box appears. Click this and you will see a pop-up dialog box in which you can name this new variable (see Figure 12-1).

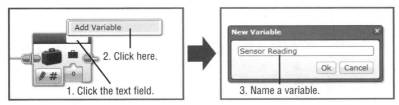

Figure 12-1: Adding a new variable

Name the variable **Sensor Reading**, and then click OK. The text field will show the name of the new variable. When you click the variable's name, you will see it listed, as well, like in Figure 12-2.

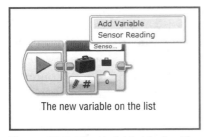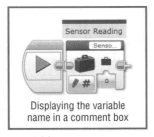

The new variable on the list

Displaying the variable name in a comment box

Figure 12-2: The Variable block with a new variable name

TIP Because the text field is too small to carry a long name, I used the comment tool to leave the variable's name fully visible. You can find the comment tool in the upper-right corner of the window. When you have a number of variables in your program, you may want to use this method to tell them apart. Alternatively, you may give the variables a shorter name that fits within the text field.

Congratulations! You've just created your first variable. You can access this variable from any program that is in the same project. It is now time to set up a data-accessing mode.

Selecting Read or Write Modes

As mentioned previously, a variable allows two ways in which to access the value that it carries (in the briefcase). In the Variable block, the two options appear as modes: Read and Write. When you click the mode selector, you will see them as options.

Let's take a look at the Sensor Reading variable. Currently, it has the Write – Numeric mode. (You will learn about the data type in the following section.) Add another Variable block next to it and choose the Sensor Reading variable from the list in the text field. Then, select the Read – Numeric mode so that you can have two variable blocks like in Figure 12-3. As you see here, one variable can appear in two Variable blocks.

Figure 12-3: The Variable block with Read mode (left block) and Write mode (right block)

When you see a Variable block with Write mode activated, you will find that it has one block input, meaning that the block can have a value coming in. You can set up the initial value by typing it in (in this example, you can type in any number), and that will be stored in the selected variable (in this example, the Sensor Reading variable). If the block gets input values via a data wire, the existing value in the variable will be replaced with the new value.

It is like opening a briefcase and replacing what is inside with new contents. For example, set up the Variable block so that it gets the reading values from infrared sensor via a data wire, as shown in Figure 12-4. Let's suppose that the sensor was activated three times (three sensor readings) while a program was running. If we say that these three readings were 28, 67, and 90, the value that the variable stored was updated three times: initial value to 28, 28 to 67, and 67 to 90.

When you look at a Variable block with Read mode activated, you will see that it has one block output, which means that the block can send out the value via a data wire. With this mode, you can use the value that is stored in this variable as another block's input. It works the same way as a sensor block that is sending out the sensor's reading value to other blocks via a data wire. But in this case, the value that a Variable block sends out will be its stored value. It is like opening a briefcase, copying down the value that is written inside, and using it as the input value for another block.

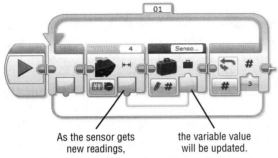

As the sensor gets new readings,

the variable value will be updated.

Figure 12-4: The Sensor Reading variable will get input values from the infrared sensor and update them as it gets a new value.

Let's continue the example with the infrared sensor. As the variable replaces its stored values (like the progression in the previous paragraph) with 28, 67, and 90, the reading value from it is updated as 28, 67, and 90.

We can build up the code so that it looks like the example in Figure 12-5. Although you directly connect the sensor block to the display block with a data wire, I am including the variable blocks to illustrate how you can pull out the stored value from the "briefcase" to use with another block. It feels a little redundant now, but once you learn more about the Data Operations blocks, you will see the benefit of using blocks in between blocks. With this code, the Sensor Reading variable stores the reading value from the infrared sensor and updates the reading value every 2 seconds. As it updates, the updated value will be displayed on the EV3 brick.

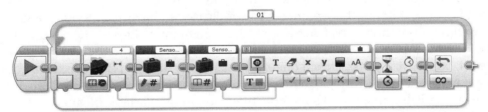

Figure 12-5: A program that makes the EV3 screen show the infrared sensor reading every 2 seconds

To try this code, have the EV3 brick ready and plug the infrared sensor into port 4. Create a project called **Data Operations** and make a program called **Variable**.

Run the program and try to move an object back and forth in front of the infrared sensor. Does the screen show different numbers?

Choosing the Variable Types

When you choose the Read or Write modes, the list of available data types will appear automatically. From this list, you can then choose which data type the variable will carry. Depending on the data type that you set up, the Variable block has a corresponding block input or output. For example, Figure 12-3 shows the numeric data type selected on the Variable block. In Chapter 11, "Programming with Data Wires and Using My Blocks," you learned about the first three data types shown here: text, numeric, and logic. You will find that there are also data types that you have yet to see: numeric array and logic array. If you understand what an array is, you will more easily understand how these new data types work.

What is an array? An array is an arrangement that a computer's memory uses to store data. The type of array that you will use in EV3 programming is a linear array, and it is structured like a line of boxes, each with its own element inside. The element in the box is a value, and in your program, that value will come in the form of a number or logic statement. Each box has an index number that counts upward from a starting point of 0 so that a program can locate the value that it carries. Figure 12-6 shows the concept of an array.

Value	Value	Value	Value	Value	● ●
Index: 0	Index: 1	Index: 2	Index: 3	Index: 4	

Figure 12-6: An array is a linear list of values.

Perhaps you will find it easier to think of an array as an organizer inside of the briefcase. Without this organizer, the briefcase can have just a single value, but with an organizer, the briefcase can have as many values as the slots that the organizer provides. The numeric array is a line of boxes with numeric values (4, 56, 7.8, 100...) inside each one, and the logic array is a line of boxes with logic values (True or False, also represented as the number 1 meaning True or 0 meaning False) inside. Let's see how they look in the Variable block.

When you choose the numeric array type, the Variable block will look like the one in Figure 12-7. When it is the Read mode, the block can send out an array of numbers, and when it is the Write mode, the block can get an array of numbers as its input.

With the Write mode, if you click the block output to put in the initial value, you will see a little window pop up like the one in Figure 12-8. You can add more boxes by clicking the + button (they will be slots within the array) and delete them by clicking the X button. You can type in a number in each box, and they will be elements that array. When you have finished making an array, you can click any blank space on the programming canvas. It will be shown in the format [value 1; value 2; ...] in the block output.

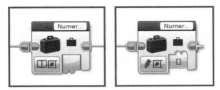

Figure 12-7: The Variable blocks with the Read – Numeric Array (left) and the Write – Numeric Array (right)

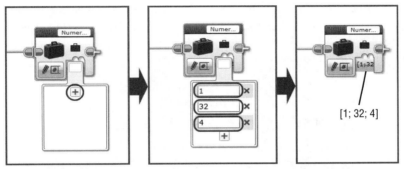

Figure 12-8: Creating an initial value in the Variable block with the Write – Numeric Array mode

The Variable block with the Logic Array mode works very similarly to the Numeric Array mode, but it carries logic values instead of numeric values. They look like the values in Figure 12-9.

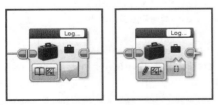

Figure 12-9: The Variable blocks with the Read – Logic Array (left) and the Write – Logic Array (right)

The process of creating a logic array for the initial value of a Variable block with the Write – Logic Array mode is same as making a numeric array. Click the block output and add slots to the array. Then you can fill these boxes with a logic value, which is either True or False. They will be symbolized with a check mark or an X. In the block output, the logic values in the array are presented as 1 (True) or 0 (False). So, if you set up a logic array as True, True, False, True, the block output will show this array: [1; 1; 0; 1] (see Figure 12-10).

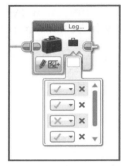 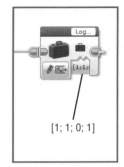

[1; 1; 0; 1]

Figure 12-10: Creating an initial value in the Variable block with the Write – Logic Array mode

If a variable has never had a value, meaning that it never received any value from other blocks or that you never set an initial value for the variable, it will automatically have a default value.

The default values are as follows:

- Numeric variable: 0
- Logic variable: False
- Text variable: Empty text (" ", nothing will be displayed)
- Numeric array and logic array: Empty array ([ ])

ACCESSING EXISTING VARIABLES

As you create new variables, they are listed up in the text field, but not all of them will show up at the same time. Depending on what type of data is chosen in the mode selector, the text field will show the list of the variables that match the chosen data type. Suppose, for instance, that you have two numeric type variables. If you select the numeric type in the mode selector and open the text field, they both will show up there. However, if you pick the text type, they won't be on the list. Keep this in mind when you want to find existing variables.

When no variables of a certain data type exist, the text field is blank. However, if you have already made some variables with a selected data type, the first one that you created will be selected in the text field as the default.

The Constant Block

The second block that comes after the Variable block in the data operations palette is the Constant block. Just as the Variable block stores values in the EV3 brick memory, this block also keeps values, which you may access at any point within your program. With the Variable block, you were able to read or write a value. The Constant block, in contrast, only allows you to read a value. In other words, a program can see and use the value that it carries several times, but you cannot change the value while the program is running. Let's see how it works in a program.

The Constant Block's Many Modes

This block has a text field and one output. When you use this block, you can define a value by typing in its text field, and this value will travel from the block output to other blocks via the data wire, as shown in Figure 12-11.

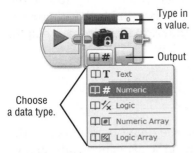

Figure 12-11: The structure of the Constant block

The Constant block has five modes, and each mode represents the data type that it can carry: text, numeric, logic, numeric array, and logic array. As you can see, they are the same data types that the Variable block can have. You choose one of the modes and then type a suitable value in the text field. For example, when you choose the Numeric Array mode, you will get to put a numeric array in the text field, such as [10; 3.14; 89; 903]. This block can prove very useful when you want to use the same data for multiple blocks' inputs, and it makes it easier to update them all at the same time. Here comes an example.

Constant Blocks in Action

Let's say you want to control the volume of the sound and the power of the motor with the same value; when the power of the medium motor is 10, the volume of the sound can also be 10. You can use the Constant block like in Figure 12-12. The Constant block has the Numeric mode and has 10 as its value. This value is plugged in to the input of the Sound block's volume and the Medium Motor block's power.

Figure 12-12: Using the Constant block to control the power of the motor and volume of the sound

When you run this code, the EV3 brick will say "Hello" very softly, with the volume value 10, and then the medium motor will turn slowly for 3 seconds with the power of 10. Because these input values are coming from the Constant block, if you want to change them, you can simply give a different value to the Constant block.

Our example has only two blocks, but imagine that you have 15 blocks and that 5 blocks need the same input value. When you set up the input value for these 5 blocks, instead of typing in the same value 5 times for each block, you can use the Constant block and wire the value. When you want to update the value, you'll only need to change the value in the Constant block rather than going to each of the 5 blocks to update the value individually. This can help to make the management of your program more efficient.

The Array Operations Block

The Array Operations block is the third block in the data operations palette, and it is the block that enables you to modify specific aspects within arrays that exist in your program. Suppose, for example, that you've created an array with the Variable block. You may then use the Array Operations block to do a few things. The block can tell an array to read an element from a specific slot, to write a new element over the old one, or to see how many elements are contained within the array. The Array Operations block has four modes: Append, Read at Index, Write at Index, and Length. Each mode handles arrays differently.

Append Mode

The first mode is the Append mode. This mode basically allows you to add one additional slot to the end of the numeric or logic array. When you choose the Append – Numeric mode, the slot that is added will be able to carry a numeric value, and when you choose the Append – Logic mode, the additional slot will be able to contain a logic value. As you can see in Figure 12-13, this mode has two block inputs, which are the Array In and the Value, and one block output. In Figure 12-13, I created a numeric array variable, cleverly named Numeric Array, in the Variable block, which has [10; 4; 30]. I wired it to the array in the Array Operations block. I added 7 for the Value input, and then wired the Array Out to the Variable block so that it can update the original array. What will the updated array look like?

When this line of code runs, the Array Operations block will process the coming array, which is [10; 4; 30], to have an additional slot at the end and put 7 in its new slot. As a result, the final array that the Numeric Array variable will have will be [10; 4; 30; 7]. The Append – Logic mode will work exactly the same as the Append – Numeric mode, but the array values will be logic statements, True or False.

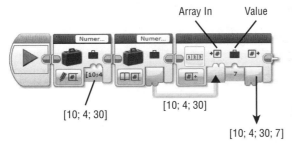

Figure 12-13: The Array Operations block with the Append – Numeric mode

Read and Write at Index Modes

The following two modes are to read or overwrite an element in a specified slot. As mentioned previously, an array has a certain number of slots, and each slot has its own index starting from 0. For example, if we use the Numeric Array variable ([10; 4; 30]) again, it has three slots, and the index will be 0 for the first slot, 1 for the second slot, and 2 for the third slot. In other words, the index will be "slot number minus 1." You need to use the index to specify which element should be read or overwritten.

As you can see in the line of code in Figure 12-14, in the Array Operations block with the Read at Index mode – Numeric, you need to set up an array through Array In ([10; 4; 30] in the example), specify the index of the element (2 in the example), and then read that element (it will be 30 in the example). The value output will carry the value of the read element.

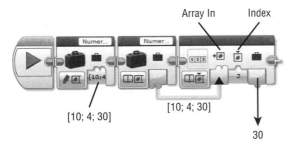

Figure 12-14: The Array Operations block with the Read at Index – Numeric mode

Similar to the Read at Index mode - Numeric, the Write at Index mode allows you to overwrite the element that you specified in the block. As you can see in the line of code in Figure 12-15, the Array Operations block with the Write at Index will have block inputs for the Array Index and Value (that will be overwritten) and a block output for the Array Out, which will carry the new updated array. In this example, the Array Operations block will get the array of [10, 4, 30] and update the element that is in index 0 with 67. Then, the array that the Array Out will carry will be the array of [67; 4; 30].

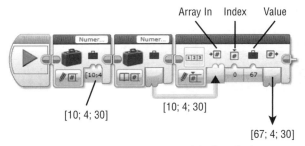

Figure 12-15: The Array Operations block with the Write at Index – Numeric mode

The Read and Write at Index – Logic modes will work in exactly the same way, but the array values will instead be logic statements. For example, if the array that is coming in to the Array Operation block is [False; False; True; True], which will appear like [0; 0; 1; 1], if you ask the block to read the element in index 1, the output value will be 0. If you tell the block to write the True value (1) in index 0, the output array will be [1; 0; 1; 1].

As you saw, you can store multiple values within an array. For example, suppose that you want to set the motor power to 55 and have it on for 3 seconds, all while making all sounds play with a volume of 80. You can make an array that contains these values (it will look like [55; 3; 80]), and then you can read the individual values and wire them to the correct block inputs in your program.

Length Mode

The last mode, Length, is for reading the length of the array that comes into the Array In. The length of the array is the same as the number of elements that the array carries within it. It can also be thought of as the number of slots. Look at the Numeric Array variable that we created, for example. It has three elements within it, [10, 4, 3]. Therefore, its length is 3. Both the Length – Numeric and Logic modes will have the Array In input and the Length output, as shown in Figure 12-16.

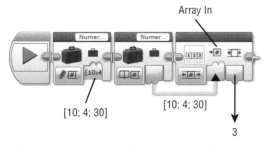

Figure 12-16: The Length – Numeric and Logic modes in the Array Operations block

The Length output will always get a numeric value because the measurement of the array's length will always be a number. If the Array Operations block gets the array of [True, False, False], the length output will send out 3 as the array's length.

The Logic Operations Block

This block will operate two logic statements: True or False. These statements will be the inputs for this block, and depending on the logical relation of these two statements, the output will also be True or False values (see Figure 12-17).

For example, this block can be set up to check whether both of its input values are True. If they both are indeed True, the block sends out its own True value; otherwise, its output value is False. There are four logic operation modes that process two logic inputs differently. Each of them is shown with the Venn diagram that represents the logical relation between two inputs that makes the result True.

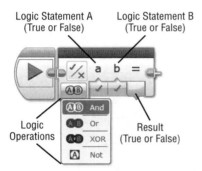

Figure 12-17: The Logic Operations block

And Mode

To get the True output with And mode, both of the test statements should be True. Otherwise, the result is False. Figure 12-18 shows an example. In this code, only one case brings the True result from the Logic Operations block: when the touch sensor is pressed and the color sensor sees red at the same time. In any other cases, the result from the Logic Operations block will be False.

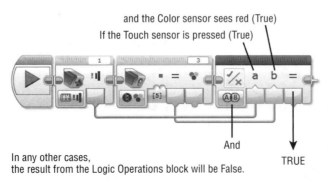

Figure 12-18: The True result from the Logic Operations block with the And mode

Or Mode

With the Or mode, it is less difficult to get the True result. The only case that gives the False result is when the both of the inputs are False. In the example in Figure 12-18, the block will provide True as its result when either the touch sensor is pressed or the color sensor detects red (or when both of these actions happen). When the touch sensor is not pressed and the color sensor doesn't see red, the result is False. See the summary in Figure 12-19.

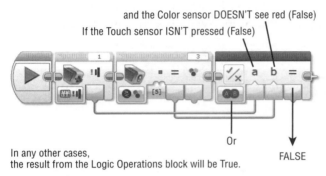

Figure 12-19: The False result from the Logic Operations block with the Or mode

XOR Mode

To satisfy XOR mode, two inputs cannot have the same value. In other words, to get the True result with this mode, only one of the inputs should have True. If both of them are True or both of them are False, the block result will be False. Going back to the example in Figure 12-18, the True case will be only when the touch sensor is pressed and the color sensor doesn't see red, or the touch sensor is not pressed and the color sensor sees red. See the summary of the True/False cases in Figure 12-20.

Not Mode

Unlike other modes, Not mode has only one input. This mode processes one True/False statement to see whether it delivers the True value or False value. As the name of the mode implies, the result of the block is the opposite of the statement's value. See the example in Figure 12-21. If the touch sensor is pressed, its compare result will be True, and this value will be the input of the Logic Operations block. Then, the result of this block with the Not mode will be False. If the touch sensor is not pressed, the result of the Logic Operations block will be True.

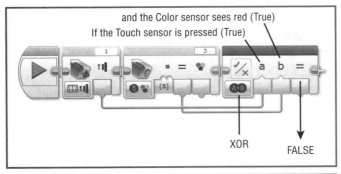

and the Color sensor sees red (True)

If the Touch sensor is pressed (True)

XOR

FALSE

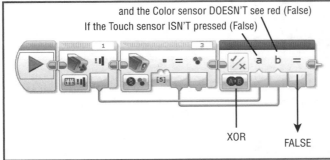

and the Color sensor DOESN'T see red (False)

If the Touch sensor ISN'T pressed (False)

XOR

FALSE

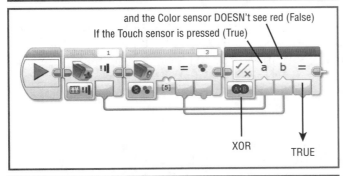

and the Color sensor DOESN't see red (False)

If the Touch sensor is pressed (True)

XOR

TRUE

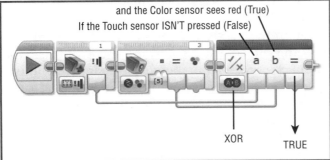

and the Color sensor sees red (True)

If the Touch sensor ISN'T pressed (False)

XOR

TRUE

Figure 12-20: The True/False results from the Logic Operations block with the Or mode

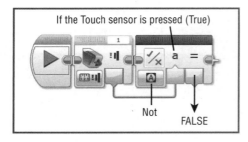

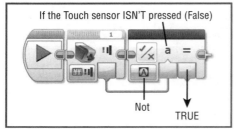

Figure 12-21: The True/ False results from the Logic Operations block with the Not mode

The Math and Round Blocks

Here come the blocks that you can use to play with numbers: the Math block and Round block. With the Math block, you can do anything from simple arithmetic to advanced calculations. With the Round block, you can make a decimal number into an integer value. Let's take a look at the Math block first.

The Math Block

The Math block has eight modes to make different math operations. The first four modes—Add, Subtract, Multiply, and Divide—have two block inputs that can have numbers. A program will process these two numbers according to the selected mode. See the summary in Figure 12-22.

The following modes contain the possibility for advanced mathematical concepts. The full extent of these blocks is beyond the scope of this book, but you will learn here about the relationship between the inputs and output result.

With Absolute mode, you can set up one numeric input, and the block will calculate how far the input value is from 0. If the input value is negative, getting the absolute value essentially removes its negative sign. If the input number is 0 or a positive number, the output is the same as what went in. For example, if the input is −34, the output will be 34; if the input is 56, the output will be 56.

With the Square Root mode, you will have one input, and the output will be the square root of that number. If your input is 4, the block will operate the square root of 4, and the result (your output) will be 2. So, 144 becomes 12, 100 becomes 10, and so on.

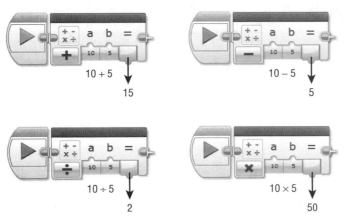

Figure 12-22: The Math block with the Add, Subtract, Multiply, and Divide modes

With the Exponent mode, there will be two inputs: one for the base number (will appear as *a* on the block), and the second will be the exponent (will appear as *n* on the block). The output will be the result of the operation. For example, if you put 3 as your base number and 2 as your exponent, the block will operate 3 raised to the power of 2, and the result will be 9 (3 x 3).

The last mode in the Math block is the Advanced mode. All the other modes process only one math operation, but with Advanced mode, you can create an equation that can handle multiple math operations. You can have four numeric inputs (which appear as *a*, *b*, *c*, and *d*) and set up the equation in the text field. The output will be the result of the equation with the input values.

Sometimes sensor readings won't really work for your program in their raw state and need to be processed. For example, let's say you have a robot with two motors in ports B and C and they need negative numbers for their power levels to move forward. Say that you want to have the motors turn one rotation forward every two seconds. If you want to use the infrared sensor readings to control the power of these motors, they'll need to be processed to be negative because the reading values from the infrared sensor will always be a positive number (0 to 100). In this case, you can use the infrared sensor value as the input value for the Math block, which will then multiply the input value by –1. The resulting output value from the Math block will always be negative. You can then wire this output to the power inputs of the Motor block. Figure 12-23 shows an example of how this program can look.

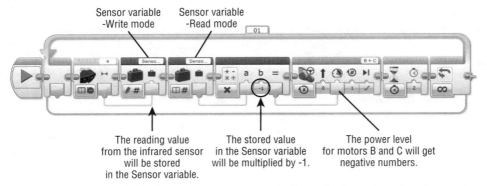

Sensor variable
-Write mode

Sensor variable
-Read mode

The reading value
from the infrared sensor
will be stored
in the Sensor variable.

The stored value
in the Sensor variable
will be multiplied by -1.

The power level
for motors B and C will get
negative numbers.

Figure 12-23: The Math block is used to change the reading value from the infrared sensor into a negative number.

In this example, you will set up the variable first, and then the reading value from the infrared sensor will be stored in a Variable block to be named "Sensor." The stored value will then be sent to the following Math block, which will multiply the value by –1. The product from this operation will be sent as the power level input for the Move Steering block that controls motors B and C. Use the Math blocks to creatively crunch data to guide your robot!

The Round Block

The Round block will refine a decimal number to become an integer or simply trim digits after a decimal point down to a certain number. The first three modes in this block show different ways to make a decimal number into an integer, and they will have one numeric input and one output for the processed integer.

With the To Nearest mode, the block follows the standard rounding rules. So, in this case, if the first decimal value is greater than or equal to 5, the last digit number of the integer part will be increased by 1. However, if the first decimal value is less than 5, the last digit number of the integer part will stay as it is. If the input value is 6.78, the output will be 7, and if the input value is 3.1, the output will be 3.

The Round Up mode means an integer will always be increased by 1 if there are any numbers past the decimal. Round Down mode means that an integer will always stay as it is and the following decimal numbers will disappear. For example, if the input is 89.2 with the Round Up mode, the output will be 90. If the input is 7.8 with the Round Down mode, the output will be 7.

The Truncate mode cuts digits off of the number from the right of the decimal. In addition to the number input, you will see an additional input on the block, which determines the number of decimals places that are allowed in the output result. If the decimal input value is 6.935 and the value for the number of decimals is 2, the output will be 6.93. Using the same input number, if the number of places past the decimal is set to 0, the output will be 6. There will be no rounding up or down. Truncating means that you are simply cutting decimal places from the number. See the summary of using the Round block in Figure 12-24.

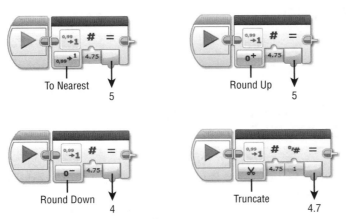

Figure 12-24: Using the Round block

The Compare, Range, and Random Blocks

Here are the blocks that you can use to compare two input values, check if an input value is in a certain range, or generate a random value. They are the Compare, Range, and Random blocks. Let's look at the Compare block first.

The Compare Block

This block evaluates two numeric values against one another (the inputs of the block) by using a certain comparison type (the mode of the block) to see whether the result of the comparison is True or False (the output of the block). As you can see in Figure 12-25, you may choose between six comparison types.

You can wire up the values from other blocks, or put in your own numbers into the block inputs. Suppose, for instance, that you want to see whether your two-wheeled vehicle-type robot made a turn. The robot has two wheels attached to motors B and C. When the robot is going straight, the motor rotations will be the same. If the robot makes a turn, however, one motor's rotation value will be greater than the other's. You can use the motor rotation values from motor B&C as the input values in the Compare block and choose the Not Equal To mode. When the robot goes straight, the output of the Compare block will be False, but when the robot makes a turn, the output of the block will be True.

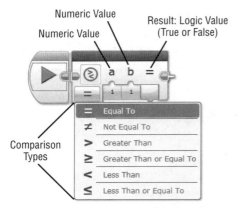

Figure 12-25: The Compare block with the six comparison types

The Range Block

The Range block will see whether the input value is inside or outside of a certain range. For example, the Range block can check if the input value is in the range of 10 and 56 or outside of that range. According to the result, the block will have True or False value as its output. As you can see in Figure 12-26, there are three inputs, from left to right—Text Value, Lower Bound (10 in the example), and Upper Bound (56 in the example)—and one logic output (the result). Two modes of the block, Inside and Outside, determine the area of the range.

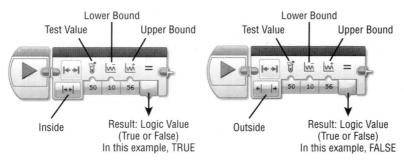

Figure 12-26: The Range block with the Inside mode and the Outside mode

When you choose the Inside mode and set up the Lower Bound as 100 and Upper Bound as 200, if the Test value is 178, the result will be True. If the block is getting 290 as its Test value, the result will be False. If you change the mode as Outside, the block will get the True value with the Test value 290.

The Random Block

The Random block will make a program that generates a random value within a certain numeric range. For example, you can set up your program to set the power level of your robot's motors to a number that falls within a range of 30–100. As a result, whenever you run this program, your robot's motors will run at an unexpected power level between 30–100. It is the perfect block to use when you desire a random and unexpected outcome. You can either have a random numeric or logic value (see Figure 12-27).

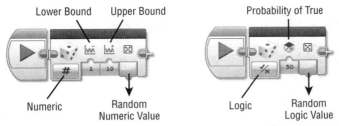

Figure 12-27: The Random block with the Numeric and Logic modes

If you want to get a random numeric value, you need to choose the Numeric mode. Then, you will get to define the range by setting up the Lower and Upper Bounds. The block picks a random number in that range as its output. If you want to have a random logic value, you want to choose the Logic mode. With this mode, you get to set up the probability of True, which means, how likely you will get the True value. For example, if you put 50, the changes that the block gets the True value will be 50 percent. Play with this block to have some unexpected, fun behavior from your robot.

The Text Block

The last Data Operations block that we have is the Text block. Unlike other blocks, with this block you will get to combine text strings. It has three text inputs (A, B, and C), and the output will be a merged string of text inputs in order (ABC). You can type in the text directly into the block inputs but also wire the value from other blocks. If the block input gets no text, when the block merges all the inputs, it will skip the empty input (see Figure 12-28).

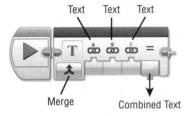

Figure 12-28: The Text block

It will be useful to print out the sensor reading values on the screen. For example, the first input can say Motor A, and the third input can say Degrees. Then, you can plug in the motor degrees values in the Motor Rotations block from motor A to the second input of the text block. Wire up the output to the Display block to see the value on the screen. When motor A is turned 89 degrees, the screen will show Motor A 89 Degrees.

The Data Operations blocks open up a whole new way to use the data in your program. As you get used to them, you will find more and more interesting possibilities that you can try with your robot.

Summary

In this chapter, you learned about the following:

- What a variable is and how to create it in EV3 programming
- How to use the Variable block
- What an array is and different types of arrays
- How to use the Constant block
- How to use the Array and Logic Operations blocks
- How to use the Math and Round blocks
- How to use the Compare, Range, and Random blocks
- How to have a text displayed with the Text block

CHAPTER 13

Building the Big Belly Bot:
A Robot That Eats and Poops

You worked hard to learn all the new EV3 programming skills, so now let's build another fun robot. This chapter introduces you to a new robot that you can feed. His name is the Big Belly Bot. When he is full of food, he reacts in a funny way. Follow the building instructions to make the robot, and make sure to take note of my program examples. They will help you to understand how the Big Belly Bot works. Later, you can modify the program samples to create your own program, like you did with the other projects. So, without further ado, meet the Big Belly Bot.

Understanding the Big Belly Bot

Big Belly Bot is a stand-up robot, and as his name implies, the Big Belly Bot has a big stomach. He also has a big mouth that you must open and close to help him eat. Check him out in Figure 13-1.

As you can see by his big mouth and belly, this guy loves to eat. How lucky you are that you are the one that gets to make him happy by feeding him. Let's see what kind of robot he is and how he functions.

Figure 13-1: Meet the Big Belly Bot.

The Big Belly Bot's Personality

It would have been really nice if you could invite Big Belly Bot to dinner and share your food with him, but unfortunately he can't eat human food. What he can eat are the red balls that come with the EV3 set, but the three balls just aren't enough to make him full. In addition to these balls, you can feed him with other small object whose size and shape is comparable to the small LEGO ball, such as marbles or wooden balls. If you don't have these on hand, consider making some balls out of foil (like aluminum foil) to feed him, like the ones in the left photo of Figure 13-2. As the right photo of Figure 13-2 shows, you can open his mouth and drop the foil balls right in. You'll need quite a few food balls.

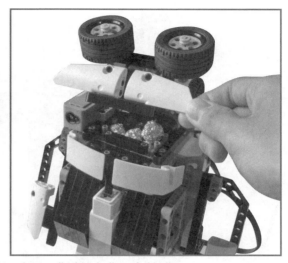

Figure 13-2: You can feed him the small LEGO balls or foil balls.

Whenever you feed him, close his mouth to see whether he is full. If he is still hungry, he won't give you any reaction, other than his look of desire for more food. Note that he needs a great deal of food to make him full. You need to stack the balls right up to the top of his mouth. When he is full, he will say, "Uh-oh." Can you guess what happens next? Yep. He will throw his hips forward and poop. Yikes. He will release the food out that he just ate and shake his body a little bit for good measure. He will close his back end and, yes, that means he is ready to eat again. He certainly can eat his fill, but he is also smart enough to know when he is full and how to empty his belly. How does he do that?

The Mechanisms of the Big Belly Bot

The Big Belly Bot has two sensors that help him realize when he is full: The color sensor and the infrared sensor. As you can see in Figure 13-3, the color sensor is located behind his upper lip, and the infrared sensor is in his throat.

The infrared sensor in his throat will see whether his belly is full. If he still has some space left in his belly after you feed him, the reading value from the infrared sensor will stay the same. However, when his belly fills all the way up to his throat, the infrared sensor's reading value changes. Then he will know it's time to let things out of his stomach. Wait, but when you feed him, the food has to pass the infrared sensor as it goes into his belly, right? We want him to recognize the difference between times when food is going down his throat (the action of eating) and others when it is piling up to the top of his throat (he is full). To do this, we need to use the color sensor.

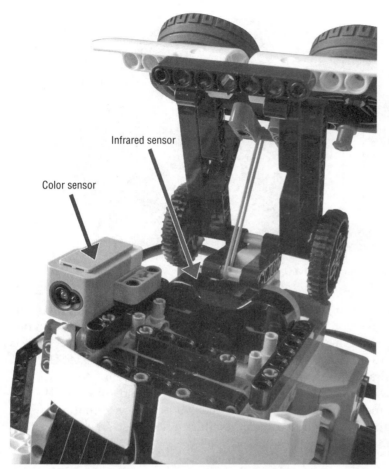

Figure 13-3: Color sensor and infrared sensor on the Big Belly Bot's mouth

The color sensor can tell whether his mouth is open or closed. When his mouth is closed, the color sensor gets the reflected light from the back of his upper lip. However, when his mouth is open, the color sensor does not see a reflection. This function allows the Big Belly Bot to know when to collect the value from the infrared sensor. When the mouth is open, the food is coming in, and at that point, he does not use the reading value from the infrared sensor to judge if his belly is full. When his mouth is closed, he knows that feeding is done. Then he will see whether the infrared sensor's reading value has changed. If the food went down to his stomach, the sensor reading value will be the same as before; he knows then that he is not yet full. However, if the food has piled up to the top of his throat and stays there after his mouth is closed (meaning that the food is blocking the infrared sensor), the reading value from the infrared sensor will change. When this happens, he knows that he is full and moves to the next action.

His pooping mechanism is simpler than his eating mechanism. His belly is designed in the shape of a hopper, so that all the food can gather in one spot. This spot has a hole that is blocked by a trap door. When he is eating, the bar on the medium motor holds the door closed. When he is ready to poop, the bar releases the door. He then lets out the objects inside of his belly and closes the door. Sometimes, after he poops, some objects remain in his belly (because they can get jammed together in the hopper). But don't worry, he can handle a little bit of constipation. After he eats and moves his body again, these objects should eventually come out.

Now that you know how he functions, let's build him and see just how well he eats and poops.

Assembling the Big Belly Bot

Collect the parts shown in Figures 13-4 and 13-5, and then follow the step-by-step building instructions detailed in Figures 13-6 to 13-34 to put the Big Belly Bot together.

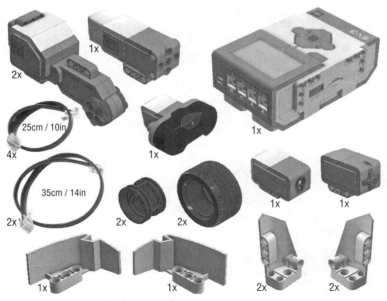

Figure 13-4: Parts for the Big Belly Bot, 1

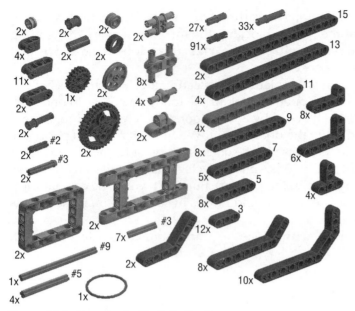

Figure 13-5: Parts for the Big Belly Bot, 2

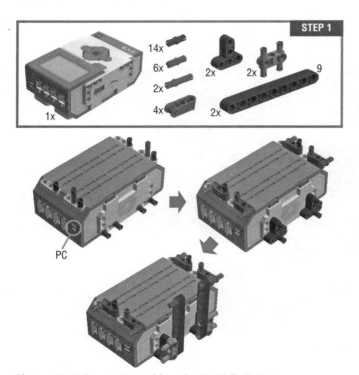

Figure 13-6: Step 1. Assembling the Big Belly Bot's torso

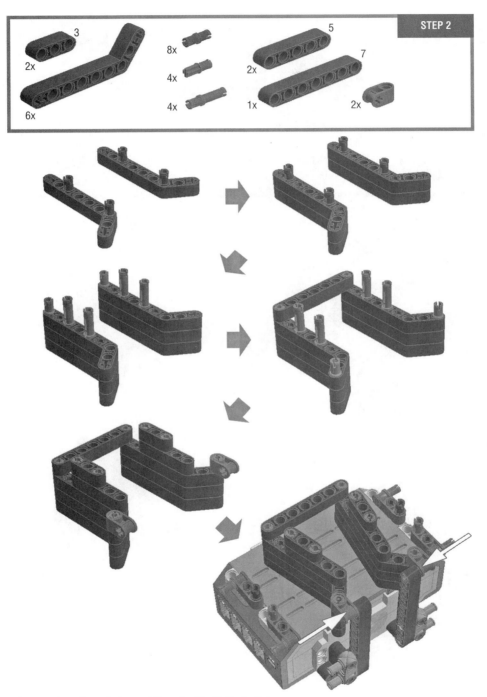

Figure 13-7: Step 2. Assembling the Big Belly Bot's torso

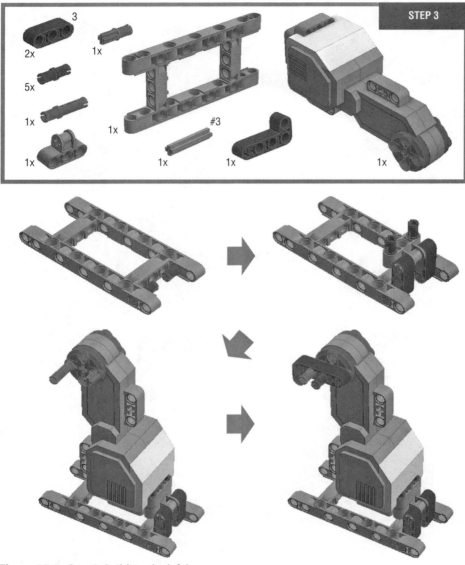

Figure 13-8: Step 3. Building the left leg

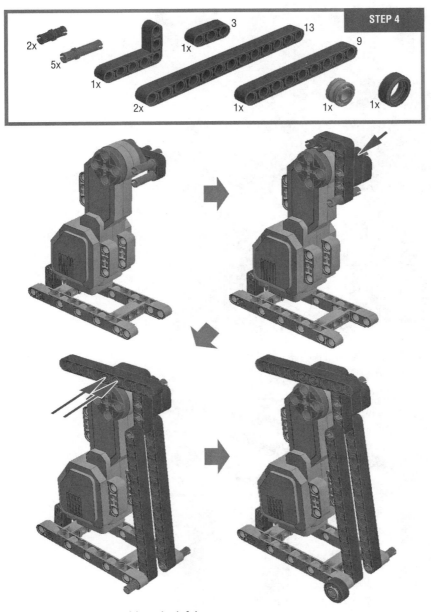

Figure 13-9: Step 4. Building the left leg

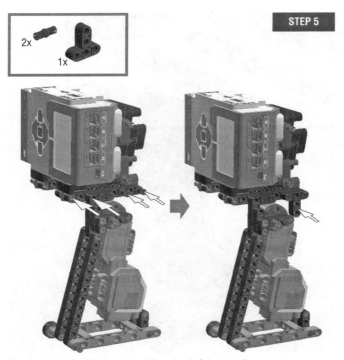

Figure 13-10: Step 5. Attaching the left leg to the torso

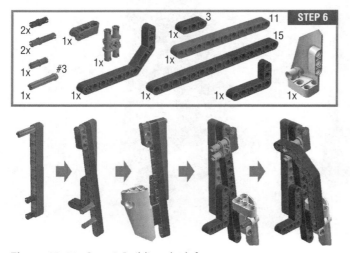

Figure 13-11: Step 6. Building the left arm

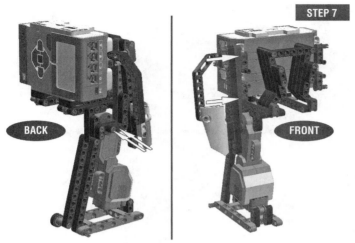

Figure 13-12: Step 7. Attaching the left arm to the torso

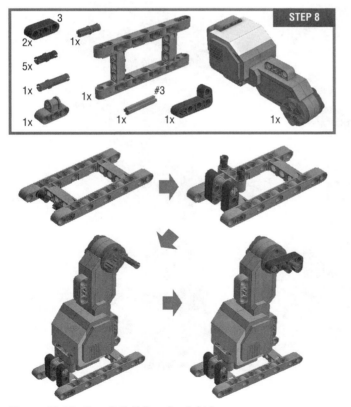

Figure 13-13: Step 8. Building the right leg

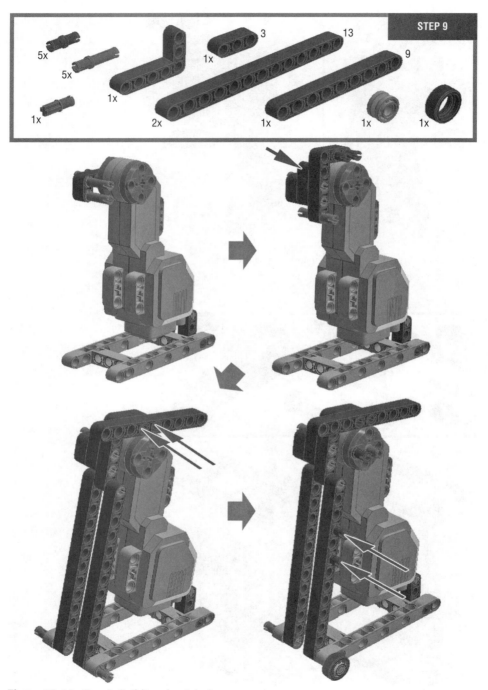

Figure 13-14: Step 9. Building the right leg

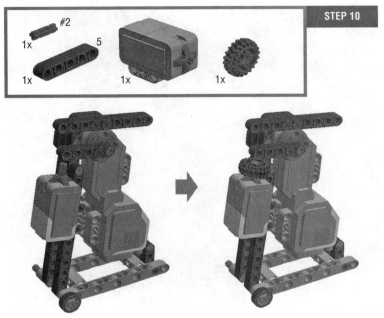

Figure 13-15: Step 10. Adding the touch sensor to the right leg

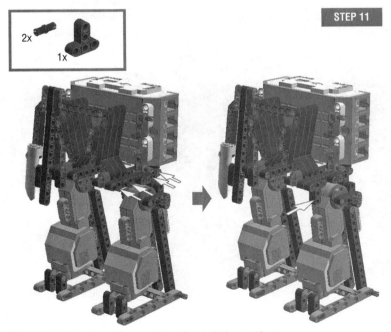

Figure 13-16: Step 11. Attaching the right leg to the torso

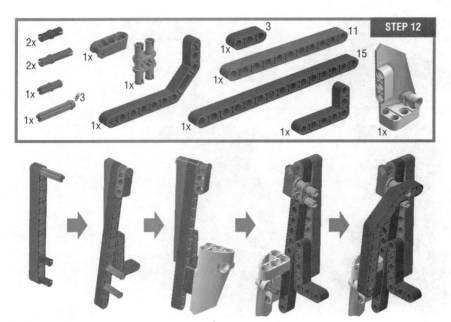

Figure 13-17: Step 12. Building the right arm

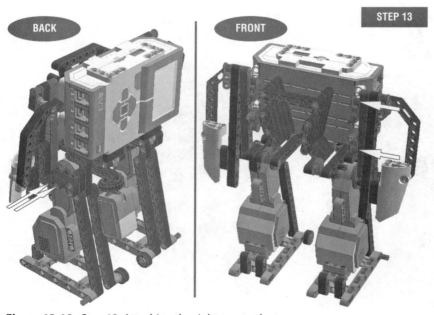

Figure 13-18: Step 13. Attaching the right arm to the torso

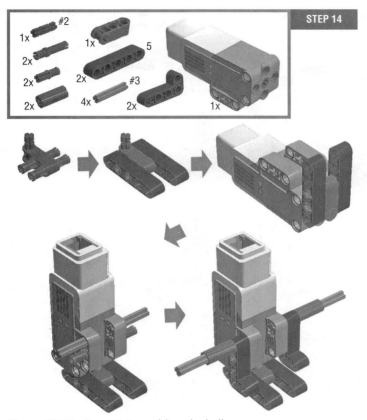

Figure 13-19: Step 14. Assembling the belly

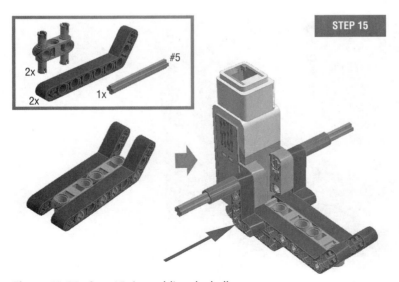

Figure 13-20: Step 15. Assembling the belly

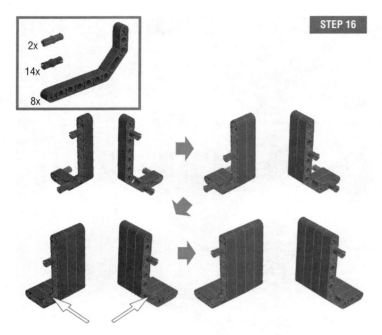

Figure 13-21: Step 16. Assembling the belly

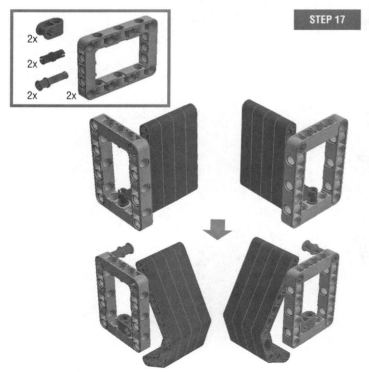

Figure 13-22: Step 17. Assembling the belly

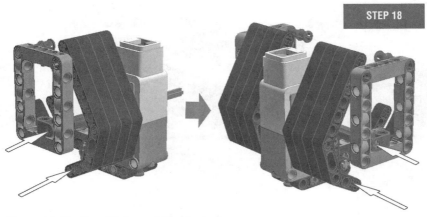

Figure 13-23: Step 18. Assembling the belly

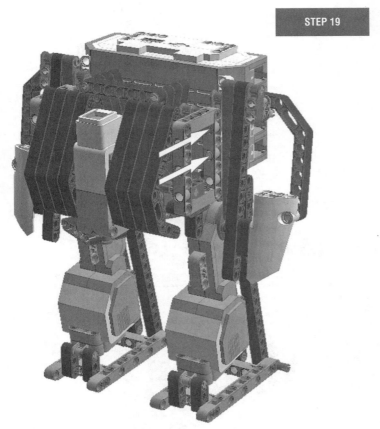

Figure 13-24: Step 19. Adding the belly to the torso

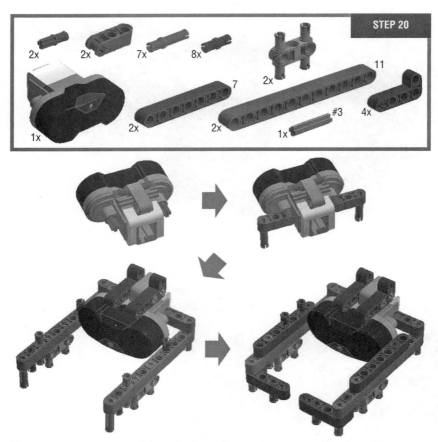

Figure 13-25: Step 20. Building the Big Belly Bot's jaw

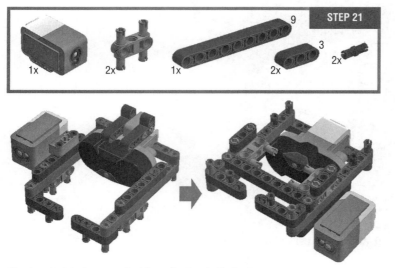

Figure 13-26: Step 21. Building the Big Belly Bot's jaw

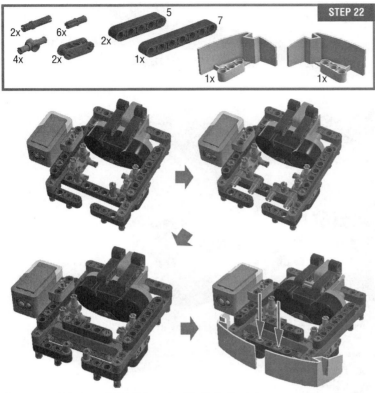

Figure 13-27: Step 22. Building the Big Belly Bot's jaw

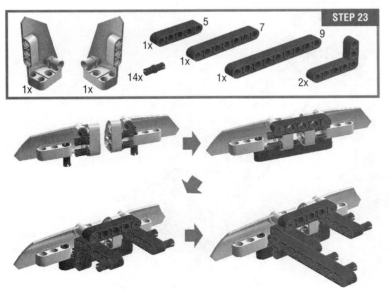

Figure 13-28: Step 23. Assembling the Big Belly Bot's upper head

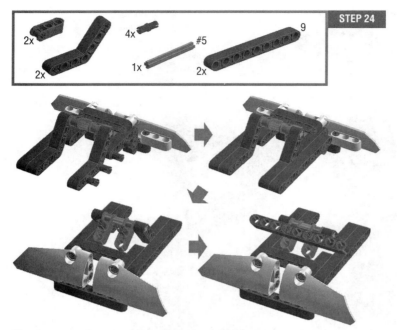

Figure 13-29: Step 24. Assembling the Big Belly Bot's upper head

Figure 13-30: Step 25. Assembling the Big Belly Bot's upper head

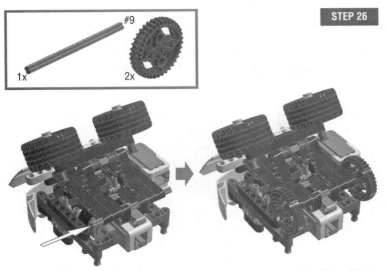

Figure 13-31: Step 26. Combining the Big Belly Bot's upper head and his jaw

Figure 13-32: Step 27. Adding the Big Belly Bot's head to the torso

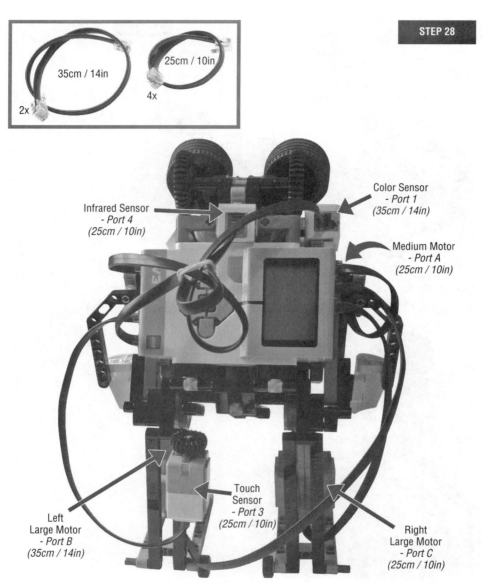

Figure 13-33: Step 28. Connecting the sensors and motors with the connector cables

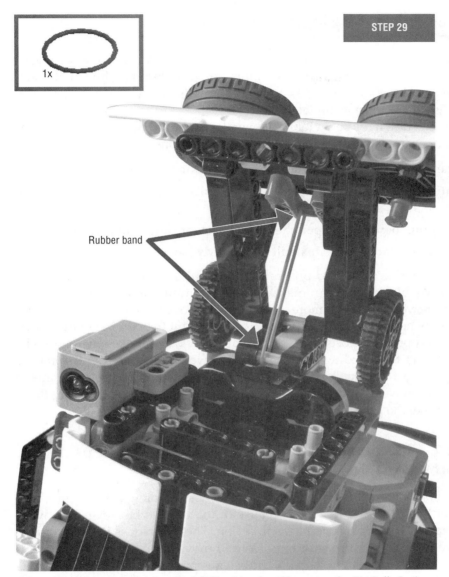

STEP 29

1x

Rubber band

Figure 13-34: Step 29. Adding the LEGO rubber band between the Big Belly Bot's upper head and jaw

Programming the Big Belly Bot

You just finished building the hungriest robot in the world. He is ready for your gentle, nonjudgmental care. Before we jump into programming him, make sure that you have his food (small LEGO balls/foil balls) ready. You need about 20 to 25 balls to make him completely full.

Let's break down his behavior into several actions and make each of them as a My block. You want to program the following actions:

1. **Standing Up Straight**: Lean backward to improve posture.
2. **Eating**: Check to see whether his belly is full after the food comes in. When he feels full, say "Uh-oh."
3. **Pooping**: Bend over, open the back end, poop, and shake the body.
4. **Close the back end**. (This will not be a My block.)

Let's follow this order and program him for all the actions. However, after we make My blocks, you can make different combinations of performance. Furthermore, you can design more actions for him. For example, you can program him to know how many times he gets to be fed (count the number of times that his mouth is open and closed with the Variable block) and make him angry if he is not full after four feedings. The actions that we program in this chapter are the basic things that you can do with him, and you will find more programs in the companion website for this book. Create the new project named **Big Belly Bot** and make the program called **BBB-basics** to get started.

Action 1 – Standing Up Straight: Lean Backward to Improve Posture

As mentioned before, his upper body is pretty heavy. You will sometimes find his upper body leaning forward because of the weight. However, you want him to stand up straight when he is in action. The two blocks in the program in Figure 13-35 make him stand up. He will move his body backward until the touch sensor that is on the back of his leg is pressed. I added more blocks afterward to make him say "Hello," bow gently, and stand back again.

When you have this program ready, select all the blocks except the Start block, go to Tools and click My Block Builder. Give it a proper name that describes the action (I named it Standing, for instance) and choose an icon. You will find this new My block in the My block palette. We will continue the program after the Standing block.

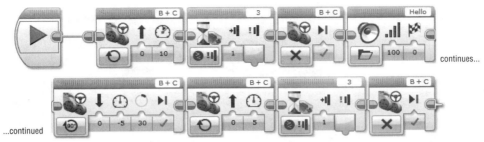

Figure 13-35: The program that makes the Big Belly Bot stand back, say "Hi," and gently bow

Action 2 – Eating: Check If His Belly Is Full When the Food Comes In. When He Feels Full, Say "Uh-Oh"

The second action is to make him react after he is fed and check to see whether he is full. We will use the Switch block with the color sensor in Compare – Reflected Light Intensity mode to see if his mouth is open or closed. The program will go like this: If the color sensor receives a value of less than 10, which means the mouth is open, the program will run the code that is in the top container of the Switch block. When the color sensor gets a value of more than 10, which means the mouth is closed, the program runs the code that is in the bottom container of the Switch block.

In the top container in the Switch block, we'll write code that dictates his reaction to getting fed. There will be the Wait block with the infrared sensor in Change – Proximity mode to see whether the food is passing his throat, another Wait block with the color sensor in Compare – Reflected Light Intensity mode to see whether the mouth is closed after feeding, and a Sound block that makes a crunching sound. When he is not fed, his mouth will stay closed, which means the program will run the code in the bottom container of the Switch block. We want to have him continue to stay still when he is not fed, so we do not put any code in the bottom container.

This Switch block is placed in the Loop block with the infrared sensor in Compare – Proximity mode to check whether the food is piled up to the top of his throat after feeding and that his mouth is closed. When the food piles up at the top of his throat, it will completely block the infrared sensor that is placed at the top. The infrared sensor will get a value of 0. When the sensor gets the 0 reading and the Big Belly Bot's mouth is closed, it means his belly is full. The program will escape the loop and make him say "Uh-oh." However, if the infrared sensor doesn't get blocked by piled up food when his mouth is closed (meaning that the sensor is getting a value that is greater than 0), the program will go back to the beginning of the Switch block, and the Big Belly Bot will wait for more food. Figure 13-36 shows the code for the second action.

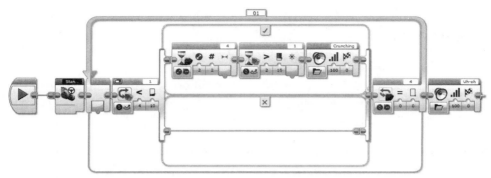

Figure 13-36: The program that makes the Big Belly Bot react to feeding and check whether his belly is full. An enlarged version of this figure appears on page 320.

Just as you did for the first action, select all the blocks except the Start block and the Standing block and make them into a My block. (I named mine Eating.) After you make this My block, there should be only three blocks on the canvas: the Start block, Standing block, and Eating block. Isn't it neat? This is the power of the My block.

Action 3 – Pooping: Bend Over, Open the Back End, Poop, and Shake the Body

The programming that we have written will let Big Belly Bot know when he is full. Now, let's make him release the food from his belly. The pooping action starts with him bending his body forward slightly. It can be done with the Steering block that moves both of the large motors 40 degrees with the power of −5. Then, he needs to open his back end. For this action, you want to program the medium motor to rotate the blocker that is connected to it and let the trapdoor swing open. When that happens, you will see the food balls dropping out from his back end. Sometimes, the balls inside of his belly get stuck. To help manage the food traffic in his belly, we will make him shake his body back and forth a couple of times. Continue with the program after the Eating block and insert the code that looks like what you see in Figure 13-37.

Figure 13-37: The program that makes the Big Belly Bot poop

Again, select the blocks that you just created and make them into one My block. (I named mine Pooping.) When you finish this process, you should see only the Start, Standing, Eating, and Pooping blocks.

Action 4 – Close the Back End

The final action of this code is to make him close his back end. Continue the program where you left off after the Pooping block. After you have the Big Belly Bot shake his body, you want to tell him to wait for a second before he closes his back end so that the balls inside of his belly can have a little more time to come out. You can simply use the Wait block for this action. Then, program the medium motor to rotate the blocker so that it closes the trapdoor on his back end. After the Medium Motor block, I added the Move Steering block to program the large motors to make his upper body lean backward. When all these actions are done, he will say, "Fantastic." I also put all the blocks in the Loop block so that he can repeat his behavior, which means after pooping he will want more food. Figure 13-38 shows what the final code looks like.

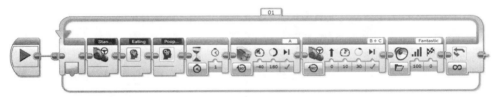

Figure 13-38: The final program for the Big Belly Bot

Congratulations! You've just made a robot poop. The program that you made shows the basic performances that the Big Belly Bot can make. Expand the program to give him more fun sounds and actions to perform before, during, and after the eating/pooping process. How's that for input and output?

Summary

In this chapter, you learned about the following:

- The Big Belly Bot's personality and what he does
- How the Big Belly Bot functions
- How to build the Big Belly Bot
- How to program the Big Belly Bot

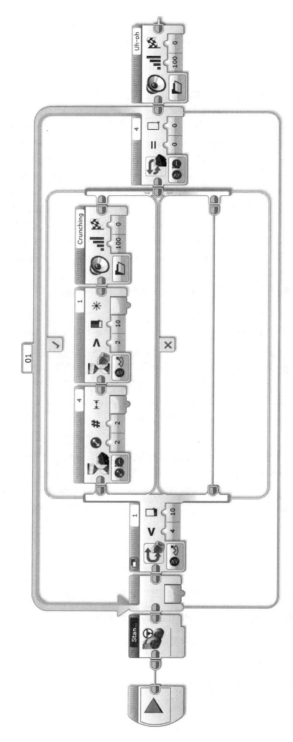

Figure 13-36: An enlarged version of Figure 13-36

CHAPTER 14

Design Your Own Robot: How Did Guapo, the Robotic Puppy, Come to Be?

So far, you've followed many different sets of building instructions to make several robots. Now you may be ready to create your own robot. This chapter introduces some tips for how to begin your own robot by sharing my process for designing and building robots. Let's get down to business: I have another robot for you. His name is Guapo, and as you can see in Figure 4-1, he is the robotic puppy. I will take you through his development from his start as an idea to becoming an actual robot.

Many builders and artists have their own process for making their projects, and, depending on the project, the building process may vary. This means that there isn't only one right way to do things. The process you will learn in this chapter works for me, and I hope that it inspires you to start your own robot.

Build Guapo, the Robotic Puppy

Before you learn how I built Guapo, let's bring him to life. Then, I will tell you the story behind how Guapo came to be. In this section, we build Guapo first. Collect the parts shown in Figures 14-2 and 14-3 and follow the step-by-step building instructions in Figures 14-4 to 14.43. Then, throughout the rest of this chapter, you learn how each of his various sections work. Follow the building instructions and prepare yourself for the story of Guapo.

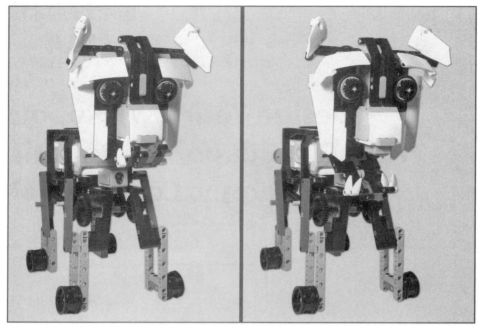

Figure 14-1: Meet Guapo, the robotic puppy.

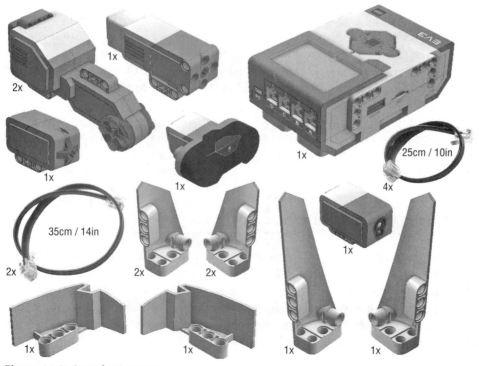

Figure 14-2: Parts for Guapo, 1

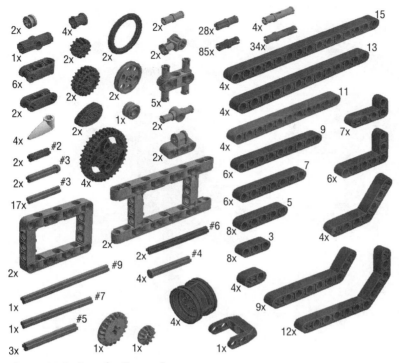

Figure 14-3: Parts for Guapo, 2

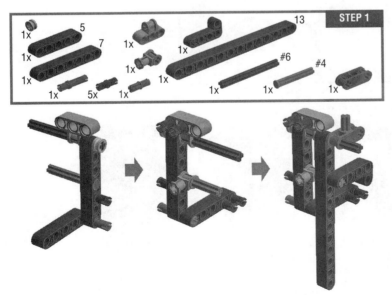

Figure 14-4: Step 1: Building a right side of Guapo's head

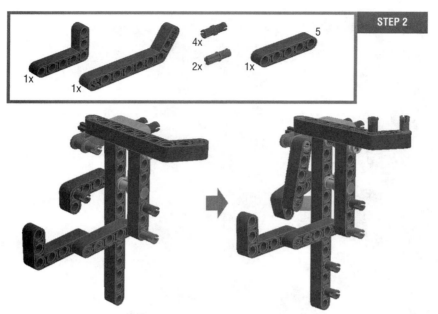

Figure 14-5: Step 2: Building a right side of the head

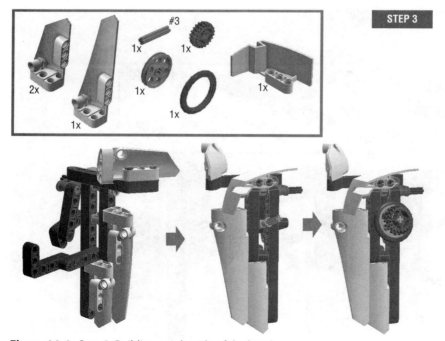

Figure 14-6: Step 3: Building a right side of the head

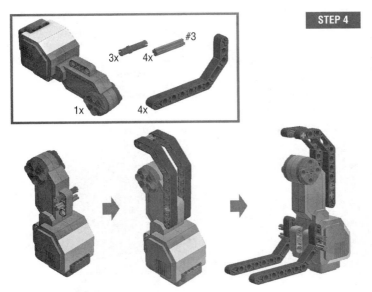

Figure 14-7: Step 4: Building the nose

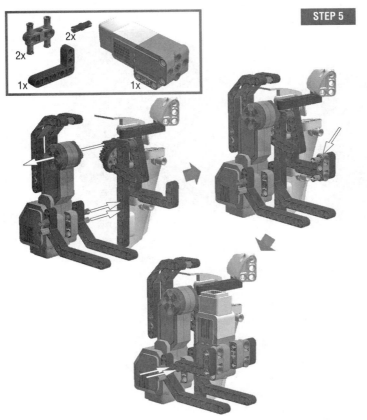

Figure 14-8: Step 5: Attaching the nose to the right side of the face

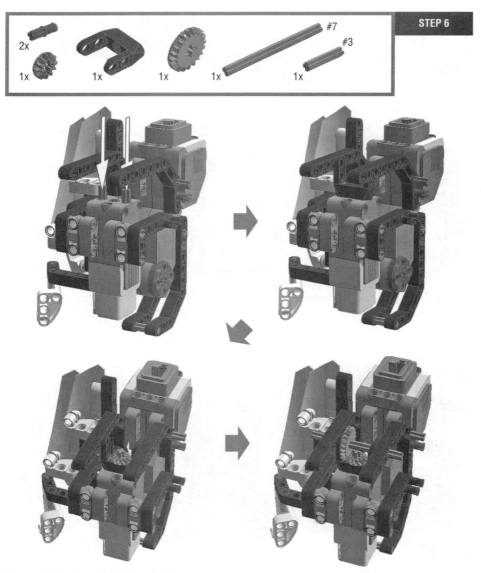

Figure 14-9: Step 6: Adding the jaw

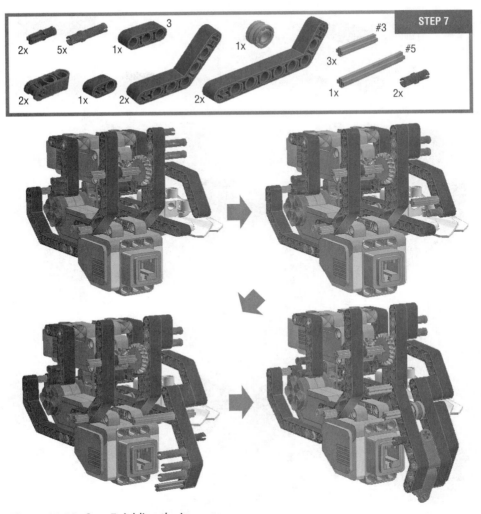

Figure 14-10: Step 7: Adding the jaw

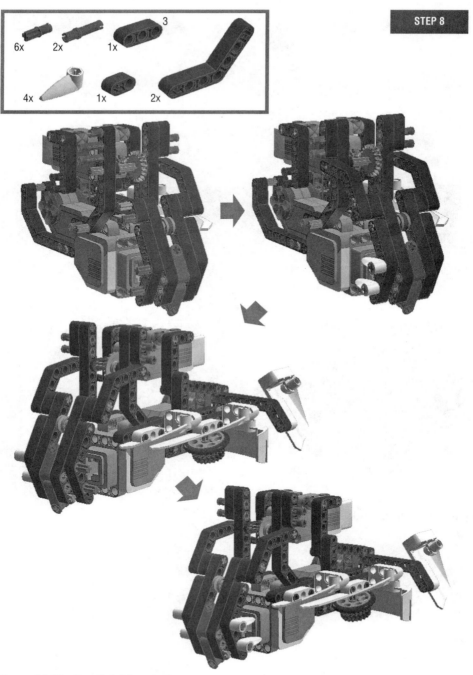

Figure 14-11: Step 8: Adding the jaw

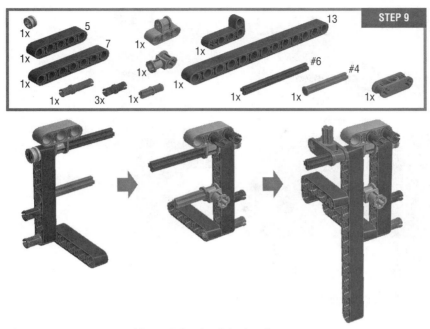

Figure 14-12: Step 9: Building a left side of the head

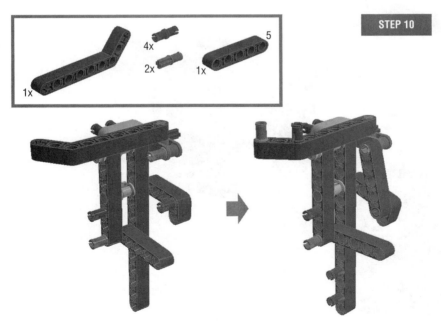

Figure 14-13: Step 10: Building a left side of the head

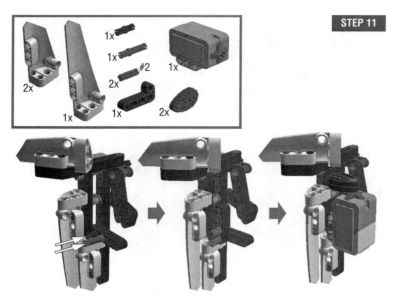

Figure 14-14: Step 11: Building a left side of the head

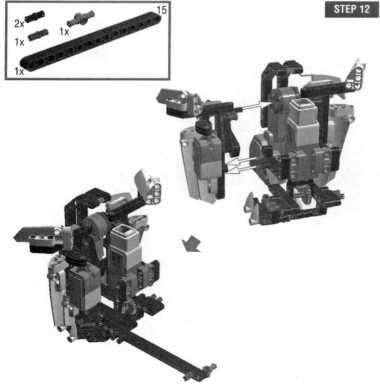

Figure 14-15: Step 12: Completing the head

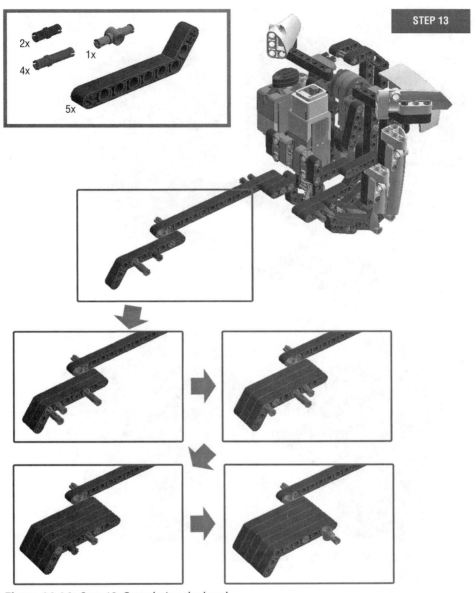

Figure 14-16: Step 13: Completing the head

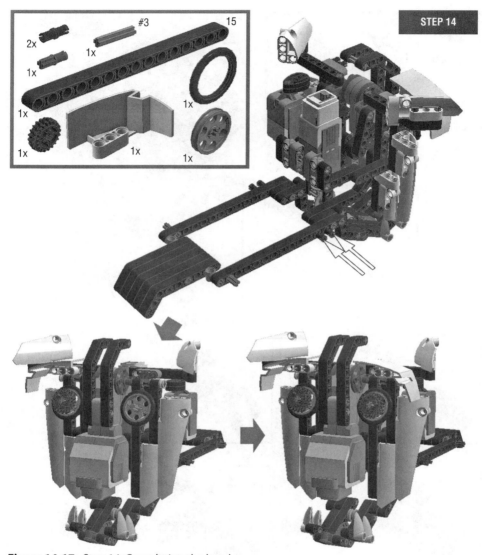

Figure 14-17: Step 14: Completing the head

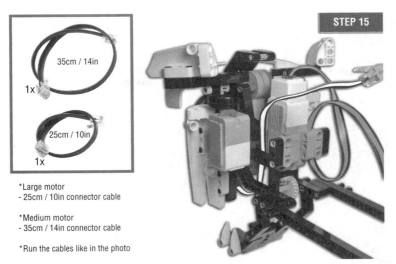

*Large motor
- 25cm / 10in connector cable

*Medium motor
- 35cm / 14in connector cable

*Run the cables like in the photo

Figure 14-18: Step 15: Plugging connector cables into the medium and large motor

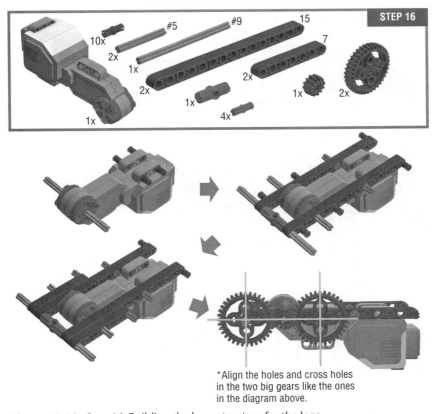

*Align the holes and cross holes
in the two big gears like the ones
in the diagram above.

Figure 14-19: Step 16: Building the base structure for the legs

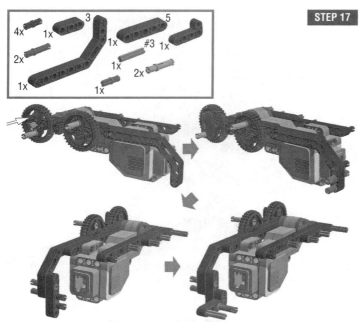

Figure 14-20: Step 17: Building the base structure for the legs

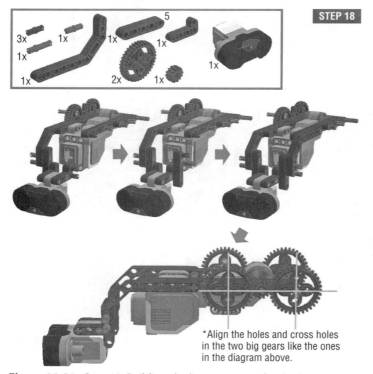

*Align the holes and cross holes in the two big gears like the ones in the diagram above.

Figure 14-21: Step 18: Building the base structure for the legs

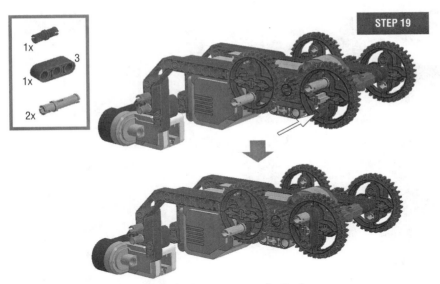

Figure 14-22: Step 19: Building the base structure for the legs

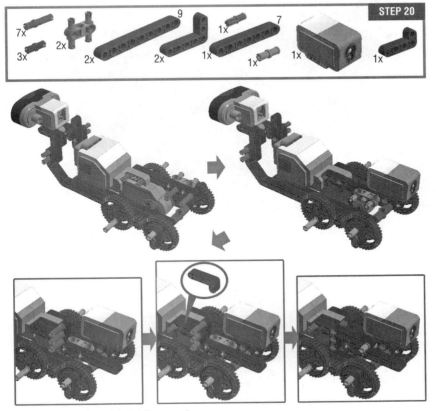

Figure 14-23: Step 20: Adding a color sensor

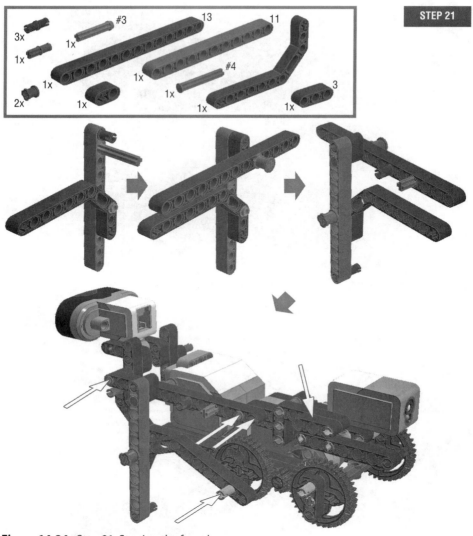

Figure 14-24: Step 21: Starting the front legs

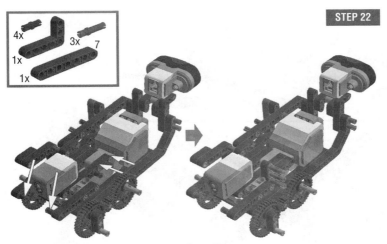

Figure 14-25: Step 22: Starting the front legs

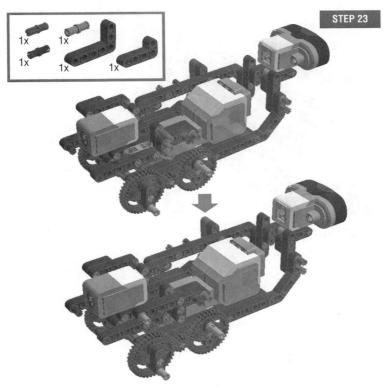

Figure 14-26: Step 23: Starting the front legs

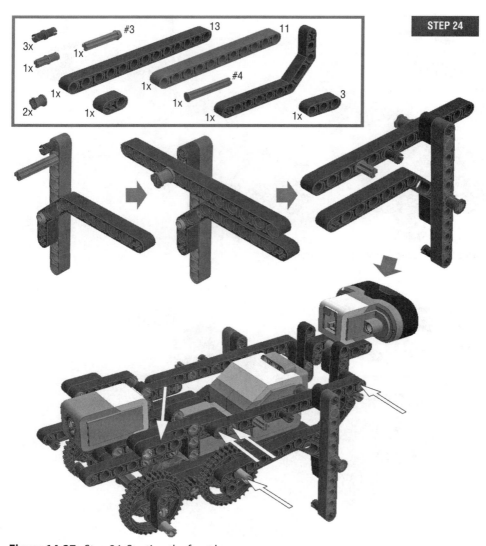

Figure 14-27: Step 24: Starting the front legs

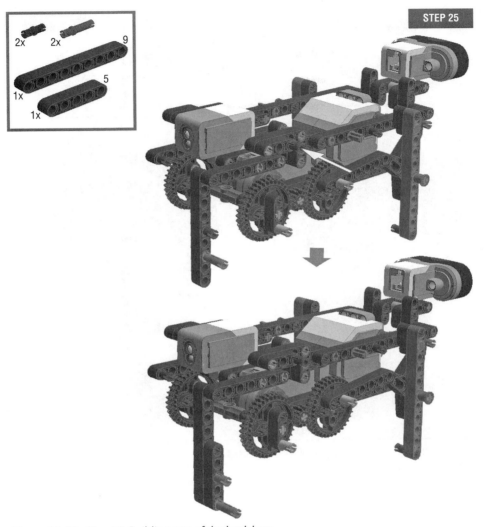

Figure 14-28: Step 25: Building one of the back legs

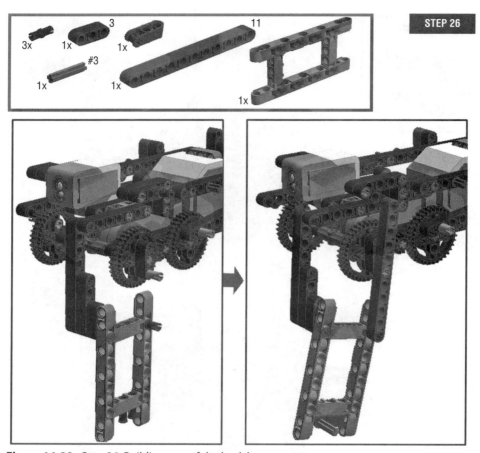

Figure 14-29: Step 26: Building one of the back legs

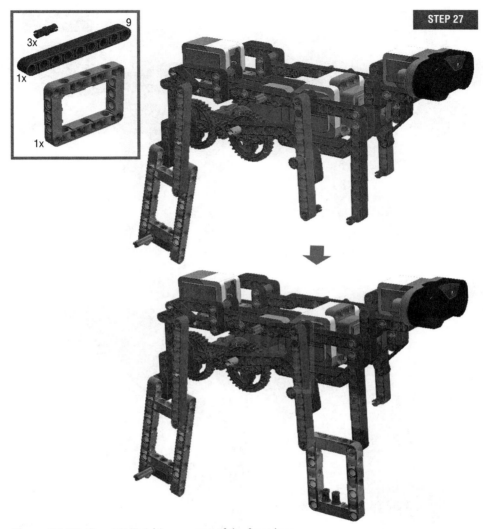

STEP 27

Figure 14-30: Step 27: Finishing up one of the front legs

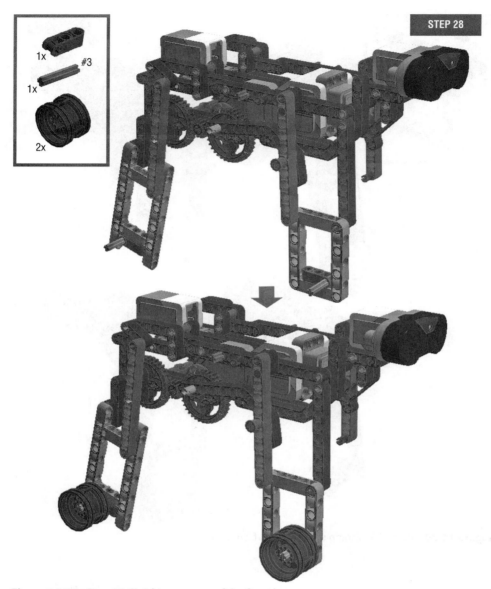

Figure 14-31: Step 28: Finishing up one of the front legs

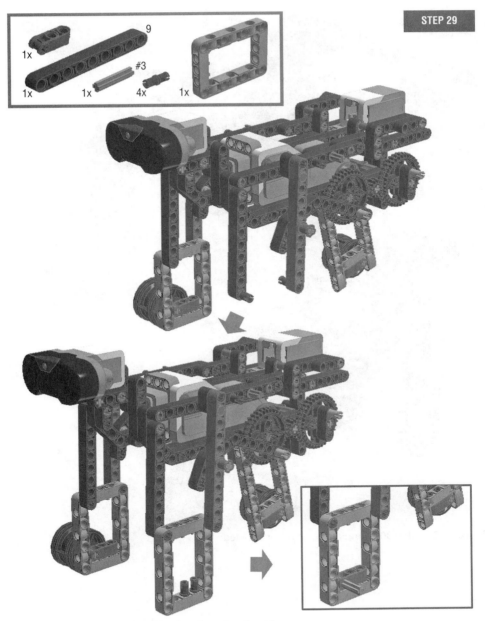

Figure 14-32: Step 29: Finishing up the other front leg

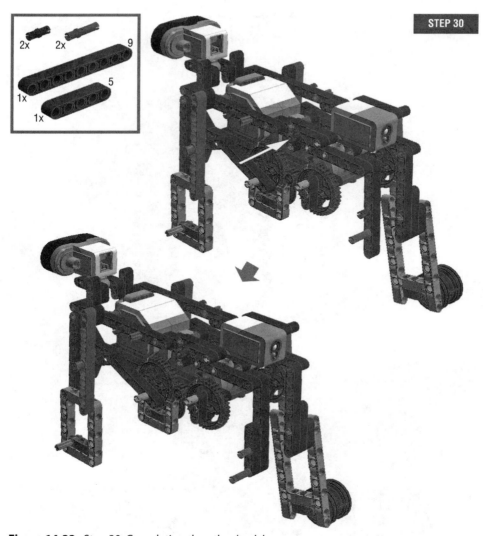

STEP 30

Figure 14-33: Step 30: Completing the other back leg

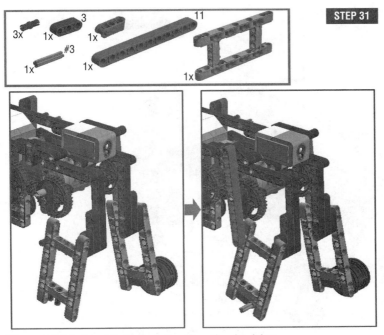

Figure 14-34: Step 31: Completing the other back leg

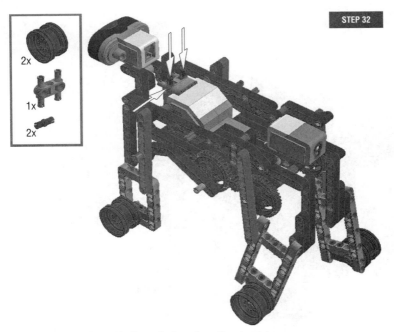

Figure 14-35: Step 32: Completing the other back leg

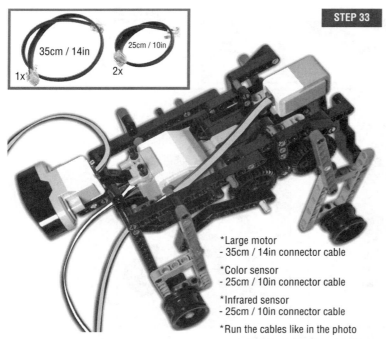

Figure 14-36: Step 33: Connecting connector cables to the infrared sensor, color sensor, and large motor

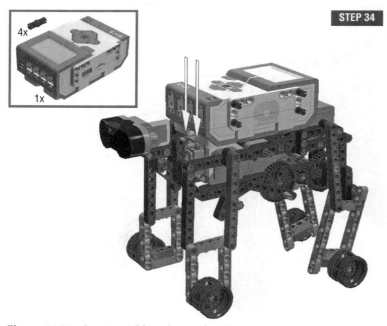

Figure 14-37: Step 34: Adding the EV3 brick

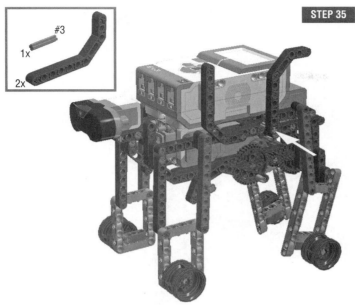

Figure 14-38: Step 35: Adding the head on the legs

Figure 14-39: Step 36: Adding the head on the legs

Figure 14-40: Step 37: Adding the head on the legs

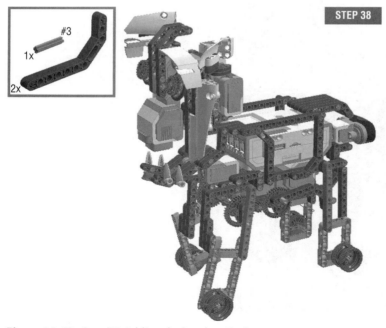

Figure 14-41: Step 38: Adding the head on the legs

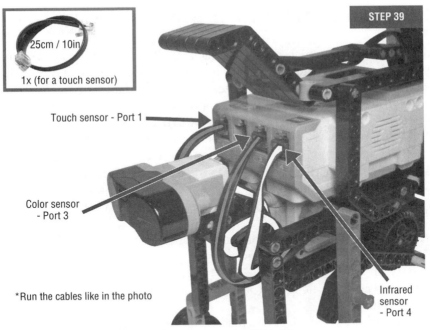

Figure 14-42: Step 39: Wiring the sensors to the EV3 brick

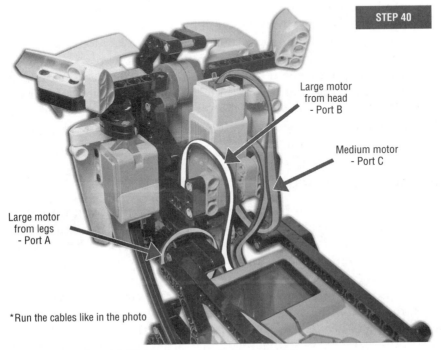

Figure 14-43: Step 40: Wiring the motors to the EV3 brick

Set a Goal: What Do You Want to Build?

Robots all do something, which is to say that they all serve a purpose. When you design your own robot, it is important to know what it will be and what it will do. You can just start putting some pieces together and adding motors and sensors, but it won't always turn out to be a robot. Knowing what you want the end product to be will help you to figure out how to break down a large process into smaller sets of plans. Also, when something doesn't work and you feel lost, you can always go back to your goal and review what you were trying to do and perhaps try a different direction to get to that goal. Now for your first step!

Collecting Inspirations for the Goal

If you already have a clear idea of what your robot will be, go for it. That can be your goal. However, if you are not sure what you want to do, don't worry; there are plenty of ways to brainstorm. The ideas for your robot can be something specific such as a robotic gorilla, a car that can steer itself, or even a LEGO piece-sorting machine.

The inspiration for your project can also come from some of the behaviors that you want your robot to exhibit. You could decide that you want a walking robot, a jumping robot, or a laughing machine. When I worked on the Big Belly Bot, my inspiration was to build a pooping robot.

Inspiration can also come from what you want to try. Do you want more practice programming a project that uses the color or infrared sensors? Do you want to try to use all three motors for your robot? Do you want to try gearing? Pick a thought that is most attractive to you and start from there.

When I started Guapo, I wanted to try building a four-legged creature. It was a pretty broad idea, one that required me to fill in a lot of details later on down the line. While you are proceeding with your idea, your goal will become clearer. The following sections show you how Guapo went from being just a four-legged creature to a cute robotic dog.

Defining Your Robot's Actions: What Does It Do?

Once the inspiration for your robot is clear, try to decide what you want it to do. For example, if your idea already refers to a specific image, such as a robotic gorilla, you'll need to decide how you want him to perform. Do you want your gorilla to dance by shaking his body from side to side? Do you want him to roll forward on four legs? Should he be able to stand up?

If you plan to use an infrared sensor on your robot, think about what the robot will do when the infrared sensor sees something close by. Perhaps your robot has two arms that will be activated by the infrared sensor. What about using these two arms as drum sticks so that they can beat a drum? Then, your robot can be a drummer. If your robot has two arms that can make a clapping motion, perhaps it can be a clapping monkey. As with the examples here, if your idea is broad, give it shape while you figure out your robot's action. Follow this line of thinking to add features that support the purpose of this robot. When you are in this step, try to define your robot like this: My robot does X, Y, and Z. This then is your goal.

When defining the actions of my four-legged robot, of course I wanted to have it walk using its legs, but simply making it walk didn't satisfy me. I wanted to add something to give it more character. I like to build robots with personality, so I decided to make a head that moves its eyes, eyelids, and mouth so that it can make facial expressions. At this point in the process, I wasn't sure whether it would be a dog or something else. Keep in mind that if you can see the big picture of what your robot will do, you can fill in the smaller details at a later time.

Decide on Moving Parts and Sensors

Once you have the big picture of your robot and how it will operate, it's a good time to decide which parts it actually needs to move to complete the actions that you've planned. If you want to make a clapping monkey, what parts of him need to move? You might want to have his arms open and close side to side. If you want your robot to beat a drum, his arms need to move up and down. I suggest beginning this step with a simple sketch of your robot.

Planning by Sketching: The Way to Decide Which Parts Will Move

Sketching your project idea is always a good idea. The first reason that I like it so much is that it is cheap and available. Let me explain. When I get a good idea, I make a little sketch. I can use whatever is handy to draw. Scrap paper works well, notebooks are great, and a whiteboard is amazing. The thing that they all have in common is that they provide a quick and easy way to take the idea that is in my mind and make it exist in the real world. Then I can look at it with my actual eyes as opposed to my mind's eye. Now I can use my critical thinking skills to decide where the moving parts will be and how I can place the sensors to get the most out of them.

> **NOTE** I can be anywhere when an idea strikes me, so I will write down my idea on whatever I have available to me at the time. As I write this, I can glance up at the wall behind my desk and see all the notes and sketches that I have made while writing this book. These sketches keep me striving toward the goal that I set at the beginning of the project.

While visualizing your design, try to break down the design into individual sections and then decide what parts you want to move. Next, mark moving points and add arrows to point how they move. Also, think about where motors should go and how to convert a rotation (spinning) motion from a motor to another type of motion like up and down or side to side. In addition, consider whether you can achieve more than one motion at the same time.

Sometimes it's hard to figure out what needs to move to make a certain motion work, and you may question if it is even possible to make the movement that you planned. For this reason, research is necessary. As you do your research, sketch out the individual moving parts of the robot and think about how you can make them move. Are you going to use linkages to connect two sections and move them together? Are you going to use gears to make the motion slower or faster? Improve your sketch with what you learn. Also, if your robot's movements should happen in a specific order or if the motors need to work in concert with the sensors, write down the steps in order. All this information will prove helpful when you program the robot.

When I started working on Guapo, I took time to research the movement of four-legged creatures. I watched online videos that depicted walking robots. I flipped through books that showed how different walking mechanisms worked. I tried sketching out how I could link the legs together, where the power source could be, and how to translate the rotation motion from a motor into a walking motion. I also made a list of the things that I wanted to try. For example, I wanted to move Guapo's eyes and eyelids together, which means when the eyes point up, the eyelids should point up and vice versa. To do this, I needed to figure out how to connect them. Another goal was to make his mouth open and close, so I needed to decide whether his jaw was going to move up and down like an elevator or perform more like a trapdoor when it opened and closed.

When you feel like you have a clearer idea about how your robot's moving parts will work, try to assign motors for each action. Remember that whenever you decide to place a motor, you must also consider how much power you need to make that movement and how well the placement of a motor fits in your design. Also, try to think where you can put the EV3 brick. The EV3 brick is big and heavy, and when you are still sketching you should consider where it will go.

I chose to design the mechanism to move all four legs concurrently (at the same time) with a single power source. I assigned a large motor for this movement because the power of a motor should be strong enough to move the weight of his entire body. I also decided to use a large motor for Guapo's eyes and eyelids because the shape of a large motor fit in really well as a nose.

Finally, I had one medium motor left; so, I assigned it to move Guapo's mouth. Before I even started putting pieces together, I knew how I wanted to position the two large motors. I wasn't yet sure how I would place the medium motor at this point.

TIP Keep in mind that it's okay to have some uncertainty in your sketch. You can postpone making decisions for some parts when you are still unsure. Your design in a sketch can seem almost perfect before you started building, but it may still evolve while you are building and fixing your project. The purpose of a sketch is to have a guide that you can follow when you are building that also reminds you which parts need more work and which parts may need a second look.

Adding Sensors: Where Sensors Will Be Most Useful

If a sensor is an important element of your robot, you may already have a plan for how to use it and where to put it. However, if you haven't already thought about sensors, now is a good time to do so. When I build a robot, I mostly focus on moving parts before I get around to using sensors. Once I have a good vision of the moving parts, I decide where sensors will fit the best in my design and how I want to use the data from the sensors for my robot's actions. Sensors can be used casually to give your robot an additional feature, but sometimes it is necessary to use them to control essential movements of your robot.

If you are building a clapping monkey that will be activated by an infrared sensor, try to figure out where you want to put the sensor when you sketch. Can it be a part of the monkey's face? Perhaps you can place it on his back? You might brainstorm how you want to collect data from an infrared sensor to control the motion of the monkey's arms.

Your goal may not include sensors now, but try to think where sensors can be useful for enriching your robot's behavior. If you are building a robotic gorilla, can you use the data from an infrared sensor to control his movement? Maybe you can add a color sensor so that he can follow a line? What about using a touch sensor for his lips so that he can react to a kiss? When you think about using sensors, you might get some new ideas for your robot. With that in mind, it's good to be open to adding sensors to any design.

As mentioned earlier, it is sometimes necessary to use sensors to make moving parts function correctly. When I built Guapo, I figured that I would need sensors to control his mouth and eye/eyelid movements. Unlike the movement of a rotating wheel (continuous motion), the mouth's movement uses an alternating motion that goes back and forth between two directions, such as opening and closing. When you design this kind of movement, it is important to know when the motion should stop and change its direction; after all, we don't want to force a motor to keep going when something is blocking its way. For example, Guapo's mouth should stop opening when it hits his body, and it should stop closing when his jaws are together. So, as the model on the right image in Figure 14-44 shows, I added a color sensor behind his jaw. The jaw blocks the color sensor when his mouth is fully open, and it changes the amount of reflected light that the sensor gets. You won't see the color sensor on the left image in Figure 14-44 because his mouth is opened and the color sensor is blocked by his jaw. When the mouth is open, the sensor does not get any reflected light, but when the mouth is closed, the sensor gets reflected light from the jaw.

Now I know when the mouth is open all the way, and I can also figure out (by using the Port View app on the EV3 brick) how many degrees the motor needs to move to have the mouth fully closed. I opened the mouth wide and went to the Port View menu, selected the port that has the medium motor plugged into it, and manually closed the mouth. The number of degrees that the Port View shows here is the number that you want to use for the motor when you want to program the completely open mouth to close all the way. When I measured the number of degrees to close Guapo's mouth, I found that I needed to move the medium motor −70°, which meant that the motor should move backward 70°. With this data, you can position the mouth wherever you want within in its movable range. Suppose, for example, that you want to have him open his mouth halfway. First you can program his mouth to be fully open from wherever it was (open until the color sensor gets more amount of reflected light) and then move the motor backward 35°.

It is important to set the mouth to a default position. I recommend that in the beginning of the program you make it so that his mouth is either fully open or fully closed. Why is that? Let's say you want to have his mouth open all the way and close all the way two times. In your program, you can say fully open − fully closed − fully open − fully closed. But what if the mouth was already halfway closed or already fully open when you run this program? Then, this program won't work. You can avoid this problem by setting up the default position at the beginning of the program. You will know that the mouth will always be placed in a certain position, and then you can plan the rest of the program for the mouth based on this default position.

For the same reason I planned to use a touch sensor to control Guapo's eyes/eyelids. When his eyes/eyelids point all the ways up, the touch sensor will be pressed, and it will stop the motor. Later, I also measured how far his eyes/eyelids can angle all the way down, which told me that the motor should turn backward 100°. So if you want to have his eyes/eyelids point straight forward, you want to move the motor backward 50° after the touch sensor is pressed. Figure 14-44 and Figure 14-45 show how a color sensor and a touch sensor work for Guapo's mouth and eye/eyelid movements.

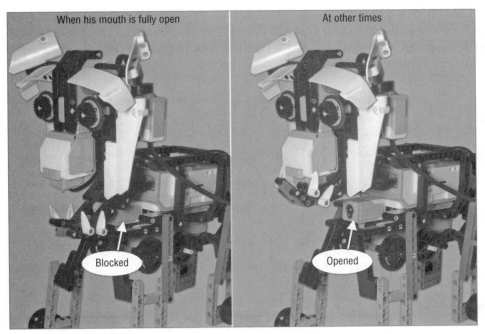

Figure 14-44: How Guapo's mouth works with a color sensor

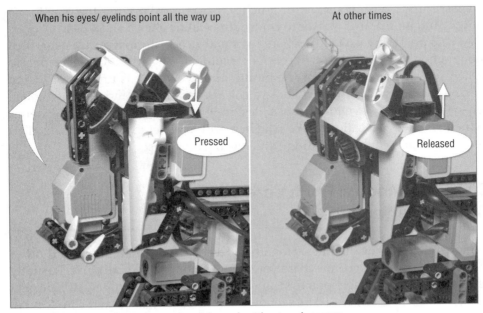

Figure 14-45: How Guapo's eyes/eyelids work with a touch sensor

I also decided that the default position for the mouth would be fully closed and for the eyes/eyelids it would be pointing straight forward. Figure 14-46 shows a program that I made to set up the default position of Guapo's mouth and eyes/eyelids.

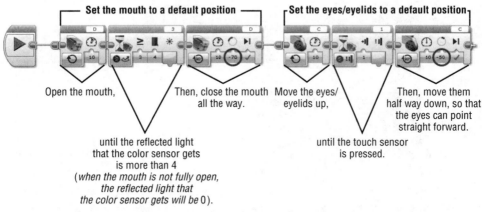

Figure 14-46: A program to set up Guapo's mouth and eyes/eyelids at their default position

You don't need to figure out detailed programs for sensors in this step, just as long as you know how you want to use them for your robot. My plan included sensors in this way: a touch sensor (or color sensor) for calibrating the position of eyes/eyelids, a color sensor (or touch sensor) for calibrating the position of mouth, and an infrared sensor to control his walking with an IR beacon.

At this point, I wasn't sure where I wanted to add an infrared sensor. So, I thought maybe it could be on his back or it could be his tail. I didn't even decide which sensor I would use for the mouth and eyes/eyelids until after I tried placing them here and there. I chose a color sensor for the mouth and a touch sensor for the eyes/eyelids because, design-wise, they ended up fitting better in their respective locations. Like I did here, you will get to make more detailed decisions while you are building, which is the next step.

Build and Modify: From Core Sections to Decorative Sections

Now it's time to put the pieces together. Keep your sketch, notes, and other parts of your research somewhere you can see them. When building, I usually assemble individual sections first, and then I put them all together. The first section that I try is always a core section of my design. When I say a core section, I am referring to the main section of the robot or the section that works like a base for all the other sections. If you are building a clapping monkey, his torso with arms can be a core section. When I feel satisfied with the core section, I move to the secondary sections.

Whenever I am done with each individual section (if it contains moving parts), I try programming it to see whether it moves the way I planned. If its movement is smooth and stable, that's great. Sometimes, though, things don't work the way you envisioned. Then it's time to modify the design and try some different things. This might require more research and brainstorming, and you might find the process time-consuming and frustrating.

> **NOTE** It is important to remember that you will learn the most when you try to work through problems. Also, you will feel very proud of yourself after you get through this process.

I highly recommend that you program the individual sections of your robot before you assemble everything because once things are all put together it is very difficult to find what is causing trouble. Again, the building process is not only the process of following the plans that you made but also modifying and improving your initial design. Other than facing problems, there is a good chance that you may discover new mechanisms and movements.

When you feel satisfied with the individual sections, it's time to put the whole thing together. You should ask yourself several questions when you assemble them all together:

- Do the sections function as well together as they did individually?
- Do you find the whole structure to be sturdy?
- Does the robot keep its balance when all the sections are in action?
- Do the sensors work as they were intended to work?

After troubleshooting, you might need to change some designs again or reposition motors or sensors. Try writing a simple program that can test basic movements of each section before you write a more complicated program.

When I started making Guapo, I built the four-legged walking mechanism first because the legs and motor are the core section of this robot. I changed the design of the legs and feet several times to get the movement that I wanted. When I felt happy with it, I moved on to build the head. I started with a large motor that powered the eyes and eyelids. Then, I tried to figure out the position of a medium motor. When I first finished the head, a medium motor wasn't mounted vertically like it is now. It was originally placed horizontally so that it was perpendicular to the face, but later on I had to change it because that position didn't really work out after I had connected it to the leg mechanism. I added the EV3 brick on the leg mechanism before I started programming because it was important to know whether the leg structure was strong enough to carry the heavy weight of the EV3 brick. I tested out the leg mechanism multiple times with the EV3 brick and tried to find the best structure to boost walking performance. I did the same thing with the head, too. In this step, I decided to use a touch sensor to control the eyes and eyelids and placed it in a position where it can be pressed when the eyes and eyelids are pointing up. I also tried to find a suitable position for a color sensor where it could be blocked by the mouth when it opened.

After I tested the individual sections, I put the head and the leg mechanism together. It wasn't easy to find a position for the head that gave the robot a good balance. When I attached the head so that it was far from the leg mechanism, the legs weren't moving properly because it was such a heavy structure. I changed the position of the medium motor so that the head could be close to the rest of the body. It was then that I also decided to use an infrared sensor as his tail. I checked to see whether it still got the signal from an IR beacon even though it was pointing backward. Most of the time the infrared sensor got the signal from a IR beacon just fine with this placement, but I found that sometimes when I tried the same thing in a small area, the communication between the sensor and IR beacon wasn't stable. It may be because the IR signal was being reflected off surrounding walls, and I had to keep it in mind when I programmed them.

After you finish assembling the sections, it is a good time to add some decorative parts. Decorative parts are, by definition, just for looks. So, they are not really necessary for the robot's motion, but they are important for expressing the characteristics of the robot. Be creative. You can give your clapping monkey a set of wings or you can decorate your gorilla with a funny face. As you go, make sure that your robot performs well despite all the decorative parts. Sometimes additional components can make a robot really heavy or can get in the way of moving parts.

After I finished working on the core structure of my robot, I started getting serious with adding decorative parts. The core structure work didn't leave Guapo with any ears or cheeks, so as I began adding these elements, I decided to make him into a dog. I chose a dog robot because I like dogs and, hey, it was fun to make him into a dog. Moreover, the robot's range and style of movements do pretty well in representing those of a dog, in my opinion. At the end of the day, it will be your robot, so feel free to add things that you like and that keep you creative.

Time to Program

When you finish building, you will have a working model of the project, and you may begin experimenting with the model's programming. Earlier I suggested that you test some of the programs as you build each section of the model. That way you will know that when the project is complete all the sections will move as intended, which then allows you to focus on programming the entire robot. Remember your goal as you write your program. After all, the code that you write moves the motors, which drive the other sections and allow you to achieve your vision of what your robot would do. You may use trial and error with different power levels for each motor to find something that works best for your robot's performance. The same advice applies when you are setting the thresholds for the sensors.

You can do several things with Guapo. We can make him walk forward and backward simply by using the IR beacon with the IR Control app. I wouldn't use the IR beacon to move his eyes and eyelids or mouth because the IR Control app does not give you control over the power of the motors; in addition, at the default power level, the motor will be too strong to make those features perform well.

We can program combined actions by using the software. Guapo can walk up to you, look up at your face, and then bark as if asking for food. When you program his mouth and eyes, begin the program with the program shown in Figure 14-46 so that you can put them into their default positions. Once this program is running, his mouth will close, and his eyes will point straight ahead. From these default positions, his jaw can drop in a range of 70°, which means that you can move a medium motor for 70° to completely open his mouth. If you only want to have his mouth open a little bit, you can use any number of degrees that is less than 70°. I recommend using 10 (or –10, when you program the mouth to close) as the medium motor's power level. For his eyes, the large motor that powers them can move in a range of 100°. From the default position, his eyes can point 50° up or 50° down. I also recommend using 10 (or –10, when you program the eyes to point down). See the code example in Figure 14-47. In this code, I made the code that Figure 14-46 shows as a My block and named it Reset.

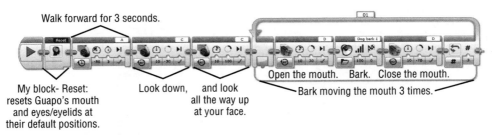

Walk forward for 3 seconds.

My block- Reset: resets Guapo's mouth and eyes/eyelids at their default positions.

Look down,   and look all the way up at your face.

Open the mouth.   Bark.   Close the mouth.
Bark moving the mouth 3 times.

Figure 14-47: A program that causes Guapo to walk up to you, look up at your face, and then bark

Try putting together some more programs to have more fun with Guapo. You can create more facial expressions by combining his eye and mouth movements. Can you also make him walk faster or slower? How would you make him start walking just by rubbing his tail? (You can program him to start walking when the infrared sensor says that your hand is really close, like within .5 inches.) Guapo is ready to play with his buddy!

Summary

In this chapter, you learned about the following:

- Steps for building your own robot
- How Guapo came to be
- How to build Guapo
- How to program Guapo

Using Bluetooth and WiFi with the EV3 Brick

Instead of using a USB cable to connect the EV3 brick and a computer together to download programs, you can do it wirelessly via Bluetooth or WiFi. Using these connections will give you more flexibility in downloading a program from your computer to the brick because you won't need to plug in a USB cable to do so. Deciding how to assemble your robot will come with fewer restrictions because you won't need to worry about your design blocking the PC port on the EV3. Note that Bluetooth or WiFi connections are possible only if the computer that you are using has Bluetooth or Wireless built in or connected as an accessory. In addition to computers, Bluetooth connections will allow the EV3 brick to communicate with Apple iOS devices such as iPhone, iPad, and iPod.

Using Bluetooth with the EV3 Brick

Depending on whether you want to download a program to the EV3 brick (computer to robot) or use an iOS device as a remote (iOS to robot), you must configure your Bluetooth setup accordingly. To avoid problems, make sure that you do not enable Bluetooth settings for the computer *and* the iOS device at the same time.

Connecting the EV3 Brick to a Computer

To connect the EV3 brick to a computer, follow these steps:

1. Turn on the EV3 brick and go to the Settings screen. Choose the Bluetooth option by clicking the Center button. A new dialog box will pop up with four options: Connections, Visibility, Bluetooth, and iPhone/iPad/iPod.

2. If the Visibility option is not checked, navigate to that option by using the Up and Down buttons and select it by clicking the center button. Then, go to the Bluetooth option and select it as well. To come back to the main menu, use the Down button and select the check mark button at the bottom of the dialog box. Once Bluetooth is turned on, you will find a left-arrow symbol (<) with a Bluetooth symbol in the upper-left corner of the screen (see Figure A-1).

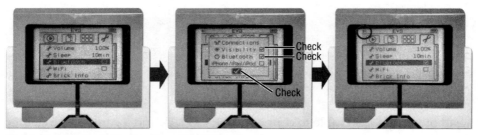

Figure A-1: Activate Bluetooth on the EV3 brick.

3. Make sure that your computer's Bluetooth option is turned on.

4. Open or create a project with the EV3 software.

5. In the lower-right corner of the software window of the Hardware page, click the Available Bricks tab. After doing so, click the Refresh button (see Figure A-2).

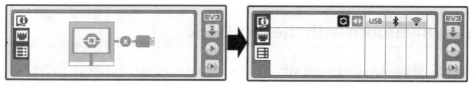

Figure A-2: Check available bricks.

6. When the software gives you a list of Bluetooth devices, find your EV3 brick. If this is your first time connecting the EV3 brick with this computer,

you will see the Pair button. Click that button, and then you will get a dialog box that asks whether you want to make a connection with the computer on the EV3 screen. When you accept the computer's request to connect on the EV3 brick's screen, you need to enter the passkey, which is set to 1234 by default (see Figure A-3). Click the Enter button.

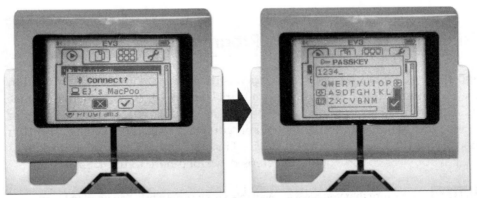

Figure A-3: Accept a Bluetooth connections request on the EV3 brick.

TIP If you are mainly using your EV3 brick at home, I suggest keeping the passkey as the default, as to avoid any future confusion.

NOTE If this isn't your first time, the software will remember the Brick that was connected before. You may refresh the available bricks on the Hardware page and choose the EV3 brick that you want to use from the list of Bluetooth devices in the pop-up window. If that brick has been connected before, the software won't ask for a passcode, and the brick will be connected.

7. Come back to the computer. If the window with a list of Bluetooth devices is still on the screen, select your EV3 brick. The Hardware page will show your EV3 brick under the Available brick tab. Click that brick and you will get a pop-up window that asks for a passcode. Type in **1234** and click the Pair button. Your EV3 brick will then be connected to the computer, and the < symbol with a Bluetooth symbol in the upper-left corner of the EV3 screen should change to a pair of arrow symbols (< >). If <> does not appear in the upper-left corner of the EV3 screen, you might see an error message instead.

The process of establishing a Bluetooth connection may produce an error message. If this happens, try restarting the EV3 brick and software. Also, you may want to delete other EV3 devices that you are not currently using from the list of Bluetooth devices on the pop-up window that appears when you refresh available bricks. Close the window and refresh available bricks again before trying again to connect the brick.

Using WiFi to Download a Program to the EV3 Brick

One of the new features of the EV3 brick is that it can make a WiFi connection. Keep in mind that you'll need to buy a WiFi USB dongle to activate this feature; LEGO recommends that you use the NETGEAR N150 Wireless USB Adapter. So that you can plug in the dongle when you want to make a WiFi connection, ensure that the USB host port on the EV3 brick is available and not blocked by any part of your robot. Follow the steps described here to use this feature.

NOTE   Make sure that you have an available wireless network. You need to know the name of the network and its password.

1. Close the EV3 software on your computer and plug the USB dongle into the USB host port on the EV3 brick. Then go to the Settings screen on the EV3 brick and select the WiFi option.

2. You will get a pop-up dialog that has three options: None, Connections, and WiFi. Navigate to the WiFi option by using the Up and Down buttons and select it by clicking the center button. The box next to WiFi will be checked, and you will see the WiFi icon in the upper-left corner of the screen.

3. Go to Connections by using the Up button and select it by clicking the center button. You will get a window that shows the available wireless networks from which you may choose the one that you want to access.

4. Select Connect on the next window that pops up. You then choose between network encryption modes: None or WPA2. The type of encryption of the network that you are connecting to will depend on how it is configured. You may need to experiment between the two if you are unsure. If the network asks you to enter a password, use the Up, Down, Left, and Right keys to navigate the virtual keyboard, and then type in a password for the network. Click the Enter button when you finish typing in the password.

5. The check mark at the bottom of the dialog window will take you back to the previous window. Click the check mark again and you will find yourself back at the main menu. When the connection establishes successfully, you will see arrow symbols (top arrow pointing to the right and bottom arrow pointing to the left) next to the wireless icon in the upper-left corner of the screen.

6. Now the EV3 brick is connected to your preferred wireless network! Make sure that your computer is connected to the same network and launch the EV3 software and open or create a project. Refresh the available brick on the Hardware page (see Figure A-2 in the Bluetooth section of this appendix); you will see the EV3 brick that you just connected to the wireless network.

You can also enable a wireless connection on the EV3 brick from a computer, as follows:

1. First you need to follow steps 1–2, and then open the EV3 software.

2. Connect the EV3 brick to the computer with a USB cable.

3. Click the Tools menu and choose Wireless Setup. You will get a pop-up window with a list of network names.

4. Click the one that you want to use, and then click the Connect button.

5. If necessary, type in the password for that network.

Once a wireless connection is established, you may unplug the USB cable. The EV3 brick will be connected to the computer via a shared wireless network.

Using Apple iOS Devices with the EV3 Brick

To use Apple iOS devices to control your EV3 robot, you need to download the free app called LEGO MINDSRORMS robot commander from Apple's App Store. You can find this app by searching for "EV3 commander." After you download the app, you will see the Commander app icon on your iOS device. To use this app with your EV3 robot, follow these steps:

1. First you need to enable both Bluetooth and the iPhone/iPad/iPod from the dialog box that appears when you choose the Bluetooth option on the Settings screen. See Figure A-1 to find how to get to the dialog box.

2. On your Apple iOS device, go to Settings and activate Bluetooth. Once Bluetooth is on, the device shows the list of the available devices. Choose your EV3 brick. Then, go through the pairing process by accepting the

pairing request on both on the device and on your EV3 brick, like in the previous section.

3. Launch the app. There are premade controllers for the robots that you see in the Lobby area on the software. If you slide the screen to the left, you will see the display that says "Create & command your own robot." When you click either this display or the "play" symbol on the bottom, it will bring you a blank page with a + symbol. Click one of the signs, and you will then be able to navigate different controller options such as joystick, horizontal slider, or switch by sliding the screen or using the arrow on the sides of the screen. Choose whatever you like, set up configurations, and then click the + symbol at the bottom.

4. Repeat this process to add more controllers.

LEGO MINDSRORMS robot commander provides many control options that you can use with your robot. Design your own controller that works the best for your robot and have fun.

Index